AKHENATEN

THE HERETIC KING

AKHENATEN

THE HERETIC KING

Donald B. Redford

PRINCETON UNIVERSITY PRESS

PRINCETON, NEW JERSEY

Copyright © 1984 by Princeton University Press
Published by Princeton University Press,
41 William Street,
Princeton, New Jersey 08540
In the United Kingdom:
Princeton University Press, Guildford, Surrey

ALL RIGHTS RESERVED
Library of Congress Cataloging in Publication Data
will be found on the last printed page of this book
ISBN 0-691-03567-9

This book has been composed in Linotron Bembo
Clothbound editions of Princeton University Press books are
printed on acid-free paper, and binding materials
are chosen for strength and durability.

Printed in the United States of America by
Princeton University Press
Princeton, New Jersey

Frontispiece: Decoration on dias of Queen Nefertity (L. Greener)

TO SUSAN
with love, respect, and gratitude

CONTENTS

Figures   xi

Plates   xiii

Preface   xxi

Abbreviations   xxv

Introduction   3

Part One: Imperial Egypt

ONE   The Extended Boundary   9

TWO   Glimpses of Imperial Egypt   21

THREE   Amenophis III, The Sun-King   34

Part Two: The Reign of the Heretic Pharaoh

FOUR Amenophis IV and the Puzzle of the Reign 57

FIVE The Excavation of East Karnak 86

SIX East Karnak before Amenophis IV 95

SEVEN The Gm·(t)-p³-itn 102

EIGHT "The Horizon of the Sun-disc" 137

Part Three: The Great Living Sun-disc

NINE The Spiritual Milieu of Akhenaten's Reaction 157

TEN The Object of Akhenaten's Worship 169

Part Four: Sunset

ELEVEN Of Politics and Foreign Affairs 185

TWELVE Symbiosis: The Reign of Tutankhamun 204

THIRTEEN Egypt and Khatte: A Tale of War and Peace 212

FOURTEEN Epilogue 222

FIFTEEN "The Beautiful Child of the Sun-disc" 232

Glossary 236

Suggested Reading 242

Index 245

FIGURES

1. Map of Egypt to the First Cataract
2. The Great Kingdoms of West Asia c. 1375 B.C.
3. Plan of Karnak
4. Facsimile of chariot scene from *Rwd-mnw* (A. Shaheen). The king in blue crown and with riding whip in his chariot, about to move off to an unspecified destination. The text reads: "Appearance in glory [. . . on (his) char]iot, by His Majesty like the Sun-disc in [the midst of heaven], brightening the Two Lands. . . ." Behind the horse's plumed heads is a band of text that seems to name them: "its (the team's) beautiful name (is) 'Made by the (Sun-disc).'"
5. Facsimile of foreign dignitaries, greeting the king (TS 4917, A. Shaheen). Two rows of Amorite princes are depicted, with typical clubbed hair, filets, and wrap-around gowns, each with his arm raised in adoration of pharoh. The bald heads in the lowest preserved register may

ix

represent Hittites. Note the Egyptian company commanders, each with the standard of his company, in close attendance on the foreigners.

6. Reconstruction of an interior gateway in the *Ḥwt-bnbn* (R. Aicher)

7. Reconstruction of part of the "Nefertity Colonnade." Many *talatat* comprising a series of pillars were recovered by Chevrier in the core of the second pylon. It was possible to reconstruct, in part, twelve of the piers, but the many remaining blocks clearly from similar pillar construction argue the presence of many more. The scene on each "long" side shows Nefertity and Meretaten offering to the Sun-disc identified as "residing in *Gm·(t)-p³-itn*"; on the other three sides similar scenes are repeated in four superimposed panels. The architrave texts are restored from the fragmentary architraves extracted from the ninth pylon and presumed to come originally from this colonnade. The text reads "she pure of hands great king's wife whom he loves, Lady of the Two Lands, Nefertity, may she live! beloved of the great living Sun-disc who is in jubilee, residing in the House of the Sun-disc in Southern Heliopolis." Other fragments of the same architraves also mention the king.

8. Cross-section through quadrant BB, facing east. The surface at the bottom represents the open court of the *Gm·(t)-p³-itn* temple, onto which at the moment of the final destruction of the temple fell the charred *temenos* wall (II, 41, 52b, 53b; III, 16, 17, 19, 20, 21). Further debris fell to the north, and was added to over the centuries as the area was used as a garbage dump (II, 42, 51b, 52b, 53b). At last, at the close of the 8th century B.C. the site was leveled up (I, 37–38; III, 12, 13, 14, 15) and houses were built (wall 11a, 14, 15; see Chapter 5). These were twice rebuilt, once in the middle of the 6th century, and again around 400 B.C.; but before the coming of Alexander the Great (331 B.C.) the area had been abandoned (II, 11, 12, 13), and wind-blown ash was allowed to accumulate (II, 8, 9). This remained the surface until 1925 when Chevrier dug his huge trench (right), flinging the earth to the north to form his own dump over the rest of the site (IV, 1–6).

9. Plan of excavation in East Karnak (grid squares 20m. on a side). The quadrants are lettered in bold type. Those of A, B, and E series (upper right-hand corner) are exposed to the level of phase N (14th century B.C.), viz. that of the *Gm·(t)-p³-itn* temple, showing south and west colonnades. The F series (center left) is exposed at phase B (4th century B.C.)

10. Section through the south colonnade of *Gm·(t)-p³-itn*, facing west. Sur-

viving masonry, brickwork, and earth are shown in solid line, restored in broken line. Small statues and steles are known to have been set up in the colonnade.

11. Elevation of the south colonnade of $Gm\cdot(t)-p^3-itn$ facing south in the reach of quadrants A and AB. The colossi are designated according to Chevrier's original numbering scheme. The back wall of the colonnade is shown decorated with a facsimile of TS 238 which we now know to have stood here. Additions not attested in the matching, but proven to have been present by fragments recovered in the excavations are 1) the palace on the left; 2) the dado of bull-slaughtering; 3) the adoring foreigners.

12. Area F, Phase N. The partly preserved *talatat* wall (left) and the two rows of pier-bases probably constitute part of the western approach to the $Gm\cdot(t)-p^3-itn$. Near here were found the fragmentary inscriptions pictured in Pls. 4.5 and 7.17. The structure indicated by the broken lines at the top belongs to the 4th century B.C. and stands at a higher level.

13. Facsimile of bowing courtiers (TS 5594; A. Shaheen). Rows of civil servants, with characteristic flounced sporans, bow before the king, each group led by a supervisor.

14. Facsimile of the party of priests (god's-fathers) greeting the king upon his arrival at the temple with sweet-smelling bouquets (R. Aicher).

15. Facsimile of palace and temple (K. Bard). This collage of blocks, originally from the north wall of $Gm\cdot(t)-p^3-itn,$ shows the point of join between two "processional scenes." On the right is the temple, with its many small kiosks among which the king is moving. On the left is the palace, with servants and wine jars. Both complexes are surrounded by "wavy" lines, possibly depicting sinusoidal walling systems.

16. Facsimile of palace scene (A. Shaheen). The scene divides horizontally in the center into two nearly identical depictions of the palace, the lower representing the feasting prior to the departure for the temple, the upper the feasting after the return. To the left in each is shown the "window of appearance" and a storage area for wine, beer, and food. A servant is busy with a fan cooling the liquid and driving off flies. To the right is the large dining hall with king and queen at separate tables, and a platoon of servants bustling about. At the bottom an orchestra entertains.

17. Isometric projection of the "window of appearance" (L. Greener). The

tall pillars support a light canopy before the window; in the center are the pillars of the dining hall behind.

18. Plan of Akhetaten

19. Facsimile of a sun-disc from *Rwd-mnw* (J. Clarke). The Sun-disc is always shown with a rearing uraeus serpent at the bottom facing the viewer (erased in this example). Around the creature's neck an ankh-sign is suspended. The original epithet of Reharakhty is now squeezed into two cartouches, always vertical, flanked on the inward side by a new, second epithet, usually in columns. This latter reads "the great living Sun-disc, who is in jubilee, Lord of heaven and earth, residing in . . . (temple x)."

PLATES

Frontispiece. Decoration on dais of Queen Nefertity (L. Greener)

2.1. Talatat from the ninth pylon showing Amorite and Sudanese auxiliary troops. Throughout Egyptian art Amorites are easily distinguished by their long beards and clubbed hair, tied round with a filet.

3.1. Relief from the tomb of the Vizier Ramose showing the chariotry general and the king's ambassador, Maya, and his wife, Urol.

3.2–3.5. *Talatat* from *sd*-festival representations from the second or ninth pylons.

3.2. Two columns of text, with part of an elaborate vessel, representing an array of foreign tribute. Column on the left: "[Bearing trib]ute to the king by the ch[iefs of . . .]"; column on the right: "[the chiefs of Na]harin (Mitanni), the chiefs of Ku[sh . . .]."

3.3. Representation of foreign emissaries proferring jars of produce to the king. Text: "Lo, the children of the chief(s) of every foreign land were bearing [tribute to His Majesty . . .]."

3.4. *Talatat* showing Amorite chieftains with arms raised in adoration of the king. A large matched scene has now grown from this single fragment: see Fig. 5.

3.5. Nubian chiefs adorned with feathers, praising the king.

4.1. Trial piece, limestone from Amarna, showing the grossly exaggerated style of carving the king's profile, usually associated with the earlier years of the reign.

4.2. Head and shoulders of one of the royal colossi from the south colonnade of $Gm\cdot(t)\text{-}p^3\text{-}itn$ in East Karnak (see Figs. 10, 11).

4.3. Aerial View of Karnak. The rhomboidal enclosure of the Temple of Amun lies to the left (north), and once communicated with the Nile (bottom) by a canal now occupied by the tree-lined street. To the right stands the enclosure of Mut, Amun's consort, with its curved lake, and in the lower right the houses of the modern village of Karnak. The excavated areas and the "dig-house" of the East Karnak expedition may be discerned in the upper left-hand corner, beyond the Amun enclosure.

4.4. Large sandstone block from the tenth pylon, originally part of the southern gateway decorated by the king in the first year of his reign. The traditional representation of the falcon-headed sun-disc, with scepter, faces the king (now lost) who makes an offering. The long name of the god is inscribed in columns before him, and was later reduplicated in two small cartouches.

4.5. Large sandstone block from the tenth pylon, originally from the southern gateway decorated by the king in the first year of his reign. The falcon-headed god with the large sun-disc on his head is Re-Harakhty, the sun god, identified by the long epithet in columns above his head. The final column contains his words to the king (who stood to the right): "Utterance: 'I grant thee [all] valor and victory. . . .'" On the extreme left is the right-hand portion of the adjacent scene showing the king in the *atef*-crown (a monstrous headdress composed of ram's horns and tall feathers). Unlike the divine figure, his has been savagely hacked.

4.6. *Talatat* from the second pylon depicting part of the decoration of a pylon, possibly the southern gateway. On the right are parts of two columns of text, probably flanking the entrance: 1) "[. . . exalted(?)]

. . . to the height of heaven [. . .]; 2) [. . .] Lord of the Two Lands Neferkheprure Wa^c-en-r^c [. . .]." In the center panel, which would be upon the left massif of the pylon, the king is shown "giving various herbs" to the anthropomorphic sun god; while on the left the contiguous panel depicts the offering of the trussed bulls. The mode of representation of the sun god reflects the practice of the first year of the reign; but the style has been influenced by the new canon of art. Note especially how the sun god's belly and torso approximate those of the king.

4.7, 4.8. Stacks of *talatat* from the second and ninth pylons. Of particular interest are the palaquin bearers, servants, and bowing courtiers.

4.9. Rows of servants, seen in echelon, carry trestles laden with flat bread. The scene (TS 5410) depicts the preparation for one of the feasts of the *sd*-festival.

4.10.–4.15. Nefertity. Nefertity as she appears in the offering scenes in the *talatat* reliefs. Two types of headdress are depicted, the long blue wig topped by the modius and feathers (4.10, 4.11, and 4.15) and the short "Nubian" wig (4.12, 4.13). Her costume, a sheer pleated linen gown drawn in and tied beneath the breasts, never varies in such scenes. Behind her stands her eldest daughter, identified in most examples by the stereotyped caption "king's bodily daughter whom he loves. Meretaten, born of the great king's wife whom he loves, mistress of the Two Lands, Nefertity may she live!" Only in 4.10 does a variant occur, which is susceptible of the rendering "king's wife, king's daughter . . ."; but it could also be translated "daughter of the king's wife. . . ." The elaborate offering table in the artist's facsimile (4.15) piled high with edibles and equipped with a small statuette of the queen holding a conical loaf, is provided with a band of text identifying recipient and celebrant: "the great living Sun-disc, Lord of heaven and earth, who is in jubilee, who resides in the Mansion of the *benben*-stone in *Gm·(t)-p³-itn*; the king's wife Nefertity, may she live!"

5.1. Modern view of East Karnak, facing north. The *temenos* wall of the Amun enclosure is on the left, the drainage canal in the center, and the site of *Gm·(t)-p³-itn* beyond the trees on the right.

5.2. Piers of the south colonnade (quadrant AB), facing north. Immediately behind the piers, excavating has begun to reveal the foundations of the wall. A tumble of broken sandstone blocks in the foundation trench is coming to light.

5.3. *Talatat* fragments recovered in the A and AB quadrants showing palanquin bearers conveying the king to the temple (probably part of the great progress of TS 235, now known to have stood in A).

7.1. Matching of *talatat* (TS 28) recovered from the ninth pylon, originally from *Rwd-mnw*. The king wears a white bag-wig, as in Pl. 7.6 below, and a flowing gown whose pleats are discernible on the extended arm. The flesh tone is a beautiful reddish-brown.

7.2. Remains of piers along the south colonnade of the temple. A colossal Osiride statue of the king, like the one pictured in Pl. 4.2 and Fig. 11 at one time stood against each of these piers, facing right (north) into the open court of the temple.

7.3. The southwest corner of the temple in quadrant AD facing north, surrounded by the shattered *talatat* from the destruction of the temple.

7.4. The southwest corner of the temple facing east. The remains of the vertical torus-roll, a common device used on the exterior of a right angle in Egyptian architecture, is the feature that betrayed the nature of the *in situ* remains. Note the pattern of the block-laying.

7.5. Section through the southwest corner, facing south. Note the depth of the foundations, as well as the irregular laying of the *talatat* at the corner. The exterior face of the wall inclines inward at the expected angle of 3°.

7.6. *Talatat* recovered in 1978 from Area F on the slopes of the drainage canal, close to the point where probably the eastern gate of *Gm·(t)-p³-itn* was located. The face of the king and his bag wig are in evidence on the left. He appears to be leaning forward slightly, and his shoulder partly overlaps his neck, as though he were engaged in arranging or handling objects at a lower level than himself.

7.7. Recovering the Destruction Level of the Temple. Encountering the first tumble of *talatat* in trench III of E quadrant, December 1977.

7.8. E quadrant (facing east), as finally cleared down to phase L (the destruction level) of the *Gm·(t)-p³-itn* temple (Summer 1978). In the background are the emplacement beds for the piers of the west colonnade.

7.9. Removing *talatat* in quadrant EE, May 1979.

7.10. *Talatat* fragments recovered in A and AB quadrants, showing a bull in the process of being thrown preparatory to trussing and slaughtering.

7.11. The Jubiliee Processional (L. Greener). The king in white crown is born along on his basket palanquin, to be followed by the queen in her chair and the "royal children" (stand-ins playing a role, rather than blood offspring) in their hooped palanquins. The artist has caught the moment when the day's ceremonies are ended and the cortege has set out once more for the royal palace. A joyous crowd waits to cheer the royal family while in the background priests and courtiers libate toward the procession in a veritable forest of offering tables. The musicians in the lower left have for once appeared out of doors; usually their functions are fulfilled in the dining hall.

7.12. Part of a matched cultic scene of blocks from the *Gm·(t)-p³-itn*, showing the king (on the right), about to proceed out of his palace through a colonnade and into his waiting palanquin. In front of him, backing away down the steps, is the high priest of the sun, burning incense before his lord; while the prostrate figures in the colonnade are accompanied by the text "kissing the earth by the chamberlains"; from one of the royal progresses from palace to temple (R. Aicher).

7.13. Matched scene (TS 5521) showing the bearers of the queen's sedan chair, seen in part at the left. (The walking sphinx forms the arm of her chair). The head between the last two men in the row is that of a sunshade carrier. As there are five men shouldering the pole at the rear, and since they are paralleled on the other side by an equal number, we may estimate the total complement of bearers at twenty.

7.14. *Talatat* from the excavations in E-quadrant in 1978, showing the heads of palanquin bearers and the front of the large basket palanquin which bears the king; from a scene showing a royal progress from palace to temple.

7.15. *Talatat* from the excavations in E quadrant in 1978, showing a bowing priest shouldering a sacred standard; the two hieroglyphs above his head identify him as "prophet"; from a scene showing the king's entry into the temple (cf. Pl. 7.16).

7.16. *Talatat* from the second pylon showing part of a row of bowing priests shouldering sacred standards, in procession in front of the king. The text identifies the whole as coming from the *Gm·(t)-p³-itn*; from a processional scene showing the king's entry into the temple (cf. Pl. 7.15).

7.17. *Talatat* from the second pylon, originally from the north wall of *Gm·(t)-p³-itn*. King in red crown elevates jars, within the context of the *sd*-festival. Note the defacement of the king's features.

7.18. Matched scene (TS 5517) showing a procession of priests carrying sacred paraphernalia. In the upper register two priests carry sacred standards (cf. Pls. 7.15, 7.16) away from a kiosk containing an offering table, toward another edicule with closed doors, the sides of which are decorated with rearing uraeus serpents. In the lower register a row of priests carry door-hinges and the holy image of the goddess Selkit, the scorpion.

7.19. Titulary of Nefertity from Karnak. The text reads: "Heiress, Great of Favor, Mistress of Sweetness, beloved one, Mistress of Upper and Lower Egypt, Great King's Wife, whom he loves, Lady of the Two Lands, Nefertity".

8.1. Text from a representation of an offering table in $Gm\cdot(t)$-p^3-itn. The prenomen and nomen of the king on the left are flanked by the name of Nefertity on the right. Note "Akhen[aten]" carved over the earlier "[Amenophis], the divine, ruler of Thebes". At a later date someone took exception to the epithet in the prenomen w^c-n-r^c, lit. "unique one of Re," and carefully effaced the glyphs for "unique one" leaving the sun-disc undamaged!

8.2. Fragment of an alabaster offering table, excavated in 1979 in the area of the western gate of the temple. As in Pl. 8.1, the two cartouches of the king are grouped with that of Nefertity. The nomen of the king has been carefully abrased, and the name "Akhenaten" carved in as a replacement.

12.1. Sandstone block from a dismantled structure of Tutankhamun at Karnak. The name of the building occurs on the right in the epithet of the god of whom the king is said to be beloved, viz. "the Mansion of Neb-kheperu-re in Thebes" wherein the god is said to be residing. Tutankhamun's Horus-name and double cartouche were once inscribed on the left and in the center respectively; but after his death these were carefully shaved off with the result that the surface of the stone was lowered. The corresponding names of Ay were then carved in the appropriate spaces, but these too were erased almost beyond detection with the coming to power of Horemheb. Such accommodation of the *reigning* pharaoh at the expense of the deceased ancestors on standing monuments is characteristic of ancient Egypt.

13.1. Architrave block from the building of Tutankhamun mentioned in Pl. 12.1. The text refers to the Beautiful Festival of the Valley, a celebration held yearly in the spring when Amun crossed to western

Thebes to visit the mortuary shrines of the ancestors and "to rest in his temple." The lower line refers *inter alia* to "Nubians" and "the tribute of every foreign land," possibly an allusion to the activity in the south and north which marked the closing years of Tutankhamun's reign.

14.1. Part of a large matched scene (TS 165) showing the king in the blue "war"-crown and holding the crook and flail, proceeding from his palanquin into the temple. The fans which dispel the heat and at times shade the monarch, are visible at the rear. While none of the texts has been tampered with, vandals have dealt a couple of hammer blows to the king's face.

PREFACE

Laity often suffer under the delusion that "scholars" constitute a special interest group that stands united whenever any of its members is attacked, and refuses to allow any without the Ph.D. "union card" to participate in its activities. Nothing could be farther from the truth. The quest for knowledge (a pompous but apt phrase) through the application of reasoned scholarly method employs far more simple common sense than most people realize, and is therefore open to all. If professionals generally do it better, that is simply because they have had more practice; but it sometimes transpires that in a particularly thorny problem it is an unbiased amateur that makes a breakthrough.

A case in point is the establishment of the Akhenaten Temple Project, and the final cracking of the problem of Egypt's heretic pharaoh. In 1965 a retired U.S. foreign service officer, Ray Winfield Smith, became interested in the thousands of standard-size blocks called *talatat* that came from the ruined temples of Akhenaten. Mr. Smith, incredulous at being told that no scholar was then engaged in a serious study of the material, resolved to make an effort himself with the aid of the most modern methods available. Convinced that the human hand and eye alone could not effect the reconstruction of the jumbled blocks into the original relief scenes, Ray wisely enlisted the help of the computer. IBM agreed to assist the fledgling project, and Mr. Froh Rainey, then director of the University Museum of the University of Pennsylvania, lent academic sponsorship. Funding at first came from private contributions, but soon the Foreign Currency Program administered by the Smithsonian Institution in Washington gave a sizable grant. Smith next managed to recruit a number of academic consultants to provide expertise in art history and archaeology, including the late Professor John Wilson of the Oriental Institute, University of Chicago; Professor Abu Bakr of Cairo University; Mr. Gerhard Haeny of the Swiss Institute, Cairo; and the writer from the University of Toronto. A staff of assistants was assembled, made up largely of students from Egypt and Great Britain, and by early 1966 the "Akhenaten Temple Project" as it has ever since been known, was ready to take the field.

There could be no question of physically reassembling the blocks first, as other abortive attempts in the Forties had proved this approach time-consuming and unproductive. Rather Ray opted for a campaign in which all blocks would be photographed to scale, and the details of the reliefs coded in preparation for feeding into the computer. Then, with the computer's guidance, the photographs could be matched on paper into collages, and with hope the relief-covered walls of the original sun temples would soon begin to take shape. Physical reconstruction of the temples might follow eventually, but this was not to be the initial goal of the exercise.

Ray and his team proved indefatigable. For extended periods in the late Sixties blocks were photographed in their storage sheds, both in color and black and white, at the rate of several score a day. James Delmege, a former officer of the British Eighth Army during the North African campaign in World War II, supported the work with both his time and his money. When not in residence at Luxor, Smith was ranging far and wide over Europe, finding and photographing those blocks that had found their way out of Egypt and into European museums and private collections. Back in Cairo an office and laboratory had been set up, and here the staff busied itself with analyzing and matching the scale photographs which were now coming in steady streams from Luxor and Europe. Dr. Sayed Tawfik and Mr. Ahmed

Sanadili, both of the Faculty of Archaeology of the University of Cairo, lent their special assistance to the work, and soon, to everyone's gratification, the giant jigsaw puzzle began to go back together. It is impossible to overemphasize the importance of the flood of light hereby thrown on the "dark" period of Akhenaten's reign.

The present work takes a fresh look at the figure and program of Akhenaten and the twilight of the Thutmosid house, using the results of current research at Karnak, Amarna, and elsewhere in the Middle East. I have avoided the use of the term "Amarna" when referring to the site of Akhetaten; and for the sake of historical consistency have employed "Akhenaten" for the king only after year 5. The name "Jati," which is occasionally alleged in the scholarly literature to be Akhenaten's name for his god, I reject; not only is it an incorrect transliteration but the idea of a "god Jati" stems from a misconception of how Akhenaten viewed deity. Terms asterisked in the text are explained in the Glossary at the end of the book. To smooth the text for the nonscholar, I have largely dispensed with footnotes: those interested in further study in greater depth are referred to the section on Suggested Reading.

The names of Egyptian temples, and occasionally toponyms, have been transliterated but not vocalized. The reader will understand that, while scholars can (and do!) make intelligent guesses as to the vocalization of the ancient Egyptian language, vowel quality (if not quantity) remains speculative. On the other hand, I felt that supplying the usual "e" vowels between the consonants results in pronunciations that are *known* to be erroneous. For those interested, the temple of Akhenaten at East Karnak was probably pronounced something like Geéna-paten (*Gm.p³-itn*).

My special thanks are due my wife and assistant, Susan, who was a site supervisor and drew site plans on the East Karnak excavations (See Figs. 1, 2, 9, 12, and 18), and who labored long to type and correct my manuscript. Mrs. Diane Grazioli is responsible for the elevations in Figs. 10 and 11, and Ms. Adella Shaheen for the drawings in Figs. 3, 5, 13, and 16. The photographs of Pls. 2.1, 3.2–5, 4.1, 4.2, 4.5, 4.7, 4.8, 4.10–15, 5.2, 5.3, 7.1, 7.3–9, 7.14, 7.15, 7.17, 8.2, and 13.1 were taken by the expedition photographers J. Delmege, J. Hoffmeier, H. Assaad, and G. Allaby. I should also like to register my gratitude to the Egyptian Antiquities Organization, especially to Dr. Ahmed Kadry, Director General, to Dr. Gamal Mukhtar, his predecessor, and to Dr. Aly el-Kholy, sometime Director of Excavations for Upper Egypt, for the permission and cooperation which made possible the excavations in East Karnak. Warm appreciation is also tendered to my former student and friend Hani Assaad and his family, for hospitality and assistance on several research trips to Hermopolis and Amarna.

The ATP was funded originally by Foreign Currency grants from the Smithsonian Institution, Washington D.C. The continuation of the Project after 1975 and the excavations were made possible by grants from the Killam Program of the Canada Council and from the Social Sciences and Humanities Research Council of Canada, Ottawa, Ontario. Throughout our work we also received generous financial support from Mrs. Mari Milholland of Richmond, Virginia and Mr. J. Delmege of Mallow, County Cork, Eire.

Finally, I trust the reader will tolerate the digression in Chapter 15, which may seem like an exercise in self-indulgence. For over twenty-five years I have been studying this fascinating heretic, and I think it is time that I allowed myself a personal appraisal.

July 3, 1982

ABBREVIATIONS

ANET	J. B. Pritchard, ed., *Ancient Near Eastern Texts Relating to the Old Testament*, 3rd ed. (Princeton, 1969)
ASAE	*Annales du Service des antiquités de l'Egypte*
BASOR	*Bulletin of the American Schools of Oriental Research*
BIFAO	*Bulletin de l'Institut français d'Archéologie Orientale*
CdE	*Chronique d'Égypte*
EA	J. A. Knudtzon, *Die el-Amarna-Tafeln* (Leipzig, 1907–1915)
GM	*Göttinger Miszellen*
JAOS	*Journal of the American Oriental Society*
JARCE	*Journal of the American Research Center in Egypt*
JCS	*Journal of Cuneiform Studies*
JdS	*Journal des savants*
JEA	*Journal of Egyptian Archaeology*
JEOL	*Jaarbericht, Vooraziatisch-Egyptisch Gezelschap: Ex Oriente Lux*

ABBREVIATIONS

JNES	*Journal of Near Eastern Studies*
JSSEA	*Journal of the Society for the Study of Egyptian Antiquity*
LdÄ	*Lexikon der Ägyptologie* (Wiesbaden, 1972–)
MDIAK	*Mitteilungen des deutchen Instituts für ägyptische Altertumskunde in Kairo*
MIOF	*Mitteilungen des Instituts für Orientforschung*
RdE	*Revue d'Egyptologie*
ROM	Royal Ontario Museum
SAK	*Studien zur altägyptische Kultur*
Urk.	*Urkunden des ägyptischen Altertums* (Leipzig, 1903–)
ZÄS	*Zeitschrift für ägyptische Sprache und Altertumskunde*

AKHENATEN

THE HERETIC KING

INTRODUCTION

We are in a pre-Biblical World. Isaiah, Elijah, Solomon, David, Moses—all are yet to be born, and the world has no inkling of what is to be wrought through their agency. If Biblical "patriarchs" roam the misty periphery of this 15th-century society, they are wholly different (except perhaps for their names) from the figures who stride confidently through the Book of Genesis. And, similarly, our European roots have yet to be planted in the 1400s B.C. No Socrates or Pericles, no Alexander the Great, no Athens of the philosophers or Rome of the lawgivers has yet appeared even in embryo. Athens is a brute town in the boondocks, the site of Rome a fen for livestock not yet considered fit for human habitation.

Yet the 15th Century B.C. in which we find ourselves is remarkably "civilized." If we dare to try to get inside the minds of these Egyptians of Memphis, or these Canaanites of Shechem or these Hurrians of Ugarit, we will find them beset by the same problems, hopes, fears, and putative solutions we know thirty-five centuries later! The basic human aspirations remain personal freedom, self-fulfilment, health, gratification of the aesthetic sense. And, *mutatis mutandis*, a citizen of the Middle East in the reign of a Shaushatar (c. 1450 B.C.) or a Thutmose IV (c. 1426–1416 B.C.) had as much chance at successfully realizing these aspirations as a tax-ridden city-dweller in the "democratic" 20th century A.D.! There were labor strikes, and we have the dossier of the fact-finding committee set up to investigate them; there was inflation, and we have the price lists and the written complaints. There were taxes and tax-evasion; we have the tax returns to prove it. People got married and divorced, changed jobs or were fired, bought and sold property and left detailed wills. People said, as we do: "times aren't what they used to be, and the young don't respect their elders anymore." People also said: "better live it up now, because you can't take it with you." People went to parties and drank too much. When times got bad some said: "I wish I were dead." They read love poems and short stories, devotional works and horoscopes, books on "How to Win Friends and Influence People" and the occult. The farther back in time we glimpse our ancestors, the more like ourselves they become!

But what of Akhenaten? Is this misshapen individual in any way like us? One thing that must be remembered is that the "reformer" has been over the past century and a half subjected to a wide variety of interpretations depending largely on the fashion of the decade or quarter-century. To the early scholars in the field Akhenaten was a disguised female or a eunuch from the south (at a time when such were still common); to Breasted (after the German and British excavations at Amarna) he became "the first individual in History"; to the perspicacious classicist Toynbee his sun-cult was a prototype of the Roman imperial Sol Invictus of the 3rd century; to Freud (bent on "explaining away" Mosaic monotheism) he becomes a mentor of the Hebrew lawgiver. To some he is a forerunner of Christ, to others a great mystic whose teaching is still relevant.

A vast literature has taken shape and moved farther and farther away from primary sources, feeding and building on itself. Such a state of affairs has only disastrous results for those seeking historical reality; to tell history "as it really was" may sound simplistic, but it is hard to know how else to begin. One must constantly return to the original sources, the hieroglyphic inscriptions and the archaeological remains of Akhenaten's period, in order to avoid distortion. No one is absolved, of course, from using critical faculties in evaluating these sources; but to ignore them in favor of flights of fantasy is utter folly.

Besides bringing the reader face to face with the primary evidence and the original texts, the present work will attempt to place Akhenaten in his time. Akhenaten was not at all an isolated phenomenon, divorced from his time and place. In every way was his movement a product of past centuries, a cult that could only have come into being at the height of a great empire.

Much of the material in this book is based on the work of the Akhenaten Temple Project which has, since 1966, concerned itself with the remains of the heretic pharaoh at Karnak and Luxor, the ancient Thebes. As Akhenaten spent only the earliest years of his reign at this "Southern City," the book may appear to skimp on the longer span he spent at the new capital Amarna. But this imbalance, if such it really is, may prove salutary. The early years are a time of inception and experiment, and a correct presentation of them will be crucial for the interpretation of the entire movement.

Is Akhenaten really like us? Let us marshal the evidence, and in the last chapter we may be prepared to hazard an answer.

PART ONE

Imperial Egypt

CHAPTER ONE

The Extended Boundary

In the year 1560 B.C. Egypt was experiencing an exhilaration the like of which had never before buoyed the spirits of her people. Her armies had achieved a tour de force: they had expelled the hated regime of foreign rulers of Canaanite stock who for 108 years had lorded it over Egypt from Middle Egypt to the Mediterranean, and were about to overwhelm their Nubian adversaries on the African frontier at Aswan. This was not a false feeling of triumph: a signal victory had been won. Everywhere along the Nile optimism prevailed, and people rightly saw the times as a new beginning.

It is difficult to direct the gaze of the mind's eye upon these remote middle decades of the 16th century B.C. So many of the monuments and buildings that were shortly to be erected in the royal centers of Thebes and Memphis by the imperial Thutmosids★ obliterated the modest structures of their immediate forebears, Ahmose the Liberator and his son Amenophis I (*regnabant* c. 1573–1529 B.C.). In any event we can be sure that it was at first a modest

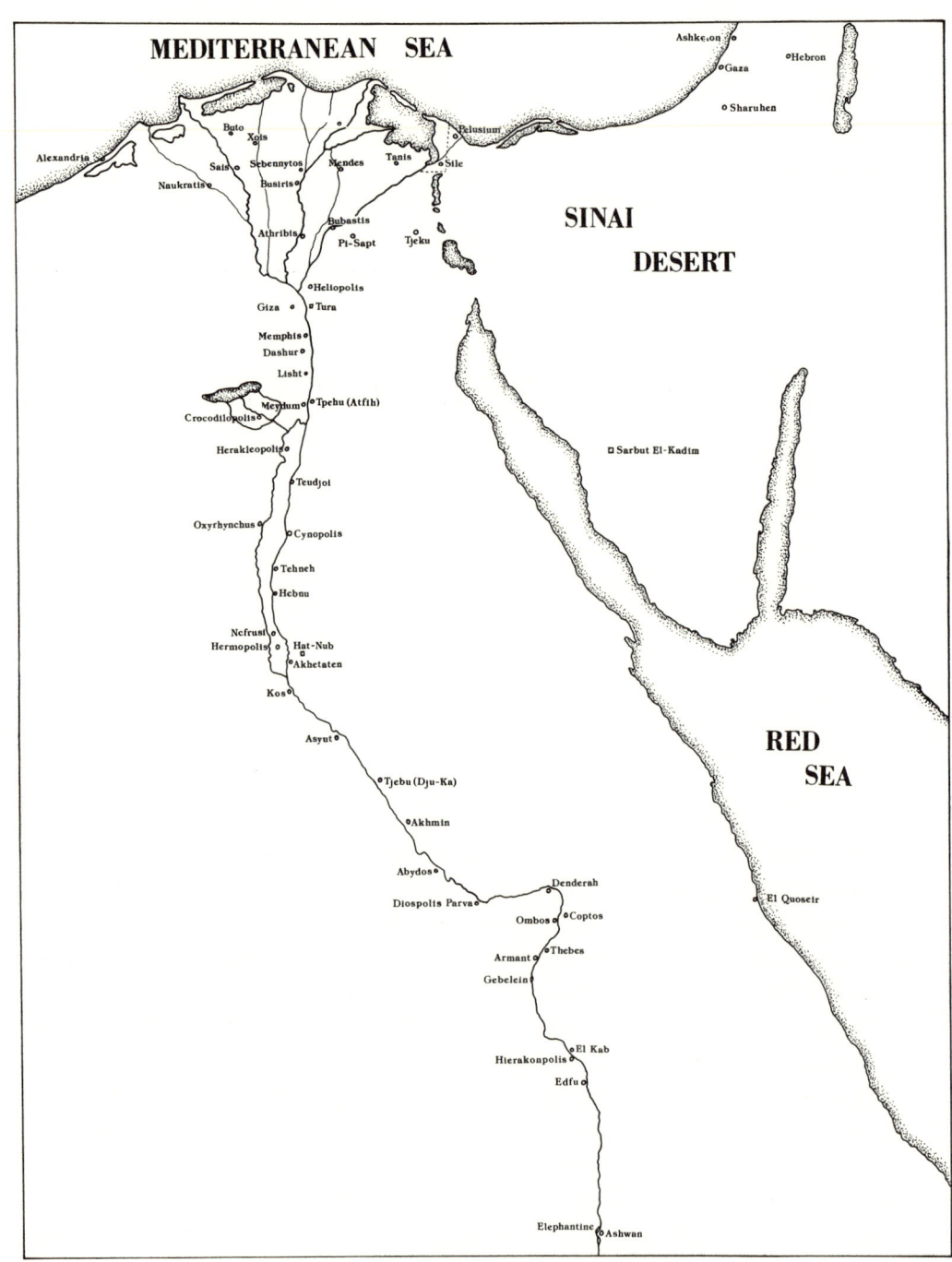

1. Map of Egypt to the First Cataract

and provincial court that the pharaohs of newly liberated Egypt could display to the world. Thebes, their town of origin and their erstwhile residence, lay in the hot southland, some 600 miles from the Mediterranean, in a part of Egypt known then as today for its rusticity. Here, in the 4th township of Upper Egypt, the eastern desert recedes to leave a broad fertile plain. Ahmose's Thebes we must imagine as a scatter of impoverished towns of mud-brick dotting this plain, each focused upon a small shrine dedicated to a local god. One such shrine, built originally by Senwosret I (c. 1971–1925 B.C.) as a royal chapel, was called 'Ipt-swwt, "(Kheperkare, i.e., Senwosret is) Most Select of Cult-seats," and was dedicated to the god Amun ("the hidden one"). Two miles to the south lay a sort of suburb, 'Ipt-rs'it, "the Southern Select (place)," where Amun was also worshipped; and five miles to the northeast was the town of Madu (modern Medamud) built around the shrine of Montu, the hawk-headed war god. Across the river, directly opposite 'Ipt-swwt, the mortuary temple of the great Montuhotpe I (c. 2061–2011 B.C.) could clearly be seen nestling against the golden cliffs of the Sahara. Montuhotpe had succeeded in reuniting Egypt after a protracted civil war; and Ahmose may well have divined that his, Ahmose's, memory would be linked by historical tradition with that of his great forebear because of their military achievements. Two miles north on the same western bank stood one of the oldest settlements in the area, dating back to prehistoric times. Latterly the houses had clustered here around the large tombs of Montu-hotpe's ancestors, the three Antefs, who had initiated and fought in the aforesaid civil war.

None of these towns, however, could claim the status of a nation's capital. The houses were poor mud-brick structures, the streets narrow, and the population small. The temples, especially those of 'Ipt-swwt and Madu, might proudly display steles and votive offerings dedicated by the kings over the four preceding centuries; but their *temenoi* were by no means as large nor their appointments as luxurious as those of temples of the Old and Middle Kingdom in northern Egypt.

Egyptian society in general during the twenty-five-year reign of Amenophis I had a distinctly conservative stamp. Egypt saw itself as the prosperous giant of the 12th Dynasty redivivus; in fact the early 18th Dynasty may be characterized as the final stage of Middle Kingdom society, delayed by four centuries and stripped of its imagination. Egyptians remained content with 12th-Dynasty models, whether for temples, pyramids, or cenotaphs, or for the relief-art and statuary with which they were decorated. In the early 18th-

GENEALOGICAL CHART

Dynasty	King	Reign
11th	Sehertowy Antef I	2134–2118
	Wahankh Antef II	2118–2068
	Nakht-neb-tep-nefer Antef III	2068–2061
	Nebhepetre Montuhotpe I	2061–2011
	Se'ankhibtowy Montuhotpe II	2011–2000
	Nebtowyre Montuhotpe III	2000–1998
	(Civil Strife 1998–1991)	
12th	Sehtepibre Amenemhet I	1991–1962
	Kheperkare Senwosret I	1971–1928
	Nubkaure Amenemhet II	1929–1895
	Khakheperre Senwosret II	1897–1877
	Khakaure Senwosret III	1878–1843
	Nymaare Amenemhet III	1843–1797
	Maakhrure Amenemhet IV	1798–1790
	Sobekkare Sobekneferu	1790–1786
13th	Sobekhotpe I	1786–1783
	Sekhemkare	1783–1780
	(13 kings)	c. 1780–1760
	Sobekhotpe II	1760–1756
	Khendjer	1756–1751
	(3 kings)	1751–1749
	Sobekhotpe III	1749–1747
	Neferhotpe I	1747–1736
	Sihathor	1735
	Sobekhotpe IV	1734–1725
	Sobekhotpe V	1725–1721
	Ya'ib	1721–1712
	Aya	1712–1700
	Merhotepre	1700–1698
	Se'ankhenre	1698–1695
	Neferhotpe II	1695–1692
	Hori	1691
	Sobekhotpe VI	1690–1688
	(18 kings)	1688–c. 1665

GENEALOGICAL CHART

Dynasty	King	Reign
15th (Hyksos)	Meribre Sheshy (Sharek/Salitis)	1665–1653
	? (Bnon)	1653–1645
	Merwoserre Ya'qob-el (Apachnan)	c. 1645–1635
	Seuserenre Khayan (Iannas)	1635–1595
	'Aqnenre Apopi (Apophis)	1595–1563
	'Asehre Khamudi (Asses?)	c. 1563–1558
18th	Senakhtenre Ta'o I	c. 1600–1587
	Seqenenre Ta'o II	c. 1587–1575
	Wadj-kheperre Kamose	c. 1575–1569
	Nebpehtire Ahmose	c. 1569–1545
	Djeserkare Amenophis I	1545–1525
	Okheperkare Thutmose I	1525–1514
	Okheperenre Thutmose II	1514–1504
	Menkheperre Thutmose III	1504–1451
	(Makare Hatshepsut)	1502–1483)
	Okheprure Amenophis II	1453–1426
	Menkheprure Thutmose IV	1426–1416
	Nebmare Amenophis III	1416–1377
	Neferkheprure Amenophis IV	1377–1360
	Onkh-kheprure Smenkhkare	1360
	Nebkheprure Tutankhamun	1360–1350
	Kheper-kheprure Ay	1350–1347
	Djeser-kheprure Horemheb	1347–c. 1318

Dynasty inscriptions we hear more than an echo, and sometimes the very words themselves, of 12th-Dynasty texts that were still on view. People wished to blot out the painful memory of the period of weakness that had intervened between the 12th Dynasty and themselves. In the list of royal ancestors used in the daily offering ceremony, the names of the 18th-Dynasty rulers follow almost immediately those of the 12th Dynasty; and, like the Middle Kingdom pharaohs, Ahmose and Amenophis I proudly display the appelative "son of Amun."[1]

1. D. B. Redford, *History and Chronology of the Egyptian Eighteenth Dynasty: Seven Studies* (Toronto, 1967), 71, 78.

Politically the early 18th Dynasty derived its inspiration from the late 12th Dynasty. Under Senwosret III (c. 1878–1843) the old social order, based on a sort of manorial system, had been weakened to the point of becoming inoperative, and had forthwith been replaced by a new, centralized system. Egypt was divided into three departments, Upper, Middle, and Lower Egypt, administered by royal heralds and "departmental officers" responsible directly to the king and the vizier. The latter, together with the chief treasurer, had specific functions and rather more powers than they had enjoyed theretofore. At the local level, the administration of towns and townships had been taken from the landed families; and though mayoralties could now be legally bought, sold, and inherited, the officeholders themselves wielded little of the power enjoyed by the feudal "barons" of old.[2]

Society in the 18th Dynasty was provincial. At its head stood the king, his chief wife, the lesser wives, and a large family of sons, daughters, nephews, nieces, and cousins at all removes. The disastrous "Intermediate Period,"★ when royal government had been weak and the country prey to invasion, had witnessed the introduction of the practice of calling military commanders by the epithet "king's-son"; now a plethora of these self-important "dud-princes" could be found throughout the realm.[3] Local cemeteries contained the tombs, not of the aristocracy, but of those who were essentially no more than municipal officials; service in the priesthood and the army were still the part-time functions of private citizens.

All this was to change beyond recall during the century following the death of Amenophis I; and to a great extent this was because of an international upheaval. The great victory of Ahmose over the Hyksos★ had flashed upon a world unchanged from the age of Hammurapi and the Mari★ archives. The descendants of Hammurapi still ruled the Tigris-Euphrates plain from their magnificent capital at Babylon, and fledgling states, among them Assyria, maintained a precarious existence on Babylon's periphery. In Syria three great states centered upon three major cities, whose political gravitational pull acted upon smaller settlements of less importance over wide areas. North Syria was dominated by Aleppo, ruling over the state of Yamkhad; while the Orontes basin owed allegiance to mighty Qatanum. In the south the cities of Galilee and the hill-country of Palestine fell within the political penumbra of Hazor, situated in the upper Jordan Valley. All

2. W. C. Hayes, *JNES* 12 (1953), 31ff.; *idem, Cambridge Ancient History* I² (Cambridge, 1961), ch. 20, 44f.

3. B. Schmitz, *Untersuchungen zum Titel S3-NJSWT 'Konigssohn* (Bonn, 1976), 255ff. 255ff.

these states, warlike in fact but respectful of an international code of honor, shared a common origin and culture. The ruling classes (and in the Levant, the populace at large) spoke West Semitic dialects often lumped together under the common rubric of "Amorite." Egyptians had become familiar with the Amorites when, from somewhere in the heart of Syria in the second quarter of the 17th century B.C., Amorite freebooters had ensconced themselves in the Egyptian Delta at the city of Avaris, to rule over the northern part of the land as "the Hyksos."

Probably as early as Ahmose's reign the security of this network of Amorite kingdoms around the Fertile Crescent was rudely shattered by the appearance of two new ethnic elements. Out of central Anatolia came a hitherto little-known group, the Hittites, who, under the leadership of their king Mursilis, descended upon Babylon and ended the rule of the Hammurapi dynasty. Turning south into Syria, the same force attacked and smashed Yamkhad, which henceforth disappeared from history. The result of these far-reaching sweeps of invincible armies was a temporary political vacuum on the upper reaches of the Euphrates. Aspirants to the rule were, however, in the offing. From the wide plains of central Mesopotamia emerged the Hurrians, a linguistic group indigenous to the region, but only lately elevated to political power. Dominated and organized by a small ruling class of Aryan-speaking nobility, a fragment of the great Aryan movement that in the middle of the millennium was descending on the Punjab, the Hurrians spread their hegemony eastward beyond the Tigris, and westward toward Anatolia and Syria. An empire was taking shape and expanding through the successful exploits of the "Hurri-host," and named for the region of its ruler's capital, "Mitanni." The Hittites were much concerned. For 200 years Mitanni and "Khatte"* eyed each other hostilely across the mountains of the Taurus.[4] But of more concern to our present purpose were the feelings of the Egyptians and the policy they adopted toward the newcomers.

Ancient Egypt's approach to what we call "foreign affairs" was in essence no different from any other nation's, in ancient, medieval, or modern times. All nations crave one or more of the following from their neighbors: their land, either for itself or for its strategic location; the raw materials or goods they can produce; the goods they can attract through trade; or the manpower

---

4. On Hittites, Hurrians, and Mitanni, see O. R. Gurney, *The Hittites*[2] (Harmondsworth, 1962); W. Hallo and W. K. Simpson, *The Ancient Near East, A History* (New Haven, 1973), 105f.

they can provide. Again, all nations have at their disposal only four ways of effecting their will: 1) amicable persuasion through agreement; 2) intimidation through the threat of force, implicit or explicit; 3) the stationing, following the application of force, of permanent military garrisons and political officials; or 4) the occupation of the neighbors' territory by large numbers of settlers. The first produces a set of international treaty relationships among equals, while the second results in what we would call a "sphere of influence" wherein the inhabitants "spontaneously" proffer their "benevolences"; the third and fourth lead to the actual subjection of erstwhile sovereign territory as either "province" or "colony." Now, during the Old Kingdom★ and the Late Period,★ Egypt's relations with her neighbors can most aptly be described as the enjoyment of a sphere of influence. Few, if any, garrisons or colonies were established: the occasional punitive raid or armed trading venture served quite well to overawe the natives of neighboring lands.

While some tentative steps had been taken during the 12th Dynasty to subjugate Nubia by establishing garrisons, the first major thrusts, both to the south and the north, that were consciously directed toward creating an empire were made by the Thutmosid kings of the 18th Dynasty. At first Egyptians honestly viewed this military activity as retaliatory or preemptive. The Asiatic enemy was "planning to destroy Egypt,"[5] and "the lands of Fenkhu★ had gone so far as to violate the frontiers"[6] of the land. Time and again the 18th-Dynasty pharaohs rationalize their empire-building as "smiting the foreign rulers who had attacked (the king)."[7] The enemy was on the march against Egypt! "All lands were gathered together, standing with one accord ready to fight. None was craven: reliance was placed in the numerous battalions, (for) there was no limit to (the numbers of) men and horses. On they came, stouthearted and without fear. . . ."[8] What else could pharaoh do but "attack all the lands as they marched against him" and "save Egypt in the breach"?[9] The Asiatics are the aggressors; Egypt is merely defending itself.

But, as time wore on, and the campaigns against the Asiatics proved successful and profitable, military activity was justified on other grounds. Pharaoh led his army northwards "in order to extend the frontiers of Egypt," a phrase that soon became the keynote of this type of imperialism. The

5. *Urk.* IV, 1254.
6. *Urk.* IV, 758.
7. *Urk.* IV, 1333.

8. *Urk.* IV, 1229.
9. *Urk.* IV, 1230.

activity was a good in itself, and carried divine sanction. God had intended the foreign lands as Egyptian territory from ages past, and he now granted pharaoh "title" to them: Amun it was "that gave him title as lord of all the foreign lands,"[10] and it was meet therefore that "all lands should labor for Egypt."

If foreign lands are Egyptian territory by legal right, any opposition by the natives toward Egypt, even if passive, is "outlawry, rebellion." "He who crushes all lands that had rebelled against him" is a common royal epithet from the middle of the 15th century B.C. And since the foreigners had broken the law, a law by implication sanctioned by the Egyptian gods, they become ipso facto "the abomination of Re."[11]

In certain traditions war, rather than being construed as an evil requiring justification, is held up as a desirable activity, a manly, robust art to be delighted in. The modern world is inclined to identify such a view of war with unsophisticated patriarchal tribal societies. Similarly in the ancient Near East the cultured city-dweller associated love of battle with the West Semitic Amorites and their kin, who are often described as seminomadic. In Egypt the warrior image of the Middle Kingdom rulers attests to the love of battle for its own sake, and in the New Kingdom it persists, principally during the reign of Thutmose I. This king speaks of his major campaign into Syria as undertaken "to slake his heart's thirst throughout the foreign lands."[12] "He found no one (i.e., on the battlefield) who could stand up to him."[13] A feeling of patriotism informs Thutmose's inscriptions, centered not simply on Egypt but on Thebes in particular; and one can sense his flush of pride in the recent reversal of the city's fortunes. He had come to the throne "in order to broaden the boundaries of Thebes, the confines of She-that-faces-her-Lord*. . . . I have made the boundaries of Egypt as far as the circuit of the Sun-disc, I have strengthened them that were in fear. . . . I have made Egypt mistress, with every land her subjects."[14]

The empire of the New Kingdom was principally the creation of three kings, Thutmose I (1525–1514 B.C.), Thutmose III (1504–1451), and Amenophis II (1453–1426). The first, though short-lived, established an ideal, the second lived up to that ideal and won an empire, the third nearly lost it.

The collapse of Yamkhad and the sudden rise of Mitanni exerted a powerful effect on the parochial Egypt of Amenophis I. Both he and his son-

10. *Urk.* IV, 184.
11. *Urk.* IV, 651.
12. *Urk.* IV, 9.
13. *Urk.* IV, 85.
14. *Urk.* IV, 102.

in-law and successor Thutmose I led ambitious campaigns which flew down the valley of the Orontes to engage the Mitannians close to home.[15] No territory was won, but a claim had been staked. Thirty years of inactivity, however, under Thutmose II and Hatshepsut allowed Mitanni to spread into North Syria, and by c. 1482 B.C. the major city-states west of the Euphrates and in the lower valley of the Orontes were bound to the Mitannian king by vassal treaty. Thus he was able to face a resurgent Egypt under Thutmose III with a powerful string of buffer states, ranging far to the south into Palestine. Two power centers in particular attracted coalitions of military might: Tunip, a large city in the lower Orontes basin, and Kadesh on the same river about 100 miles to the south. The former was probably subordinate to Mitanni by formal treaty; the latter was independent.

Kadesh organized the first strong coalition in opposition to Egypt. City-states from central Syria to the Negeb pledged troops to the king of Kadesh, and the combined forces met at Megiddo in the plain of Esdraelon intent on moving at once on Egypt. At the battle of Megiddo in the late spring of 1483 Thutmose preempted their plan and defeated them soundly. With the fall of Megiddo itself in December of the same year the coalition broke up, and Thutmose mopped up the minor pockets of resistance in Palestine piecemeal. By 1475, having reduced and garrisoned the Phoenician coastal ports, the Egyptians were able to attack Kadesh itself, and while the city withstood the assault, its power was broken.

Opposition to the Egyptian advance now gravitated further north. In 1474 an attempt by the king of Tunip to subvert certain coastal cities now vassals of Egypt was frustrated by Thutmose's timely appearance. The initiative had now passed to Egypt, and two years later came the decisive test. In the spring of 1472 His Majesty's fleet, complete with troop-transport ships, appeared off Byblos, and a party of soldiers was detailed to fell timber for shipbuilding in the nearby Lebanons. With prefabricated assault boats drawn on carts in the van, the army crossed the mountains and marched down the Orontes, heading for the great fortress of Carchemish on the Euphrates. The king of Mitanni must have realized too late the object of the campaign, and despite his resolve to hold his ground in North Syria he was compelled to retire. Three hard-fought skirmishes brought the Egyptians to Carchemish, and just when the fugitive Mitannians thought they had made good their escape across the Euphrates, Thutmose brought up his assault boats. The Mitannians bolted in panic. Their king "fled through fear

15. D. B. Redford, *JAOS* 99 (1979), 270ff.

to a far-off place," Thutmose gloats; their officers and nobles hid themselves in caves. Let the pharoah himself describe the sequel: "there was no deliverer in that land of Naharin (Mitanni) which its lord had abandoned through fear; (for) I hacked up his towns and villages and set them on fire, turning them into (ruin-) mounds which shall never be refounded. I took all their inhabitants prisoner, brought off as living captives; took their cattle without limit, and their property likewise. I took their sustenance away from them, harvested their corn and cut down all their fruit trees . . . My Majesty devastated it, and it was turned into red dust on which no foliage will ever (grow again)!"[16]

The victory seemed complete. No enemy remained on the field, and the Egyptians retired south at their leisure. As a supreme act of imperial conceit, Thutmose even took time out in the swamps of Niya★ to hunt the wild elephants who pastured there. "My Majesty took them on, in a herd of 120. Never had the like been done by any king since the time of the god, of those who of old had received the white crown!"[17]

Though Thutmose was destined to return annually to the scenes of his triumph in punitive campaigns for ten more years, a permanent empire had been fashioned. Attempts to expand it were made by his son Amenophis II: a far-flung expedition in his seventh year brought him to the plains of the modern Turkish Hatay, but his feats of personal bravery could not prevent the natural strength of the Mitannians from reasserting itself. Amenophis might rail against the Asiatics as he pleased, and even, in an act of savagery, hang seven Canaanite chiefs from the walls of Napata★ in the Sudan; but as soon as the Egyptian forces withdrew from Syria, the local city-states bowed to *force majeure* and acknowledged once again the hegemony of Mitanni. By the end of his reign Amenophis had wisely recognized the futility of continued hostility, and gave his approval to a treaty with his father's enemy. All North Syria went to Mitanni, including the lands of the lower Orontes and the Syrian coast. To Egypt went the cities of the Phoenician coast as far north as modern Tripoli. Thence the frontier crossed the Lebanons eastward to the desert and then turned south, giving pharaoh the rich lands of the central and upper Orontes, Damascus, Galilee, and territories that lay to the south. Though probably an ad hoc solution to the stalemate, this line of division between the two empires proved remarkably durable under Amenophis's son and short-lived successor, Thutmose IV (c.

16. *Urk.* IV, 1231; A. J. Spalinger, *JNES*   17. *Urk.* IV, 1233.
37 (1978), 35ff.

19

1423–1412 B.C.), when attempt was made of dubious intent and extent to involve Egypt in further military action in Syria. But there was more to gain by reaffirming the friendship with Mitanni; and, with the help of a timely dynastic marriage, the courts of Egypt and Mittani put hostility behind them and carved an alliance which stood the test of the next century.

Thutmose IV's *floruit* proved to be a harbinger of things to come. The king had, by his own admission, been helped to the throne through the agency of the sun god Reharakhte, who had appeared to him as a prince in a dream. Throughout his reign the king continued to honor the sun under the icon of the "sun-disc," a divine manifestation of which we shall hear more.

CHAPTER TWO

Glimpses of Imperial Egypt

The year was 1440. A drastic change had overtaken the rustic hamlets in the Theban district: they were now the wards and suburbs of an imperial city. Just three generations had elapsed, and old men could recall the parochial days before the empire. Those days were gone forever, and although pharaoh preferred to reside in Memphis in the north, Thebes received most of the booty of conquest. It remained the town of origin of the royal family, and the place where its members would be interred.

The Army

Not only the Southern City, but all Egypt had changed. Socially the changes centered upon the growing military class of professional full-time soliders.[1]

1. On the military in New Kingdom Egypt, see especially W. Helck, *Die Einfluss der Militärführer in der 18 ägyptischen Dynastie* (Leipzig, 1939); and A. R. Schulman, *Military Rank, Title, and Organization in the Egyptian New Kingdom* (Munich, 1964).

21

No longer had pharaoh to rely on the levies of manorial retainers: he could now draw on the "permanent armed forces" (*iwʿyt*), or the "braves" (*ḳnyt*), an elite corps commanded by a lieutenant general. Mustered as an expeditionary force, the army was grouped into divisions, each about 5,000 strong, organized by the part of the country the men came from—Thebes, Heliopolis, the Western Delta—and placed under the aegis of the appropriate god of that region. We hear of "the companies of pharaoh," each with its own standard, "brigades of archers," chariot warriors, and "marines." Titles that indicate full-time service begin to abound; transposing them into modern terminology we encounter: "commander in chief," "general of the army," "lieutenant (general)," "brigadier," "quartermaster general," "company commander" (lit. standard-bearer of the company), "ship's captain." The king's personal staff on campaign constituted a proud group: "king's barber," "king's butler," "king's armor-bearer," "king's bow-carrier," "king's charioteer."

Quite typical of Egypt, where bureaucracy permeates society, officers concerned with logistical support seem to be everywhere. There is the "chief keeper of the army registers," or draft lists as we would call them. The "quartermaster general" (lit. chief of the stable) controlled the supply of chariots and horses, while a "keeper of hostages" and a special "registry office" maintained records of the origin and present whereabouts of all POWs brought to Egypt.

Many of these military officers share a title in common, which yields a clue to the chief mechanism of organization of 18th-Dynasty society: they proudly display the appelative "child of the harem," i.e., the royal nursery. They were, in fact, the boyhood companions of the king's sons, who grew up with the heir apparent and gravitated, on the "old-boy" principle, into high military posts. Chosen, according to tradition, from the most promising and deserving children of the realm, these boys were accompanied to the court from their home towns by an entourage of relatives. Their good fortune entailed benefits especially for the distaff side of their families; we find the mothers and wet-nurses of these children holding prominent place among the ladies of the court, "the king's ornaments," throughout the dynasty.

The carefully selected childhood companions guaranteed the future king a band of followers that could be relied upon for unquestioned loyalty. One cannot mistake the note of love and pride in the biographical statement of the royal herald "who did not desert the Lord of the Two Lands on the battlefield in any northern country";[2] and time and again in the private tombs at Thebes the owner will stress that he "followed the Good God, the king of Upper and Lower Egypt . . . in every foreign land he marched through."[3] And pharaoh knew how to reward his own. Often the army was allowed to keep the spoils of battle. The king explicitly bestowed on his butler Neferperet a legal right to possess seven head of cattle the man had carried off "they shall be under your charge throughout your lifetime, and after you yourself grow old they shall pass from son to son and from heir to heir. Do not assign them to the sphere of the superintendant of cattle. As for any who may come to dispute it, do not let them have a hearing in any royal office."[4] Asiatic prisoners were sometimes assigned as personal servants to the Egyptian soldiers who had captured them. Thus, for example, the royal barber Si-Bast was favored with possession of his captive: "I have a slave who was assigned to me whose name is Yuwy-Amun. I captured him myself when I was following the Ruler [on campaign]. He is not to be beaten nor turned away from any door of the king's house. I have given the daughter of my sister . . . to him as wife. She shall have a share in my inheritance just like my wife and my sister."[5]

The Provinces

The empire this army had helped to win stretched, in 1440, over two thousand miles from north to south, an area occupied today by six independent states. The boundary steles, with which the Egyptians marked their frontiers, stood at Kenisa on the upper Nile, c. 350 miles north of Khartoum, and on the banks of the Euphrates within sight of the mountains of Anatolia. The startling demographic differences encompassed within the vast reaches now under their control were not lost on the Egyptians: a motif on the base of the royal dais during the 18th Dynasty, best seen in Nefertity's example (Frontpiece), shows a line of bound, kneeling prisoners in which Nordic blondes alternate with African blacks!

This recognition of the diversity of the provinces manifested itself also in a lenient and practical approach to the governance of the acquired territories. The inscriptions may rant self-righteously against the vile Asiatic or

2. *Urk.* IV, 1370. 4. *Urk.* IV, 1020f.
3. *Urk.* IV, 1441. 5. *Urk.* IV, 1369.

the Sudanese poltroon; in practice pharaoh suited his administration to the disparate needs of the conquered. The barren valley of the Nile south of Aswan,[6] despite a rudimentary attempt at monarchy in the 17th and 16th centuries, had never known any more sophisticated organization of society than the tribe. Early experiments at ruling through tribal chieftains were discarded after Hatshepsut's reign for a political form imported from Egypt. All the southern territory was placed under a "king's-son of the Southern Lands" who stood *in loco regis* as a veritable "viceroy" in our sense. Under him functioned two deputies, one for Nubia (Wawat), the other for Kush,★ corresponding to the bipartite vizierate in Egypt (Upper and Lower Egypt). Other institutions were imported from the home country. A department concerned with food production and supply, granaries, a treasury, a resident garrison, and a flotilla of ships for communication—all these comforting elements of orderly government began gradually to exert a "civilizing" influence over the south. Egyptian colonists assisted in the process. Great temples, often dedicated to the worship of deceased pharaohs, sprang up on the thin arable strips bordering the Nile, surrounded and served by growing cities, governed, as in Egypt, by "mayors" and scribal staffs.

The products of the south now entered Egypt unhindered. Minerals and building stone, cattle and wood were yearly transported back to Thebes by the viceroy as part of the "tax quota of Kush." Tropical products from much farther south found their way down the Nile to fill the coffers of the king and the gods. So much gold was shipped back from the Wady Allaki that for a prolonged period in the second half of the 15th century the price of the metal was substantially depressed. A better appreciation of the riches now at pharaoh's disposal may be had from a perusal of the impost of the south from the 38th year of Thutmose III:

> The labor quota of vile Kush: gold, 100[+] deben;★ 36 male and female Nubian slaves; longhorns and shorthorns, 111; bulls, 185 (total 306 [*sic*]); in addition to cargo-boats laden with ivory, ebony, and all the fine products of this land, and also the grain harvest. . . .
>
> The labor quota of Wawat: [gold], 2,844 deben★ (approximately 700 lbs.); 16 male and female Nubian slaves; longhorns and short-

---

6. On Egypt and Nubia in ancient times see especially A. J. Arkell, *A History of the Sudan to 1821* (London, 1961); W. B. Emery, *Egypt in Nubia* (London, 1965); B. Trigger, *Nubia under the Pharaohs* (Boulder, Colo., 1976).

horns, 77 in addition to [cargo-boats] laden with all the fine products of this land.[7]

Egypt's organization of her northern provinces followed markedly different lines.[8] In Canaan and Syria the Egyptians encountered city-states and small kingdoms as politically sophisticated and culturally advanced as their own land; there was no need to impose a bureaucratic framework *de novo*. The cities were kept in a state of subversion by a number of simple expedients. Most of the towns of Canaan were reduced to vassalage by demoting their rulers to the status of the local mayors in Egypt, and demanding the same taxes and services from them as from their Egyptian counterparts. The rulers of larger cities such as Hazor, Damascus, Tyre, or Qatanum might continue to refer to themselves as "king," but to pharaoh they were all designated by the common rubric "the man of town so-and-so." Internal administration remained in the hands of the natives. The Canaanite rulers kept their small feudal levies of "knights" (*maryannu*) and men-at-arms, and continued to trade and quarrel with their neighbors.

Legally all native rulers were bound to pharaoh by an oath. The Egyptian term "to cause (the vassal) to eat the *tryt*" (whatever that was) may originally have indicated some kind of ritual that accompanied the swearing ceremony; but the oath itself was a simple promise, taken in the king's name, to be loyal and not rebel. Because the obligation was personal, each new pharaoh upon his accession had to reimpose the oath, employing his own throne-name.

In practice the oath was accompanied by a polite demand that the vassal despatch some of his relatives to Egypt. Usually the male heirs were sent, but daughters, brothers, and sisters were also acceptable. In Thebes these were assigned a quarter of the town to live in under a mild sort of confinement, and during their childhood years received an Egyptian education. On the death of a vassal one of his sons in Egypt would be selected to go back to his patrimony and take over the reins of administration. These unfortunate Canaanite children, now *déraciné* and speaking only Egyptian, often found themselves completely ostracized by their own people, whose lan-

---

7. *Urk.* IV, 720f.
8. On the organization of the Asiatic provinces, see especially R. Giveon, *The Impact of Egypt on Canaan* (Göttingen, 1978); W.

Helck, *Die Beziehungen Ägyptens zur Vorderasien*[2] (Wiesbaden, 1972); J. M. Weinstein, *BASOR* 241 (1981), 1f.

guage and customs they had had no opportunity to learn. But from the Egyptian point of view, the advantage of having Egyptianized rulers in the subject states could not be gainsaid.

To faciliate Egyptian control, Palestine and Syria were divided into broad groupings of city-states, based loosely on geographical considerations. Each such provincial division was placed under an "overseer of the northern countries" (Akkadian★ šākin mâti, "territorial governor") sent out from the Egyptian court and usually headquartered in a major city. Thus Gaza was the residence of the governor assigned the oversight of Canaan north to Esdraelon, Megiddo (later Beth-shan) the headquarters for the upper Jordan and Transjordan, Kumidi in the Bekaa the district capital for Damascus, Galilee, and the Golan, and Ullaza (later Sumur) on the Phoenician coast the control center for the Phoenician coast and Amurru. Often the governor was assisted by a scribal staff and a small garrison of Egyptian archers. Although the garrisons were not numerically large—examples range from 50 to 200 troops—they had the reputation of being crack fighting forces, and Canaanite mayors and princes often vied with one another in beseeching pharaoh to supply such a peace-keeping force to their towns as well as to the district capital. The governor was responsible for the general policing of his district, the prompt despatch of taxes, and the execution of special orders from pharaoh's court.

Every year a tax assessor and his party of scribes made the rounds of the provinces, both in Asia and the Sudan, to establish the quotas to be paid in the coming months. Let the chief construction engineer and king's scribe Minmose describe this task, which he pursued under Thutmose III: "[I trod] Upper Retjenu★ after my lord (the king), and I assessed the taxes of [Upper] Retjenu★ [in silver, gol]d, lapis, various semiprecious stones, chariots and horses without number, cattle and flocks in similar multitudes; and I informed the chiefs of Syria what was their yearly labor. I (also) assessed the taxes of the chiefs of Nubia, in electrum, . . . in gold, ivory, ebony, numerous boats of dôm-wood (a kind of palm), this being the yearly quota. . . .[9] The commodities demanded varied with the natural products of the districts. The plain of Esdraelon to the northeast of Megiddo grew wheat for pharaoh's court, while Lebanon despatched cedar logs 60 cubits (100 feet) in length for Egyptian shipyards. Wine and oil were exacted from southern Palestine, lead from Syria, and copper from Cyprus. Egypt also

9. *Urk.* IV, 1442.

coveted the manufactured goods her new dependencies could produce or acquire through trade. Weapons of war, including swords, shields, armor, bows, and chariots were included in every quota set for Syrian towns. Especially sought after were the costly and elaborately crafted vases of metalwork which Syria could produce.

The reception of these taxes and tributes in Egypt was often organized as a gala event. Here is the description of a presentation of Nubian gifts during the reign of Amenophis II, taken from a monument of User-satet, the viceroy.

> His Majesty appeared on the midst of Thebes on the great dais . . . then [this] army [brought in] the tribute of the southern lands before this Good God (the king), while the entourage offered adulation and the army saluted His Majesty saying, "Great is thy power, O Good God! . . . This tribute is more numerous than (that of all other) lands, and has not previously been seen, since the time of the ancestors of former times! But it has happened unto thee, O Our Lord!" Tally of those bearing this tribute: those bearing [silver], 200 men; those bearing gold, 150 [men]; those laden with hm^3gt-stone,★ 200 men; those laden with ivory, [3] 40 men; those laden with ebony, 1,000 men; those laden with a variety of [fine] aromatics of the southern lands, 200 men; . . . those who bring a live panther, 10 men; those bringing dogs, 20 men; those bringing long- and short-horned cattle 200 m[en]; total of those bearing this tribute, 2,657 [men].

Cosmopolitan Egypt

The New Kingdom is the first period in Egyptian history since the Old Kingdom when large numbers of true slaves are found along the Nile; and this social phenomenon resulted directly, as we have seen, from the wars of foreign conquest. The principal beneficiaries were, at first, the temples. To the temple of Amun primarily and later also to the temples of other gods and the Theban mortuary temples of the 18th-Dynasty kings went large numbers of POWs. Thutmose III dedicated 1,588 Syrian prisoners to Amun from his Asiatic campaigns, while Thutmose IV dedicated the captive inhabitants of the Canaanite town of Gezer to the service of his mortuary temple. If we are to believe Amenophis II, 89,600 Asiatic prisoners were transported by his troops to Egypt and distributed to the temple estates.[10] Four generations after the founding of the empire the Asiatic slave population of Egypt was so numerous that Amenophis III could speak of his mortuary temple as "filled with male and female slaves, the children of the chiefs of all the foreign lands, the captivity of His Majesty . . . their number is beyond knowing, (the temple itself being) surrounded by the settlements of Syria."

Apart from captives of war who, of course, had no choice, Canaanites and Syrians began of their own free will to flock to Egypt. Commerce was a great attraction, and the Syrian merchant soon became a fixture in the Memphite marketplace. His strange West Semitic dialect was also heard in the streets of the major cities of the Delta, and Canaanite loanwords, especially technical terms, began to turn up in Egyptian itself. Indeed, "to do business in the tongue of Syria" is the Egyptian expression for "haggling" over a price![11] Some quarters in the larger cities were set aside for Asiatic residents.[12] Thus at Memphis we hear of the "camp of the Tyrians," centered upon a "temple of Ba'al of Memphis," and a "house of Ba'al and Astarte" at Peru-nefer near Memphis. Similarly, the Canaanite goddesses of fertility Anat and Kadesha found places on the periphery of the Egyptian pantheon; and Reshef the Canaanite god of war enjoyed a cult center somewhere in the Delta. Though the presence of these alien deities in Egypt must be set down to the religious needs of the new resident Canaanites, these strange foreign gods began shortly to exert an attraction on native Egyptians. Their names were transliterated into hieroglyphic, their representations cast in an Egyptian style, and occasionally their myths were even translated into Egyptian.

Merchant or POW the first expatriate Syrians may have been, but by the end of the 15th century B.C. Canaanites in Egypt had graduated to higher roles. They are found in the priesthood, as palace functionaries, and occasionally in the "Foreign Office." Many of them were pressed into service in the army, where we see the Syrian spearman side by side with the Sudanese black (Pl. 2.1). Those in higher offices were sometimes given Egyptian names, usually compounded with the name of the reigning king.

One class of Asiatic whose presence in Egypt, though not desired by the Egyptians, can still from time to time be detected in these halcyon days of

10. But see J. M. A. Janssen, *JEOL* 17 (1963), 141ff.

11. J. J. Janssen, *Two Ancient Egyptian Ships' Logs* (Leiden, 1961), 73.

12. W. Helck, *Oriens Antiquus* 5 (1966), 2ff; R. Stadelmann, *Syrisch Palästinensische Gottheiten in Ägypten* (Leiden, 1967).

2.1. Talatat from the ninth pylon showing Amorite and Sudanese auxiliary troops. Throughout Egyptian art Amorites are easily distinguished by their long beards and clubbed hair, tied round with a filet.

empire is the wandering bedouin with his flocks. To pasture his animals in the Delta and eat of the plentiful food produced there remained the goal of many a tribesman from the Negeb. By establishing fortifications at Sile,★ the entry into Egypt of the road from Gaza, and in the Wady Tumilat★ to the south, pharaoh's government sought to control the ingress of the no-mads. Entry quotas were set up, and entry times restricted to certain days of the month. Nevertheless it was still possible to meet sizable clans of bedouins in the Delta, tending to their flocks and carrying on their own customs, uninfluenced by their surroundings. In a New Kingdom school text, a father scolds his wayward son in a "model" letter: "you are wandering like a swallow with its young! You have reached the Delta after a long journey, where you mingle with Asiatics, and have eaten bread (mixed) with your own blood!" (a reference to a tribal ritual of blood brotherhood).[13] A renegade groom steals from his master, a military officer, then runs away: "Now he has entered right into evil (ways): he mixes with the tribes of the Shasu,★ having adopted the guise of an Asiatic!"[14]

13. J. Černý, *JNES* 14 (1955), 161ff.   14. Anastasi. i. 20.

It would be strange, in the light of the drastic changes that had overtaken Egypt in so short a time, if the image of Pharaoh did not undergo an alteration as well. And, in fact, the imperial pharaoh was considerably different from his dignified ancestors who had occupied the "Horus-throne of the Living" in centuries past. In contrast to the austere and remote king of the Pyramid Age who rarely appeared outside his palace, the Middle Kingdom had created the image of the "strong-man" king who "acted with his own arm." The Amenemhets and the Senuserts were mighty warriors who personally led their troops in battle. They revealed their divine nature in their ability to lay detailed plans without help from their courtiers, and then to put plans into effect through their own (physical) strength.

This aspect of the king as administrative and military genius was all but lost during the 13th Dynasty and the Hyksos period, but it reappeared with the rise of the new Theban dynasty in the south. The ideal was enhanced by the international situation: the Thebans were involved in a life-and-death struggle with the Hyksos. The prolonged period of hostility, when their efforts were directed solely toward winning the war, profoundly shaped their attitudes. Small wonder, then, that with the emergence of the victorious 18th Dynasty, the ruler should have assumed once again the mantle of the Middle Kingdom warrior-king. The military aspect of kingship thus continued, but with a new and important element added: the image of pharaoh as a healthy athlete and sportsman, with a perfect physique.

There is evidence that Ahmose had already cultivated this physical ideal of kingship, and its roots may in fact be found in the practice of fishing and fowling of the Middle Kingdom monarch;[15] but we first see the "sportsman-king" as a full-blown motif in literature during the reign of Thutmose III. The chatty, first-person narrative by a court scribe, describing the mighty acts of strength of the king, whether on the battlefield or in the hunt, had by this reign become a full-fledged literary genre. One of the earliest examples, the Armant stele of Thutmose III, runs as follows:

(This is) a compilation of the deeds of mighty valor that this Good God performed, viz. every successful deed of (personal) bravery. . . . If they were recounted individually they would be too numerous to

15. R. A. Caminos, *Literary Fragments in the Hieratic Script* (Oxford, 1956).

be put into writing. He used to shoot at a copper target . . . in fact His Majesty put one such in the temple of Amun (on display): it was an ingot of beaten copper, three fingers thick, with his arrow stuck in it, having passed through and protruding on the other side by three handbreadths. . . . I speak accurately of what he did . . . there is not fabrication—after all, it was in the presence of his entire army!—there is not one word of exaggeration in it. Whenever he spent a little time in relaxation, hunting in any foreign land, the number of animals he bagged would be more than that of the entire army. He shot seven lions in the space of a moment, and bagged . . . twelve wild bulls in one hour![16]

The sporting tradition was taken up and exploited to the full by Thutmose's son, Amenophis II, the true "muscle-man" of the dynasty. The mummy and statuary of this king show him to have been very much a scion of the Thutmosids: a thickset man, relatively short, with a round fleshy face and a boyish, cherubic appearance that belied his ferocity. He never tires of telling us in his inscriptions that no one else in the kingdom could match him in feats of strength and endurance. "There was none like him among the vast numbers of troops. Not one of them could draw his bow; none could outrun him. Strong-armed was he, one who never got exhausted when he took his oar: He could row in the stern of his 'Hawk-boat,' the equal of twenty men."[17]

Like his father, Amenophis excelled in archery. But one senses from his statements a gnawing desire to surpass his sire.

He drew 300 stiff bows, while comparing the work of their makers, in order to distinguish the incompetent from the competent. Now after he came out from doing what I have just told you, he entered his northern garden, and found set up for him four targets of Asiatic copper, (each) one palm thick, and spaced twenty cubits (a little over thirty-three feet) from each other. Then His Majesty appeared upon his chariot like Montu in his power. He seized his bow, grabbed a fistful of arrows, and drove north shooting at each one like Montu in his regalia, his arrows passing right out the backs of them. . . . It was a deed never seen before, nor heard of in gossip, viz. shooting

16. *Urk.* IV, 1245.   17. *Urk.* IV, 1279.

an arrow at a copper target, (an arrow) that went right through it and dropped to the ground. . . .[18]

Amenophis II was the first king born to empire, and in him we detect a congenital "imperialist" spirit. His contempt for "lesser breeds without the law" is as manifest as his pride in his strength. Yet withal he shows a trace of commendable wit. A letter, fascinating because of its lack of convention, which he sent to the viceroy of Nubia, was set on stone by this flattered worthy, and has luckily survived. The date is the twenty-third anniversary of his accession (November, 1428 B.C.) and the venue the harem. The king, the text tells us, was drinking wine (which in part explains the tenor of the missive). After complimenting himself on his total victory, and his viceroy on his prowess as a faithful warrior, the king proceeds to characterize himself as "[the slaughterer of the] Naharinian, he who sealed the fate of the Hittite, and the [owner?]" of various cities in Syria. Each is contemptuously identified metaphorically as a female: Sangar is a slave-girl, Byblos a maidservant, Alalakh★ a little girl, and Arapkha an old woman. "And the Takhsians,"★ continues Pharaoh, "they have nothing at all! Really, what are they good for? . . . Don't have any truck with the Nubians! Beware of their people and their magicians. See to the tax of the sharecroppers . . . don't listen to their words and don't meddle in their affairs!"[19]

It is difficult to criticize or advise a god-king whose every scheme and feat of strength succeeds beyond the wildest dream. How ludicrous in the mouth of Amenophis II is the solicitation of counsel from his court, a formula that the literature of the times demanded! Something of the impossibility of the situation seems to come through in the text describing the investiture of Ken-amun as steward of Peru-nefer:

> [His] Majesty [appeared] upon the great [seat] on the dais of electrum, [and the princes] and courtiers [were ushered in] in two rows on either side of him. Then [His Majesty] said to them . . . "My desire is that a [steward] be appointed . . . on whom my heart can rely. . . . Let each man say what he knows, and the king himself shall do what he suggests." Then they said to the king: ". . . shall Horus who is in heaven be led and guided across the sky? Shall directives be given to the acquaintance of Ptah,★ the patron of crafts? Shall Thoth★ be taught

18. *Urk.* IV, 1280.   19. *Urk.* IV, 1343f.

about speech? . . . If thou givest thine attention to him who knows nothing, by the next day he is cleverer than the wise. . . . Thou art Re, and nothing fails that thou hast ordained![20]

The contemporary perception of kingship had indeed created some brittle icons! The roles the king and his court were forced to play were virtually those of *opera buffa*; shallow, narrow, and comic. Had the "Horus-throne of the Living" been reduced to fit the rump of a macho, posturing pooh-bah?

20. *Urk.* IV, 1385f.

CHAPTER THREE

Amenophis III, The Sun-King

Forty years after the death of the great conqueror, Thutmose III, his great-grandson sat upon the throne of Egypt. Three generations had sufficed to bring to fruition the dream of the early potentates of the 18th Dynasty: Egypt was the unrivaled leader of the known world. Her messengers ranged un-impeded over the Middle East to Babylon, the Hittite Kingdom, Mitanni, and Cyprus; her merchant fleets sailed unmolested by pirates to Byblos, Tyre, Ugarit,★ Crete, and Aegean Greece. Untold wealth poured in from the gold mines of the Sudan and the far-flung lands of central Africa; tribute came annually from the north, borne on the backs of cowed Canaanites and Hurrians (Fig. 2).

Amenophis and His Family

Amenophis III reaped the benefits of the conquests of his enterprising pred-ecessors. No king in such circumstances could have failed to play a majestic

34

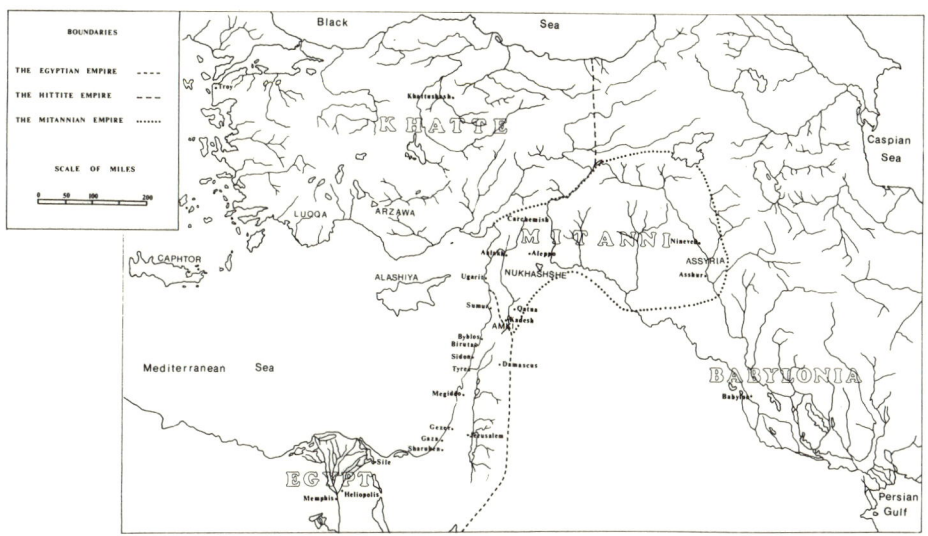

2. The Great Kingdoms of West Asia c. 1375 B.C.

role but Amenophis III took full advantage of the status and wealth of the country to fashion a court, a society, and an artistic taste that became proverbial for elegance. Amenophis became Egypt's "Sun-king" in truth, adopting the sobriquet "the Dazzling Sun-disc"; before the close of his reign he had attracted the epithet "Horus" par excellence, and later generations remembered him as the great "Hor." "King of kings, Ruler of rulers," ". . . he who lays Egypt's foundations . . ." these epithets, bombastic though they seem, were not far off the mark: Amenophis III and the Egypt he ruled never had been, nor would be again, in such a position of absolute power in the world.

As did all pharaohs upon their accession, Amenophis III took a title consisting of five names: "1. Horus, Mighty Bull, appearing in truth; 2. the Two Ladies [the patron goddesses of Upper and Lower Egypt]: mighty and strong, subduer of the Asiatics; 3. Golden Horus: ruler of truth, developer of the Two Lands; 4. King of Upper and Lower Egypt. Nebmare; 5. Son of Re, Amenophis the Theban Ruler." On all formal proclamations of the king this fivefold name would appear; but equals or favored magnates could address him by his praenomen, Nebmare (pronounced at the time *Nimmu^ca-ri^ca*★).

Probably at the outset of his reign Amenophis, who could have been no more than a teenager, took a young lady in marriage. It is unlikely that the

35

marriage would have taken place during his father's lifetime, or that court traditionalists would have arranged a marriage to a commoner. And that was precisely the young monarch's choice: a girl named Tiy from a village in Middle Egypt, daughter of a foreigner named Yuya who had become a lieutenant general of chariotry in the Egyptian armed forces, and an officiant in the temple of Min★ at Akhmim.[1] In spite, however, of her nonroyal origin, Tiy became "Great King's Wife" (i.e., the chief of all the king's spouses) and wielded considerable power in the kingdom. Though in part traditional, her epithets convey something of her exalted standing: "the Heiress, greatly praised, Mistress of all lands, who cleaves unto the king . . . Lady of Rejoicing, Mistress of Upper and Lower Egypt, Lady of the Two Lands." The marriage announcement of the young couple (the so-called "Marriage" scarab) reflects what it meant for a young woman to be married to the great king of kings: "the Great King's Wife Tiy: the name of her father is Yuya, and the name of her mother is Tuya. She is the wife of the mighty king, whose southern frontier is at Karoy [central Sudan], and whose northern is in Naharin [northwestern Iraq]."[2]

This early union with Tiy, though probably fraught with mutual affection, did not prevent Amenophis from entering into other liaisons. Besides his many Egyptian mistresses, he is known to have married two Syrian princesses, two princesses from Mitanni, two Babylonian princesses, and a princess from Arzawa (southwestern Asia Minor). Ladies continued to arrive in grand style throughout his reign: one of the Mitannian princesses whom he married in his 10th year, a certain Gilu-khepa, daughter of the Mitannian king Shutarna II, came with an entourage of 317 ladies-in-waiting. The constant demand of the king of his provincial governors was for more beautiful servant-girls; in a fortunately surviving directive to the prince of Gezer (just south of the Jerusalem–Tel Aviv highway in modern Israel) Amenophis writes:

> I have sent you this tablet to inform you that I am sending you Colonel Khanaia, together with a consideration, to fetch beautiful women. Silver, gold, garments . . . various precious stones, a seat of ebony, and sundry other fine things: total (value), 160 deben.★ Total women,

---

1. J. E. Quibell, *The Tomb of Yuua and Thuiu* (Cairo, 1908); J. Yoyotte, *Kêmi* 15 (1957), 25ff.

2. *Urk.* IV, 1741.

40; 40 pieces of silver being the cost per woman. So send very beautiful women, but none with shrill (voices). Then the king your lord will say to you "that is good." To you life is sent. And may you know that the king is in good health, like the sun god, and that his troops, his chariots and his horses are very well indeed; for Amun has put the Upper Land and the Lower Land, the rising and the setting of the sun under the feet of the king.[3]

When foreign kings asked for Egyptian princesses in marriage, however, none was sent, not out of any fear (as has been suggested) of Egyptians dying abroad, but out of sheer political arrogance. When the king of Babylon requested a daughter of the king of Egypt he received the curt reply: "From of old a daughter of the king of Egypt has not been given to anyone." In vain the Babylonian protested, "Why do you speak so? You are a king and may do as you wish. . . . If there is any woman who is beautiful in your opinion, send her. Who shall say she is not a king's daughter?"[4] Nevertheless, no Egyptian girl was sent.

While the offspring of Amenophis III's marriages must have thronged the royal palace, it was only his six children, two boys and four girls, by the Great King's Wife Tiy that counted in the succession.[5] The oldest girl, Sat-amun, seems to have been her father's favorite, and when she had reached puberty she was elevated to the rank of Great King's Wife, like her mother. The oldest son, who stood in line for the throne, was named Thutmose after his grandfather, and was stationed in Memphis as high priest of Ptah, as were most heirs apparent during the 18th Dynasty. The second son, born perhaps toward the beginning of the third decade of his father's reign (c. 1385 B.C.), was named for his father, Amenophis.

Amenophis the Strong Man

Amenophis III had grown up in a court in which, as we have seen, the monarch was expected to fill the role of great sportsman and mighty warrior, and in the early years of his reign the "Sun-king" lived up to expectations. In the full vigor of young manhood, possessed of a vast treasury and a

3. *EA* 31a.
4. *EA* 4.

5. B. van de Walle, *CdE* 43 (1968), 36ff.

physique and personality alike attractive to those around him, Amenophis set out to establish a hunting legend. In the second year of his reign

> they came to tell His Majesty "there are wild bulls on the desert upland of the district of Shat-meru." His Majesty sailed north in the ship "Appearing-in-Truth" at the time of evening, setting a good course. Successful arrival was made at the district of Shat-meru at dawn, and His Majesty appeared in his chariot with his entire army following him. Officers and enlisted men of the entire army, along with the young recruits, were detailed to keep watch on these wild bulls. Lo, His Majesty ordered that these wild bulls be herded within a wall and ditch (enclosure), and then did His Majesty proceed against all these wild bulls. Tally thereof: 170 wild bulls. Tally of His Majesty's bag in the hunt of this day: 55 wild bulls . . .

It was a similar story with respect to other wild game: "Tally of the lions which His Majesty bagged through personal archery from year 1 to year 10: 102 fierce lions."[6]

It was more difficult for Amenophis III to find an opportunity to don the helmet and play soldier in earnest. The by-now legendary might of Egypt was sufficient to forestall invasion from without and to discourage the would-be rebel in the provinces of the empire. Hence it must have been with some ingenuity that, in year 5, month 3, day 2, a minor disturbance in the Sudanese district of Ibhat was construed by the king's advisors as an excuse to send in the army. Ibhat, a distant principality south of the Second Cataract, still only partly "civilized," had apparently fallen into the habit of raiding Egyptian settlements in the southern provinces; now it must be taught a lesson. The king's viceroy in the Sudan, Merimose, was put in charge of the operation, and it is his official stele set up at Semna that I quote: "When the time of harvest came for those vile, fallen ones of Ibhat, each man went about his own business. Then it was that Pharaoh's [army], which was under the command of the Viceroy, was mustered and the squadrons were formed . . . each man being with his (own) village, from the fortress of Baky* as far as the fortress of Taroy,* which amounts to fifty-two *itr** of sailing. The mighty arm of Nebmare got them in one day, in a single hour, and a gr[eat slaughter] was made [of the enemy. Their children,

6. *Urk.* IV, 1739f.

wives,] and cattle [were brought off] without any escaping. . . ." Yet when the captives and enemy dead are listed, one can easily see what a storm in a teapot the whole affair really was: "Tally of the booty that his Majesty brought off from the highland of vile Ibhat: living Nubians, 150; skirmishers, 110; female Nubians, 250; servants of the Nubians, 55; their children, 175. Total of the living, 740; hands (i.e., the dead), 312, added to the living (i.e., grand total), 1,052."[7]

In spite of the paltry nature of this policing action, it was blown out of all proportions in the official records. Steles were left at Buhen, Semna, and on the island of Sai to commemorate the king's triumph. As the host passed Aswan going north on the return voyage, three large and bombastic "steles of victory" were carved on the rocks. On one of them Amun was made to say: "Welcome in peace, O my beloved son! . . . My heart is greatly gladdened to see thy victories and the power of thy fame overwhelming foreign lands! I give thee the southerners as thy serfs, and the northerners abjectly submitting to thy fame . . ."[8] and so on. The repute of the event lived nearly 1,800 years: in the fourth century A.D. Eusebius could still record how the "aethiopes" in year 5 of an Amenophis had borne down upon Egypt!

Amenophis the Diplomat

But Egypt during Amenophis III's reign had no need to go to war. Her international diplomacy was carried on from a position of strength, and her will was effected through persuasion, diplomatic gift, marriage, or veiled threat. The era of the "Pax Aegyptiaca" was at its height.

The designation of nations as superpowers, middle-ranking powers, or "third-world" states, a terminology commonly thought to have been invented in the 20th century, is as old as civilized man himself! The Amorites,[9] who came to the fore politically and culturally shortly after 2000 B.C., were highly conscious of their tribal heritage, and were sensitive to the nuances of political supremacy or subordination. Their system of international diplomacy was based on a simple patriarchal model, but it survived throughout

7. *Urk.* IV, 1659f.
8. *Urk.* IV, 1664.
9. See Hallo and Simpson, *Ancient Near*

East p. 71ff. and the literature there cited; J. M. Munn-Rankin, *Iraq* 18 (1956), 68ff.

the ancient world until the coming of the Sea Peoples.★ Of rulers who were free and independent there were "great kings" and "lesser kings." Great kings were very few in number, of equal rank, and preferred to intermarry, although none was under any obligation to his peers. A strict, though unwritten, etiquette governed the relations between kings, and if such relations were particularly close, involving intermarriage, the "sharing" of possessions, or a bilateral treaty, the two monarchs were said to be "brothers." Custom then demanded a regular, and ostensibly voluntary, exchange of presents, which at times took on the dimensions of a "gift-giving" economy, based on luxury items.[10] A regular exchange of letters was also demanded, and pursuant thereto an elaborate mode of epistolary address was created, which could not vary on pain of severe displeasure.

"Lesser kings" were often vassals of great kings, and the relationship was spoken of in filial terms: the lesser king was the "son," his suzerain his "father." Brotherhood and intermarriage were all but impossible, and relations with other kings only if the suzerain permitted it. A treaty bound the little king to his "father" and laid out the former's obligations, which included taxes, trade rights, and the supply of troops to the suzerain's army.

In the world of Amenophis III there were less than half a dozen great kings, and of these Amenophis himself was preeminent. The king of Babylon also boasted a great kingship, as did the king of Mitanni, but neither was really pharoah's equal. On the periphery hovered the king of the Hittites in Asia Minor, a great king by virtue of his ancestor's victory over Aleppo and Babylon in the 16th century B.C.; but both he and the kings of Cyprus and Crete were not yet in the "mainstream" of world politics. Amenophis III's relations with all these states are spelled out in the fortunately surviving letter-files from the archives of his reign, a source that affords a more intimate glimpse of him and his "brother kings" than even contemporaries had.

Amenophis III had married at least two Babylonian princesses. The brother of one, Kadashman-enlil, shows himself in his letters to be an irascible old fellow, a complainer, and an inveterate haggler. Some of his complaining may not have been without cause: Amenophis neglected on one occasion to send a message of condolence when Kadashman-enlil was ill, and on another delayed answering a letter for six years! The Babylonian

10. Cf. K. Polanyi, *Trade and Market in the Early Empires* (Glencoe, Ill., 1957), 262; J. Van Seters, *Archaeological News* 8 (1979), 35ff.

potentate (scion of a family of Kassite extraction from the Zagros Mountains of western Iran) had agreed to marry his daughter to Amenophis, but requested a shipment of gold first, for a palace he was building:

> Now as for the gold about which I wrote you, send very much gold, as much as possible, now quickly, (even) before your (return-) messenger reaches me, . . . that I may carry through the work I have undertaken. If during the harvest . . . you send the gold for which I sent to you, then I will give you my daughter. . . . But if you do not . . . send the gold so that I cannot carry through the work I have undertaken, why should you send anything at a later date? When I have finished the work I have undertaken, why should I then want gold? Even if you should then send 3,000 talents of gold, I would not accept it, but would return it to you; nor would I give you my daughter in marriage.[11]

Indeed negotiations over this marriage took on the dimensions of an international incident. In another letter Kadashman-enlil remonstrates with his Egyptian brother-in-law: "Indeed, you want my daughter in marriage, but my sister whom my father gave you is with you there, but no one has seen her (recently), or knows whether she is alive or dead. . . . You spoke to my messengers when your wives were assembled and standing before you: 'There is your mistress before your eyes.' But my messengers did not recognize her. Is it really my sister that looks like that?"[12]

In his 10th year Amenophis III married Gilu-khepa, daughter of Shutarna II, king of Mitanni. About six years later Gilu-khepa's brother Tushratta took the throne under dubious circumstances, and at once set about to establish good relations with his brother-in-law. He was eminently successful: no other great king grew so close to Amenophis III as Tushratta did. His letters may be wordy, brimming with a friendship occasionally tending toward obsequiousness, but they are always much more tactful than those of his Babylonian counterpart:

> To Nimmuᶜariᶜa the great king, king of Egypt, my brother, my brother-in-law, who loves me, and whom I (also) love, speak as follows: thus says Tushratta, the great king your father-in-law who loves you, the king of Mitanni, your brother. Things are going well with

11. *EA* 4:36–50. 12. *EA* 1:11ff, 37ff.

41

me; may things go well with you, and with your house, my sister, your other wives, and with your sons, your chariots, your horses, your armed forces, with your land and all of your possessions may things go very, very well indeed. During your father's time they entertained very amicable relations with my fathers. . . . Now, since you and I mutually enjoy friendly relations, you have enhanced them tenfold over (what) my father (enjoyed). . . . and when my brother sent Mani his messenger with my brother's verbal message, "bring your daughter for marriage with me, to be mistress of Egypt," I did not sadden my brother's heart. . . . may (Mani) conduct her safely to my brother's land, and may Ishtar and Amun make her measure up to my brother's desire. . . .

And again: ". . . and let my brother send me exceeding much gold, without measure . . . for in my brother's land gold is as plentiful as dust . . . and let not the gold which I ask for bring dismay to my brother's heart, and let not my brother sadden my heart. . . ." And further: "I have honored Mani, my brother's messenger, and all the military escort of my brother which came with Mani. . . . when Mani comes my brother can ask him whether I have honored him very, very much. He will tell my brother, and my brother shall hear what I have done . . . forever I will do my brother's desire, and may my brother do my desire! Just as men love the sun, so may the gods grant that we for ever love each other in our hearts!"[13]

Amenophis the Publisher

A seeming awareness of the uniqueness of the reign early led to the development of a new type of document for disseminating information, the "historical scarab." Earlier (and later) kings occasionally used the scarab seal as a means of commemorating and publicizing an important construction project or a victory, but Amenophis III carried the practice to its highest stage of development. Apparently to set on record for contemporaries and posterity the major events of his reign, he had published at intervals series of large scarabs on which were inscribed a brief record of the particular event in question. Scores, perhaps hundreds, of each issue were turned out, and

13. *EA* 19, 21.

distributed throughout the provinces and to foreign rulers. Today nearly every museum in the world possesses some specimens of each of the six or seven known issues. In this way did the king publicize, in a manner approaching the methods of a modern news medium, the public works and acts of his reign. Thus we know of his marriage to Tiy and Gilu-khepa, his bull- and lion-hunts, his construction of an irrigation basin for Tiy, a temple to Khopry,* and so on.

Before the close of the reign the fad of issuing commemorative scarabs had fallen into abeyance, but the king's divine feats continued to be disseminated abroad. On pylons, on free-standing steles, on the natural rock, inscriptions continued to noise abroad the works of this superhuman being. And for once the hyperbole of an Egyptian royal text has some warrant: "Lo, His Majesty's heart was satisfied with making very great monuments, the like of which had never come into being since the primeval age of the Two Lands."[14]

Amenophis the Builder

The reign of Amenophis III witnessed the first great building boom of the 18th Dynasty. A century later his gigantic constructions were envied and emulated by Ramesses the Great, and a millennium later his colossal statues were mistaken for images of a Greek hero, Memnon.

Already in year 2 the building program had begun: "His Majesty commanded that new quarry chambers be opened to extract fine limestone . . . to build mansions (that shall last) for millions of years, after he had found buildings . . . fallen into disrepair since days of old. It was His Majesty that began renovations."[15] And soon the whole land was humming with construction work. A new temple to Thoth was erected at Hermopolis in year 2, followed by other temples, at Elephantine (to Khnum),* Letopolis, and Elkab (Nekhbit).* An enormous temple called "the Castle of Nebmare" was thrown up at Memphis, Amenophis's residence, where both Ptah and himself were worshipped jointly. The provinces were not neglected. A most beautiful shrine, dedicated to "Nebmare, Lord of Nubia" (the king as local moon god) arose at the Nubian site of Soleb, and others at neighboring Sadeinga (to Tiy) and Wady es-Sebua.

14. *Urk.* IV, 1648.　　　　15. *Urk.* IV, 1681.

But it is among the ruins of Thebes that Amenophis's building program is most in evidence today. Although possibly born there, Amenophis had resided, like most of his predecessors, in the major center of Egypt, Memphis, to the north at the apex of the Delta. We find him still residing there in his 20th year, but as the third decade of his reign wore on, he apparently decided to move the court to the "Southern City," Thebes. The final ten years of the reign witnessed an extended program of construction and embellishment of the new southern residence. A vast mortuary temple, fronted by two colossal statues of the king seventy feet tall, rose out of the flat plain on the west of Thebes to house the mortuary service of the king's spirit throughout all eternity. About a kilometer to the south the king's engineers planned an enormous harbor-basin for merchant ships, cut out of the alluvial flats and connected by canal to the Nile. On the western side of the basin lay docks, warehouses, a settlement, and the large, rambling palace thrown up hastily for the court. Constructed of mud-brick, wood, and other light materials, when finally completed the whole complex measured about 400 meters east-west by 650 meters north-south. It contained a palace of the king with quarters for his wives, an audience hall with private apartments, a palace for Tiy, villas for officials, servants' quarters, and a small temple of Amun. Although colorfully painted, the whole must have had a slightly unsettling effect on the viewer because of its unsymmetrical, if not ramshackle, appearance.[16]

By contrast the "houses of the god" the king brought into being on the east bank of the Nile were models of orderly layout in the best tradition of the processional type of temple. Sandstone was the medium in which the splendid new temples of Montu on the north and Mut the mother goddess on the south of Karnak were constructed; and the same stone was also employed for the beautiful temple of Amun in "Southern Opet" (modern Luxor), about three kilometers south of Karnak on the Nile. It was probably Amenophis or his architects who conceived the notion of connecting the scattered foci of settlement that constituted ancient Thebes into an organic whole by sphinx-lined avenues. The avenues led, of course, to the temples, and to provide a suitable point of arrival giant pylons had to be erected. At the great temple of Amun this meant fronting the western and southern ends of the two axes of the temples with fortresslike entries. On the west fronting

16. See W. S. Smith, *Art and Architecture in Ancient Egypt* (Harmondsworth, 1958), 160ff.; D. O'Connor, *Expedition* (Summer, 1979), 52f.; *idem, Excavations at Malkata and the Birket Habu 1971–74* (Warminster, 1977).

the river, Amenophis swept away a motley welter of small shrines, way stations and steles, dating as far back as the Middle Kingdom, that had previously stood between Thutmose I's pylon (now the fourth pylon) and the temple wharf. The combined masonry of all these structures was used as filling material in the new pylon. The latter, now the third pylon, stood in front of Thutmose I's old one, and was intended to act as a final façade to the temple; in order to prevent any successor from contemplating further construction to the west, a canal and turning basin for ships was dug in front of the monumental gate. (Ironically it was here, just seventy years later, that the giant hypostyle hall of "modern" Karnak was built, concealing forever Amenophis III's mighty pylon; the latter's gradual fall to ruin has resulted in the coming to light once more of the inscribed blocks and dismembered reliefs of the earlier buildings of which it was composed). On the south of the Amun temple Amenophis erected another, though smaller, pylon, facing the precinct of Mut, and set up two colossal standing statues of himself, flanking this gate on its external face. This pylon, however, (a precursor of the later tenth) was never decorated by him, and before the end of the century had been torn down and replaced. Of the now-shattered colossi all that remains in place is a single gigantic foot.[17]

The outlay of wealth represented by all this building is unusually large. The recorded figures of the metals and precious stones that went into the Montu temple is quite staggering: 3.25 tons of electrum, 2.5 tons of gold, 924 pounds of copper, 1,250 pounds of lapis lazuli, 215 pounds of turquoise, 1.5 tons of bronze, and over 10 tons of beaten(?) copper. Such was the return on Egypt's investment in an empire!

Possession of wealth beyond measure and the willingness to spend it are not always accompanied by good taste, but in Amenophis's case a discriminating taste was most certainly present. Whether in monumental architecture, painting, relief, or in the "lesser" arts, craftsmen display a confident and complete command of their medium, which was never again equalled in the 1,500 years Egypt's pharaonic culture survived. The grace and balanced proportions of the papyriform columns of the Luxor temple, and the splendor and majesty of the Memnon colossi alike evoke a breathless awe of the skill, imagination, and ambition of craftsman and patron. If Amenophis himself set the standard of aesthetic appreciation, his court did not lag

17. C. F. Nims, *Thebes of the Pharaohs* (London, 1965); G. Bjorkman, *Kings at Karnak* (Uppsala, 1971).

3.1. Relief from the tomb of the Vizier Ramose showing the chariotry general and the king's ambassador, Maya, and his wife, Urol.

far behind. The beautiful tombs of his ministers at Thebes are decorated with delicate, low reliefs, showing elegant ladies and gentlemen at meal, and capturing the diaphanous quality of their fine linen gowns. The artist is equally adept at conveying the feel of a curvacious lady's supple flesh, or the regularity of the tight curls of which her wig is composed. Here, one feels bound to conclude, was a court of voluptuaries, to whom expense was no consideration, and who could gratify any aesthetic whim! (see Pl. 3.1).

Amenophis the "President" and His Cabinet

The king seems to have been a good judge of character. Only thus can we explain his success in surrounding himself with a group of brilliant admin-

46

istrators, famed for their wisdom and accomplishments centuries later. Each bore the title "royal secretary," which denoted the highest rank in the state, and an intimate of the king. Apart from this designation of rank, perhaps comparable to the modern "cabinet minister" or "secretary of state," each bore a specific title signifying the government department of which he was the head.[18]

A recent arrival among the portfolios represented in the pharaonic cabinet, but one of the most important during this reign, was the office of "scribe of recruits," which often entailed a paramilitary command. This was the "secretary of labor" who was in charge of "manpower." His responsibility was the oversight of the registers of labor gangs, draftees, and military personnel; he supervised recruitment, saw to it that draft-lists were maintained, and made sure that there was sufficient manpower on hand for state projects, both civil and military. His jurisdiction extended to garrisoning the forts, both in Egypt and the empire, distributing and registering state POWs, recruiting and despatching army divisions, quarry gangs, and construction levies, and even supervising customs and immigration posts at the Nile mouths. It is quite clear that, without the genius of this logistical officer, Amenophis III's Egypt would have ground to a halt.

Amenophis inherited one Horemheb, a protégé of the Amun cult, who had served as scribe of recruits under his father, but he was soon replaced by Senu, who was also the chief royal herald. Although possibly as many as six incumbents were to function under Amenophis III, the one who shortly followed Senu was the most successful and the longest in office, Amenophis son of Hapu.[19] Of humble origin, native of Athribis* in the Delta, he was early singled out by the king, "promoted because of the soundness of his counsels, elevated by the king over his peers." In one of his many inscriptions he tells us "the Good God, the King of Upper and Lower Egypt, Nebmare, the eldest son of Horakhty, favored me, and I was appointed undersecretary of the king, and inducted into the god's-book (the temple library collection). I saw the 'Tools of Thoth' (the hieroglyphs); I was well-schooled in their secrets, and delved into all their difficult passages, and my advice was sought on all their points." After education came his appointment to the cabinet: "the total population was under my supervision as king's scribe, charged with the recruits; I levied my lord's labor-draftees, my pen

18. In general see W. Helck, *Zur Verwaltung des Mittleren und Neuen Reichs* (Leiden, 1958).

19. A. Varille, *Inscriptions concernant l'architect Amenophis fils de Hapou* (Cairo, 1968).

registered the numbers of myriads . . . I taxed the estates according to their number . . . I inventoried all their chattels, I mustered recruits." Before his death he was able to say, "I am a righteous man, I have not shown partiality, I have not consorted with the malefactor . . . my character is upright; the things that I have done are visible to everyone. . . . Truly upright in old age, I have attained eighty years in the favor of the king. I shall complete 110 years."[20] Although Amenophis son of Hapu was probably thwarted in his wish to achieve the 110 years of a successful man, his fame far outlived him. A millennium after his death he was still revered as a wise man, and a demigod with healing powers.[21]

Of the other members of this privileged, inner cabinet, we may also mention the pious Khaᶜemhat, the king's scribe and overseer of granaries. Khaᶜemhat's father, Imhotpe, had, as "overseer of the storehouse of gold and silver," also been a member of this cabinet early in the reign. Charged with the supervision of the grain-growing and the collection of the harvest, not only in Egypt but throughout the empire as well, Khaᶜemhat had at his disposal a veritable army of field-scribes (to assess the yield in advance), police, and tax-collectors. In year 30 Khaᶜemhat handed in to the sovereign an exceptionally bounteous harvest-tax, and he and his staff were rewarded by pharaoh, a distinction he pictured in his tomb. Something of an erudite man, Khaᶜemhat prided himself on knowing all the gods by name, and offering regularly to the spirits of the departed, both private and royal.

The treasury was in the hands of a family that had held it for three generations. These kinsmen favored personal names compounded with the name of the crocodile-god, Sobek. The powerful incumbent under Amenophis III was the "king's scribe and superintendent of the treasury Sobekhotpe," son of the superintendent of the privy purse Sobekmose. He was concerned with the acquisition of precious metals, and consequently directly involved in mining operations. Undoubtedly a high point in his career came in the winter of Amenophis III's 36th year when "His Majesty was in the Southern City [in his palace on the west] of Thebes. Then it was brought to the attention of the king's scribe and superintendent of the treasury [Sobek]hotpe, called Panehsy ("the Southerner," his nickname) to fe[tch

20. *Urk.* IV, 1820ff.
21. D. Wildung, *Imhotep und Amenhotep* (Munich, 1977).

tur]quoise, while His Majesty was celebrating his Third Jub[ilee]."[22] This entailed a long trek to the Sinai mines with a host of workers, prospectors, miners, and support staff. But the mission was a success, and the king was liberal with rewards.

Among the most prominent of the king's scribes, to judge from the size and richness of their tombs, were the chief stewards. Second only to the secretary of labor in power and influence, the chief steward was a sort of managing director of the king's possessions, by this juncture in Egypt's history grown to awesome proportions. While still resident at Memphis in his youth, the king's eye had fallen on two young sons of a certain Imhotpe, the overseer of cattle and granaries of the estates of Amun in the Delta. The older son, Amenophis, was appointed "hereditary prince, count, seal-bearer of the king, king's scribe, and chief steward" in Memphis, and for a time also held the office of king's scribe of recruits. In his own eyes Amenophis's chief claim to fame was constructing the monumental temple to his sovereign at Memphis; he was subsequently put in charge of the temple, and before the end of his life he secured the same office for his son Ipuwy, who outlived Amenophis III. Imhotpe's second and younger son Ramose was later to become the king's Theban vizier in the south.

Also in the south one Amenemhet, nicknamed "Surer," was the chief steward. His father, Itj-towy (from the north?) had been an overseer of the herds of Amun, and his son initially followed in the father's footsteps as "superintendent of the cattle and fields of Amun, superintendent of the gates of Amun, and scribe of the god's treasury of Amun." By the time the court moved to Thebes Amenemhet had graduated to the status of "hereditary prince, count, unique friend with the right of approach to his lord, king's chief steward, king's scribe, . . . fan-bearer on the king's right hand . . . grandee in the king's house."

Though not chief stewards, two other magnates, by fulfilling a function close to the persons of the king and queen, achieved the coveted status of king's scribe. Nefersekheru, son of a lowly "esquire," and an erstwhile superintendent of the herds of Amun, turns up at Thebes as "first courtier with right of access to Horus within his palace . . . king's scribe, steward of the House of 'Nebmare-the-Dazzling-Sun-disc'" (i.e., the Theban palace). Kheruef, son of a low-ranking civil servant, became "hereditary prince,

22. *Urk.* IV, 1891.

count, . . . superintendent of the privy purse, king's first herald . . . true king's scribe, steward of the house of the Great King's-wife Tiy."

Before the end of the reign, and presumably in succession to Amenemhet Surer in the south, a certain Ria, formerly a "scribe of the grain count" under the Khaᶜemhat, became "true king's scribe, his beloved, superintendent of granaries of Upper and Lower Egypt, and king's chief steward."

Size and appointments of their burials alone would mark the chief stewards as enormously wealthy. The tomb of Nefersekheru, though imperfectly investigated, is one of the most beautiful at Thebes. Surer's Theban grotto is enormous: cut out of the living rock, it extends nearly 250 feet into the cliff, and contains a hall with seventy columns. Kheruef's tomb is one of the largest private tombs ever excavated at Thebes. It consists of a narrow corridor leading to a large colonnaded courtyard and a transverse hall with thirty columns; beyond is a long hall of eighteen columns, and more corridors and rooms. The whole was 360 feet long, and later was itself turned into a burial ground.[23] No one who has not seen these tombs can appreciate the technical excellence of the relief and the standard of taste reflected.

Yet, for all their wealth, these stewards usually had a surprisingly precarious tenure of office. More than one royal steward suddenly and mysteriously fell out of favor, and saw his monuments destroyed and his property confiscated. Possibly the handling of so much wealth proved a temptation impossible to withstand, and the relatively lowly origin of some stewards may have created a fatal jealousy among their "betters" who had been bypassed for the job. The suspicion of scandal and the envy of the influential—these are the only elements required in an eastern state, even today, to ensure the downfall of the once-loved and undoubtedly loyal officer!

The chairs in the cabinet room are not yet completely accounted for. We must mention the viceroy of Kush, Merimose, a fan-bearer on the king's right hand, who was king's scribe responsible for the gold mines of the Sudan. There was also the "king's scribe, undersecretary of the king, mayor of Memphis, Menkheper," and the "king's scribe and commander in chief of the army of the Lord of the Two Lands, Nakht-min."

The august and ancient office of vizier did not rank as a post of "king's scribe"; in fact, it was superior to all these offices, except that of treasurer.

23. C. F. Nims et al., *The Tomb of Kheruef* (Chicago, 1980).

Bifurcated into vizierates for Upper and Lower Egypt, the office was responsible for the day-to-day running of the residence city and the smooth operation of the entire bureaucracy, and its occupant was usually put in charge of all construction work throughout his half of the realm. Besides the famous Ramose, the younger brother of Amenophis the steward, who held the southern vizierate during the later years of Amenophis III and whose tomb is justly famous for its exquisite reliefs, we may mention the shadowy figure of the little-known Ptahmose, who for a time was "mayor of the Southern City," and vizier. Probably toward the close of the reign Ptahmose appears as the "steward of (the estate of) Amun . . . archibishop of Upper and Lower Egypt," and high priest of Amun. Who was this man? As archbishop, "pontifex maximus," and erstwhile prime minister, he must have been for a time the most influential minister in the realm.

Amenophis and His Jubilees

The last decade of the reign, when Amenophis III was in residence in Thebes, witnessed the celebration of three *sd*-festivals in years 30, 34, and 37.[24] To judge by the number of contemporary reliefs and paintings devoted to the commemoration of these celebrations, they must have been regarded as the most important events of the reign. All took place at Thebes "in [his] palace, [the 'House-]of-Rejoicing'" i.e., the new Malqata★ palace on the west of Thebes, which thus became a mecca for all the magnates of the empire. From the high officials of the administration were exacted "benevolences" (*'inw*) in the form of food and drink, but these worthies were willing enough to comply, especially since they felt honored to be involved in the sacred performances as celebrants. Not a few of them proudly display in their tombs among the titles and offices they held in life the designation of the fleeting role they played at the jubilee. Thus both Nefersekheru the steward and Merimose the viceroy were "controllers of the double throne," Kheruef was "palace controller," Amenophis the vizier, Amenemhet the steward, and the aforementioned Nefersekheru were "custodians of the boundary markers(?) in the Broad Hall," Kha^cemhat was "priest of Anubis," and Amenophis son of Hapu was "hereditary prince in the offices of the *sd*-festival."

24. See W. C. Hayes, *JNES* 10 (1951), 35ff.

The rites were also witnessed by foreign potentates or their ambassadors, pictured in the reliefs and identified as "the chiefs of every distant land who had not known Egypt" (cf. Pls. 3.2–5). It must have been on one of these occasions that the king of Babylon registered a complaint, by letter, regarding the absence of proper protocol where his emissaries and their chariots were concerned: "my chariots were ranged in the midst of (your) mayors' chariots, and you never gave them a glance."[25] He also complained that the Egyptian ambassador had not been sent to announce the *sd*: "when you made a great festival, you did not send your messenger saying '[eat dr]ink,' nor did you send a festival present."[26] Amenophis freely admitted the truth of the accusations, but castigated the Babylonian messengers: "on one occasion your messengers went to your father and their mouths spoke hatred; (now) a second time they go and speak hatred to you."[27] In consequence, Amenophis concludes, he has decided not to give them anything in the future, for, no matter what he does for them, they will misrepresent his intentions.

But no Babylonian complaint could dampen the enthusiasm for the festivals: the food was present in superabundance and the wine flowed freely. All rites were performed, so Amenophis proudly declares, in conformance with the most ancient order of service, prescriptions that the king had found on dust-covered "writings of the ancients" in the archives. In fact, the monarch seems to have taken a dilettante's delight in objects of remote antiquity: a primitive slate palette, from the dawn of Egypt's history some 1,600 years before, has come to light with a representation of Queen Tiy on the reverse!

Toward the close of his life Amenophis III was ailing. His mummy, though badly preserved, shows us a fat, bald old man, who had spent the last years of his life in luxury and indolence. His teeth must have caused him considerable pain, for they were found to have been badly worn, with numerous abcesses. It may have been because of his poor condition that in year 35 he sent to his brother-in-law, Tushratta of Mitanni, to see whether he could suggest any remedies. Tushratta wrote back saying that Ishtar of Nineveh had just made an oracular declaration: "to Egypt, the land which I love, I will go." So Tushratta packed Ishtar's cult image off to Egypt with the request "may my brother honor her, in joy send her back, and may she

25. *EA* 1:88ff. 27. *EA* 1:72ff.
26. *EA* 2:18ff.

3.2

3.3

3.4

3.5

3.2–3.5. Talatat from sd-festival representations from the second or ninth pylons.

3.2. Two columns of text, with part of an elaborate vessel, representing an array of foreign tribute. Column on the left: "[Bearing trib]ute to the king by the ch[iefs of . . .]"; column on the right: "[the chiefs of Na]harin (Mitanni), the chiefs of Ku[sh . . .]."

3.3. Representation of foreign emissaries proferring jars of produce to the king. Text: "Lo, the children of the chief(s) of every foreign land were bearing [tribute to His Majesty . . .]."

3.4. Talatat showing Amorite chieftains with arms raised in adoration of the king. A large matched scene has now grown from this single fragment: see Fig. 15.

3.5. Nubian chiefs adorned with feathers, praising the king.

53

return. May Ishtar mistress of heaven protect my brother and me. . . . Ishtar is my deity, she is not my brother's deity."[28]

Ishtar's therapeutic powers proved ineffective. Seven months into his 38th year, probably in January, 1377 B.C.,[29] "Horus" died in his palace on the west of Thebes. As the wording of the official obituary would have put it: The hawk has flown to heaven, and another stands in his place. Who that "other" was Egypt was soon to learn, to her ultimate consternation.

28. *EA* 23.   29. D. B. Redford, *JNES* 25 (1966), 120f.

PART TWO

The Reign of
the Heretic Pharaoh

CHAPTER FOUR

Amenophis IV and the Puzzle of the Reign

Possibly in the fifth month of the civil calendar in what had been his father's 38th year (January, 1377 B.C.), Amenophis IV ascended the Horus throne of the living. If sculptors showed uncertainty as to how to treat the strange figure of their new sovereign in art, they but mirrored a general hesitancy and puzzlement about what to expect from this young and unknown ruler.

The Young Pharaoh

In contrast to the frequent appearance of his brothers and sisters, Amenophis, the second son of Amenophis III—his older brother has died young—is conspicuous by his absence from the monuments of his father. It may well be that he was intentionally kept in the background because of a congenital

4.1. (left) Trial piece, limestone from Amarna, showing the grossly exaggerated style of carving the king's profile, usually associated with the earlier years of the reign.

4.2 (right) Head and shoulders of one of the royal colossi from the south colonnade of Gm·(t)-p³-itn in East Karnak (see Figs. 10, 11).

ailment which made him hideous to behold (Pls. 4.1-2). The repertoire of Amarna art has made us familiar with the effeminate appearance of the young man: elongated skull, fleshy lips, slanting eyes, lengthened ear lobes, prominent jaw, narrow shoulders, potbelly, enormous hips and thighs, and spindly legs. Of late the experts have tended to identify his problem with some sort of endocrine disorder in which secondary sex characteristics failed to develop, and eunuchoidism resulted.[1]

Be that as it may, it is a fact that Amenophis does not appear on monuments during his father's reign. The only certain reference to him seems

1. See C. Aldred, *Akhenaten, Pharaoh of Egypt* (London, 1968), 133f.

58

to be on a wine-jar seal from Malkata where his name appears in the expression, "the estate of the true(?) king's-son Amenophis."[2] He was, then, old enough to have his own establishment during the last decade of his father's reign, and, as we should expect, was residing at that time with the rest of the court at Thebes. That he was born at an earlier point in the reign, when the royal residence was at Memphis, is a plausible assumption, albeit incapable of proof.

Although it is best to admit our ignorance on the subject of where and by whom Amenophis IV was educated, one thing seems certain: his early training did not take him far, if at all, from his father's court and certainly not beyond Egypt's borders. There is no evidence that he remained at Memphis after his father moved south to Thebes in about his 29th year, nor that he was ever resident in Heliopolis, the center of the sun-cult. To postulate an "education" in the latter city simply to explain his devotion to solar theology is wholly unnecessary: the sun god and his theology so permeated the Egyptian cultus that it would have been hard to insulate a young prince from solar influence wherever he might be brought up. Anen, his uncle,[3] was, it is true, a high priest of the sun god, but if this was the lesser Karnak cult of Re (as seems most likely) and not the Heliopolitan, the title probably went along with Anen's occupancy of one of the first ranks in the priesthood of Amun at Karnak.

As we shall see, the changes in cultic iconography and, undoubtedly, the decision to build new structures for a new god belong to the very beginning of Akhenaten's reign. One wonders whether it was the charge to commence work that Ramose commemorates in his tomb. Certainly the king's words, and Ramose's reply, fragmentary though both are, refer to building operations: "[Words spoken by] the king who lives on Truth, 'lord' of the two Lands [Neferkheperure], given [life], to the hered[itary prince, count], mayor, and 'vizier,' Ramose [deceased! . . .] The words that I have brought to your attention, the counsels [. . .] . . . its form [?] [. . .]. I have commanded it. All that is in [. . .] than the . . . of kings since the time of the god. . . .'" Ramose replies, "'[May the] Disc [do] as thou hast commanded [. . .]; thy monuments shall last like heaven, thy monuments like the Disc which is in it. Thy monuments shall have being like the beings of heaven. Thou art unique . . . with his counsels. The mountains pour forth

2. Hayes, *JNES* 10 (1951), 172, fig. 27   3. Aldred, *Akhenaten*, fig. 18. (KK).

to thee their hidden treasures; thy cry affects their hearts as it does the hearts of men, they obey thee as men do!"[4] The directive that is implied by the king's words may be that alluded to in the Silsileh quarry inscription: "The first occasion when His Majesty issued a command to . . . pursue all work from Elephantine to Sema-behdet, and to the commanders of the army to levy a numerous corvée for quarrying sandstone, in order to make the great *bnbn* of Reharakhty in his name 'Sunlight-which-is-in-the-Disc' at Karnak. The princes, courtiers, supervisors, and baton-bearing officers were in charge of his levy for transporting the stone."[5]

Something of the totalitarian spirit that informs these early building projects can be felt in the inscriptions of Parennefer. This worthy, the king's butler and hand-washer, was appointed to the post of "archbishop" (overseer of the prophets of all the gods). Apparently a parvenu, Parennefer was fulsome in his praise of the new king: "Hail to thee, O thou child of the living Disc, *Wʿ-n-rʿ*, one without peer, who formed me and fostered me!" One scene in his tomb shows him being rewarded in a style that was to become more or less stereotyped for three and a half centuries, but the occasion for the reward is not made precise. Parennefer was put in charge of the offerings in the new temples. Already large quantities of offerings were being diverted to the Disc at the expense of other temples, and Parennefer notes laconically that those officials that did not adjust to the new conditions would be cutting their own throats: "Now Pre★ knows which is the servant who is diligent in respect of offerings. The servant who is not diligent concerning the offerings of the Disc gives himself over into thy (the king's) power; for the corn-imposts of every other god are measured (merely) by oipe,★ but for the Disc they are measured in superabundance!"[6]

Thebes at the Accession of the Heretic

When Amenophis III died the great complex of Amun at Karnak seemed to have reached a stage of structural completion (Fig. 3; Pl. 4.3).[7] On the west Amenophis III's pylon (no. III) fronted the temple if one approached by ship along the canal from the river and into the turning basin; on the south, beyond the last pylon of Hatshepsut (no. VIII), a pylon of dimensions equal

4. N. Davies, *The Tomb of the Vizier Raʿ-mose*, (London, 1941), pl. 36.

5. *Urk.* IV, 1962.

6. *Urk.* IV, 1996.

7. See E. Riefstahl, *Thebes in the Time of Amunhotep III* (Norman, Okla., 1964).

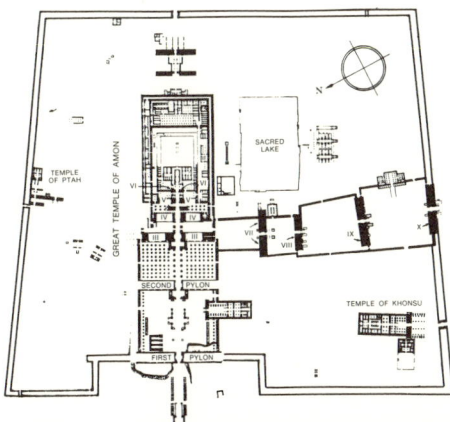

3. Plan of Karnak

4.3 *Aerial View of Karnak. The rhomboidal enclosure of the Temple of Amun lies to the left (north), and once communicated with the Nile (bottom) by a canal now occupied by the tree-lined street. To the right stands the enclosure of Mut, Amun's consort, with its curved lake, and in the lower right the houses of the modern village of Karnak. The excavated areas and the "dig-house" of the East Karnak expedition may be discerned in the upper left-hand corner, beyond the Amun enclosure.*

to those of its western mate, provided a monumental entry for those coming from the Mut-temple. To the north Amenophis's new shrine to Montu and its enclosure balanced the complex he had built for Mut on the south. Only on the east was there no construction. Thutmose IV, it is true, had here erected beyong the mud-brick enclosure wall of Amun a single obelisk which he had found in a workshed, neglected by the masons since the death of Thutmose III twenty-five years before. Thutmose IV had completed the decoration of this monument, and had dedicated it to Re-Harakhty. But no further construction, to our knowledge, was effected by either Thutmose IV or Amenophis III in this sector.

For a few months into the new reign, or perhaps for as much as a single year, sculpting and architectural decoration of a traditional nature proceeded apace. Work on the two Karnak pylons of his father, largely left undecorated at the death of Amenophis III, was continued by Amenophis IV. Pylon III received, on the north wall of its porch, a traditional head-smiting scene, in which the cartouches of the triumphant pharaoh belong to Amenophis IV. For some reason the southern pylon of Amenophis III (on the site of the present tenth) received considerably more attention. The gate was decorated with a series of registers of self-contained scenes, each showing Amenophis IV in the traditional guise of a pharaoh, offering to the falcon-headed sun god (Pls. 4.4-6). The latter's representation is unexceptional, save for his ubiquitous epithet, written in columns, which is new: ". . . he who rejoices in the horizon in his name 'Sunlight that is in the Disc.'" The gate was named after Amenophis IV,[8] and the adjacent towers of the pylon were partly decorated with traditional offering scenes.

Traditional though the *form* appeared, Amenophis was already beginning to question the norms of art and the cult with which he had been brought up. Looming large in the soul-searching the new king must have been engaged in was the prospect of a jubilee early in his reign. What motivated him to even entertain the prospect is as unknown to us today as it probably was to his contemporaries; for jubilees were not traditionally celebrated before the thirtieth regnal year.[9] Nevertheless, sometime early in his second year at the latest the intent crystallized in Amenophis IV's mind to celebrate a jubilee, a *sd*-festival as it was called, as his father had done in his last decade;

8. The name appears on a block, still in the east wing of pylon 10, on which can be read "the gate (named): 'Neferkheprure Wa-ᶜenre is [   ].'"

9. See E. F. Wente and C. Van Siclen, *Studies in Honor of George R. Hughes* (Chicago, 1976), 217ff.

and the time was set a few months hence to coincide with the third anniversary of his accession to the throne. The king gathered his chief sculptors around him, including one Bek, the son and successor of his father's sculptor Men, and issued new orders: the king's form was to be portrayed in such a way as to emphasize the attributes that differentiated him from a traditional royal subject—his youth, musculature, and beauty (Pl. 4.2).

There is a certain variety in the treatment of the king's face in the early years of his reign, which makes it difficult to say what he really looked like. The artists appear to be torn between the need to follow the king's instructions and their inclination to be true to the ideal "Thutmosid profile." If one notes those features common to all relief scenes of the king, and deems them ipso facto reliable indicators of his facial peculiarities, then the list will include the following: high cheekbones, full lips, arched brows, slender neck, and a rather supercilious expression.[10]

The decision to celebrate a jubilee sparked the commencement of an energetic building program at Thebes. We have already noted the royal edicts to quarry stone and lay down ground plans, and the surviving texts give us the identity of the buildings to be put up. There are four major structures mentioned. If relative frequency of attestation is a guide to relative importance and/or size, then the four may be ranked as follows: *Gm·(t)-p³-itn* (lit. "the Sun-disc is found"), *Ḥwt-bnbn* (lit. "the Mansion of the benben-stone," an object shaped like an obelisk said to be "in the *Gm·(t)-p³-itn*"), *Rwd-mnw-n-itn-r-nḥḥ* (lit. "Sturdy are the monuments of the Sun-disc forever"), and *Tni-mnw-n-itn-r-nḥḥ* (lit. "Exalted are the monuments of the Sun-disc forever"). Sporadic references to four additional structures, including a "Broadhall" and a "House of Rejoicing," may allude to structures already standing in Thebes upon the young king's accession. Though mentioned time and again the four buildings are nowhere described, and their purpose is never made explicit.

The Recovery of the Talatat

My account to this point has taken the form of a simple narrative. This has been possible because the evidence, though far from abundant, is at least

10. K. Myśliwiec, *Le Portrait royal dans le bas-relief du nouvel empire* (Warsaw, 1976), 75ff.

4.4. (left) Large sandstone block from the tenth pylon, originally part of the southern gateway decorated by the king in the first year of his reign. The traditional representation of the falcon-headed sun-disc, with scepter, faces the king (now lost) who makes an offering. The long name of the god is inscribed in columns before him, and was later reduplicated in two small cartouches.

4.5 (right) Large sandstone block from the tenth pylon, originally from the southern gateway decorated by the king in the first year of his reign. The falcon-headed god with the large sun-disc on his head is Re-Harakhtay, the sun god, identified by the long epithet in columns above his head. The final column contains his words to the king (who stood to the right): "Utterance: 'I grant thee [all] valor and victory. . .'" On the extreme left is the right-hand portion of the adjacent scene showing the king in the atef-crown (a monstrous headdress composed of ram's horns and tall feathers). Unlike the divine figure, this has been savagely hacked.

sufficiently representative to enable us to draw a fairly complete picture. Names, faces, and careers, campaigns, construction, and festivals—all contribute to fill out the story; and even the thinking lurking behind a particular act or policy can often be elicited by reading between the lines.

Such is decidedly not the case with the short, but important, span of time I have now to describe: the first five years of Amenophis IV's reign represent a shocking hiatus in our historical knowledge. So thoroughly were memorials of this period eradicated on the morrow of the Amarna period, whether temple reliefs, steles, or tombs, that little if anything remained on public view for succeeding generations. Without the reliefs and steles the mighty acts of pharaoh cannot be recounted; without the tombs his nobles will languish in oblivion. No connected narrative is possible here. Instead our interest will, for the time being, be centered on the search for, and the recovery of, the primary evidence, rather than the weaving of such evidence into the more elaborate fabric of narrative history.

4.6. Talatat *from the second pylon depicting part of the decoration of a pylon possibly the southern gateway. On the right are parts of two columns of text, probably flanking the entrance: 1) "[. . . exalted(?)] . . . to the height of heaven [. . .] 2) [. . .] Lord of the Two Lands Neferkheprure Wa^c-en-r^c [. . .]" In the center panel, which would be upon the left massif of the pylon, the king is shown "giving various herbs" to the anthropomorphic sungod; while on the left the contiguous panel depicts the offering of the trussed bulls. The mode of representation of the sun god reflects the practice of the first year of the reign; but the style has been influenced by the new canon of art. Note especially how the sun god's belly and torso approximate those of the king.*

Not the least element in the mystery surrounding the young king's formative years is the location and layout of the structures he erected. The bewildered visitor to modern Karnak looks in vain for any trace among the vast complexes of Amun, Mut, or Khonsu of *in situ* remains from this period. No denuded foundations protrude above the surface, no fallen columns with the royal titulary betray a lost building. So complete and thorough was the destruction wrought by pharaoh Horemheb, whose reign terminates the Amarna period, that literally no stone was left upon another. Yet the masonry from these sun-temples, for that is what they have proved to be, was by no means smashed.

For more than a century and a half evidence has been gradually accumulating toward the solution of the problem of the whereabouts of the king's temples.[11] Already in the second quarter of the 19th century investigators

11. See R. Saad, in *The Akhenaten Temple Project, Vol. 1: The Initial Discoveries*, ed. R. W. Smith and D. B. Redford (Warminster, 1977), 69.

65

had become aware of the presence in the debris which at that time encumbered the south side of Karnak of a number of small blocks bearing the cartouches of Amenophis IV with representations of his sun-disc. The great epigraphic expedition of Richard Lepsius, sponsored by the king of Prussia, identified and copied additional blocks from the same area in the 1840s. All were lying about loose and disarticulated, and all seemed to have standard dimensions of 52 by 26 by 24 centimeters. The inhabitants of Karnak dubbed this size of block a *talatat*, an Arabic word over which debate continues: is it the plural of the word "three," possibly alluding to the fact that such a block is three handbreadths long, or is it the Italian *tagliata*, "cut masonry," appearing as a loan word? In any event, the term has survived in colloquial usage, and is now well established in scholarly literature.

The sector from which early examples of *talatat* emanated was the uneven terrain around pylons IX and X. Shortly, however, it appeared that the blocks had not long lain there, but had in fact fallen from inside the ninth pylon due to earthquake and natural delapidation. Horemheb had employed *talatat* by the thousands as masonry fill inside this pylon, which he had erected in the course of his Theban building program, c. 1340–1330 B.C. The clearing of this area in 1882–1883 convinced Sir Gaston Maspero, the erstwhile director of the Service des Antiquités, that the "small" temple to the Sun-disc had stood somewhere in the vicinity of the ninth pylon, and he opined (erroneously) that it had been begun by Amenophis III.[12]

The problem, however, rapidly became more complicated. In the 1890s the clearance of the Luxor temple, about two miles south of Karnak, revealed that its great pylon, built by Ramesses II in about 1295 B.C., was also stuffed full of *talatat*, and that hundreds of additional fragments had later been built into the Roman houses surrounding the *temenos*. Georges Daressy opted for a Luxor temple to the Sun-disc, different from any that might have been erected at Karnak.[13] In similar fashion the excavators of Medamud (eight miles northeast of Karnak) in the 1920s interpreted the presence of several hundred *talatat* in their excavation as evidence for a Sun-disc temple there. Meanwhile, the early decades of the present century witnessed the clearance of the tenth pylon at Karnak, and it, too, proved to be filled with masonry of Amenophis IV; but there, in addition to *talatat*, there were also blocks of large dimensions bearing the cartouches of the aforesaid monarch. Since

12. Sir G. Maspero, *History of Egypt*, Vol. 5 (London, 1900), 80.

13. G. Daressy, *Notice explicative des ruines du temple de Louxor* (Cairo, 1893), 4.

these frequently showed the sun god in the form of the falcon-headed man, with the well-known appelative "Re-Harakhte," scholars began to conjure up an otherwise unattested "Re-harakhte Temple" of Amenophis IV.[14]

The evidence from Karnak, at least, was unanimous in pointing to Horemheb as the king who dismantled Amenophis IV's structures and used their component blocks as structural fill in his own architectural additions to the Amun temple. As early as a hundred years ago, the great historian August Wiedemann set on record the observable fact that the second pylon at Karnak which, with the great hall behind it, had been begun by Horemheb in front of Amenophis III's façade to the Amun temple, was filled to overflowing with thousands of *talatat*.[15] It looked very much as though, wherever Horemheb had built, the core and (as it turned out) the foundations of his building were likely to contain *talatat*.

At long last attempts were made to retrieve the *talatat* from their secondary resting places. The program of restoration that the Service des Antiquités devised to refurbish and strengthen the ruins at Karnak gave birth to the novel technique of dismantling the buildings of Horemheb. Once the *talatat* had been taken out, the outer skins of the pylon walls could then be reconstructed with a modern masonry fill in the core. The major part of this work fell to the lot of Inspector Henri Chevrier, whose tenure at Karnak spanned more than a quarter century (1925–1953). Using what little funds and equipment were available to him—his reports suggest he never had enough—Chevrier in the Twenties and Thirties and again in the late Forties succeeded in retrieving over 20,000 inscribed *talatat* (and many more uninscribed) from the 2nd pylon and beneath the floor of the hypostyle hall.[16] A similar program of careful dismantlement was begun on the 9th pylon, and though interrupted by long intervals, has progressed since the mid-Sixties under the supervision of the late Ramadan Saad of the Egyptian Antiquities Organization, and MM. Lauffray and Golvin, both directors of the Centre Franco-Egyptienne pour la Restoration de Karnak.[17]

The result of this labor, by 1965, was the acquisition of nearly 45,000

14. R. W. Smith, in *The Akhenaten Temple Project*, 1:45.

15. A. Wiedemann, *Ägyptische Geschichte* (Gottha, 1884), 399.

16. See the reports of M. Pillet and H. Chevrier in *ASAE* from 1922 to 1952.

17. R. Saad, in *The Akhenaten Temple Project* 1:69; S. Sauneron, *Kêmi* 19 (1969), 138ff.; 21 (1971), 145ff.; J. Lauffray, *Karnak d'É-gypte, domaine du divin* (Paris, 1979).

inscribed and decorated *talatat*. Each had once constituted a component block in a wall, carved in relief and brightly painted. Since there is no immediate visual means of telling which blocks originally had been contiguous, it is clear that we were dealing with a huge and jumbled jigsaw puzzle. The problem was to reduce this intractable conundrum to dimensions that could be handled adequately in library, studio, or laboratory. Consequently the photographing to scale of all inscribed pieces was the first step in the process of analysis.

But one element of arrangement might be postulated at the outset. All the indications are that Horemheb's men had pursued their task of taking down the temples to the Sun-disc in an orderly manner. As course upon course of *talatat* were removed, they were at once carried off to be placed in new beds in the second and ninth pylons, the hypostyle, and elsewhere. We should have expected, then, to have found the *talatat* placed in these secondary *loci* almost in reverse order; at least we might have hoped that blocks that once stood side by side still enjoyed some proximity in the core of Horemheb's pylons. From scattered hints let slip by Chevrier, such, in fact, appears to have been the case. Sadly, however, neither Chevrier nor his predecessors saw fit to keep full records of each *talatat* as it emerged, and very few photographs or precise measurements were taken. The blocks, once stored in the open air, were several times moved to other locations and restacked, so that any chance today of matching original scenes simply by observing the *talatat* in their present storage locations meets complete frustration: the blocks are in total disarray. (Pls. 4.7–8)

The apparent hopelessness of the project of piecing the puzzle together again for a long time discouraged scholars. Occasionally isolated *talatat* with interesting reliefs or inscriptions were copied and photographed, and sometimes found their way into the scholarly literature. Thanks to lax security during the early decades of this century some of the better pieces, especially those containing heads of the king or queen, were spirited away illegally to be sold on the art market in Europe and America. But well over 95 percent of the relief material remained unknown and unstudied. Thus books on Amarna art or history published before 1970 suffer from the serious drawback (of which the authors were usually aware) that they were able to examine only the tip of the iceberg.

It was only with the concentrated work on the blocks undertaken by the Akhenaten Temple Project that scholarship became aware of the full range of the epigraphic and iconographic evidence of the "Karnak years" of the

4.7, 4.8. *Stacks of* talatat *from the second and ninth pylons. Of particular interest are the palaquin bearers, servants, and bowing courtiers.*

heretic king. Examined individually the *talatat* yield considerable new information, but their contribution is enhanced many times over when seen matched into the original scenes of which the walls were composed. Hence all efforts were directed toward the solution of the jigsaw puzzle.[18]

There were certain simple clues, often found through trial and error, that assisted us in the matching. A *talatat* could show relief decoration on the long side, in which case it would be called a "stretcher," or on the short side, a "header." Seldom it might be decorated on the two long sides, or on a long and a short side. Experience gradually taught us that in the construction of the buildings Amenophis IV's masons had alternated courses of headers and stretchers, a simple technique that has helped greatly in eliminating possible but incorrect matchings. Again, scenes tend to be stereotyped, and repeat themselves ad nauseam. The offering scene, for example, will always have the same components: celebrant (usually the king but sometimes the queen), identified by titles and cartouches that never vary; offering table; sun-disc; elevated offerings, etc. Once familiar with the details of such a scene, the analyst needs only a single block with a telltale clue to be able to reconstruct the entire scene. In the same way the caption texts which give the name and titles of the king, queen, and daughters are identical wherever they are found, so that, again, reconstruction from a mere fragment becomes possible. The sun-disc, which appears ubiquitously in the decoration, is provided with a stereotyped caption (in columns) that identifies it as "the great living sun-disc who is in jubilee, lord of heaven and earth. . . ." The only variant element in this title is what comes next, namely ". . . who resides in (temple so-and-so)," and it is on the basis of this temple identification that we can sort out the relief scenes that belong to each of the four temples mentioned.

To date, the project has matched a little over 2,000 "temporary scenes" (the term used for the individual collages of the puzzle). Some number as few as two or three blocks, but many comprise several score, and the largest contains approximately 160. Often a point is reached where a temporary scene defies further additions, until someone realizes that a totally different collage actually fits on to one end of the scene. Suddenly the original scene

---

18. On the work of ATP, see, in particular, R. W. Smith, *National Geographic Magazine* 138, no. 5 (Nov. 1970), 634ff.; D. B. Redford, *JARCE* 10 (1973), 77ff; 12 (1975), 9ff; Smith and Redford, *The Akhenaten Temple Project*, 1.

expands to twice its width and one begins to acquire a view of the broader whole and the overall scheme of composition.

The separating out of the reliefs from each temple on the basis of the caption of the sun-disc has assisted greatly in clarifying the building program of Amenophis IV's early years. For one thing, it has helped to eliminate a number of early postulates, unwarranted by the evidence. There were no temples to the sun-disc erected at Luxor or Medamud: *talatat* at these sites were later carried there from Karnak, sometime after the reign of Horemheb. Likewise the supposed Re-Harakhty temple vanishes under close scrutiny: the large blocks with traditional representations of the king and god actually come from the southern gate of Amenophis III, left undecorated at his death. As noted earlier, buildings erected with reliefs in the new style date no earlier than the decision to celebrate a jubilee. The earliest appears to be the *Gm·(t)-p³-itn*, judging by the rather tentative and experimental attempts at the new canon. *Rwd-mnw* and *Tni-mnw* probably followed within a year, and finally about the fourth year, the *Ḥwt-bnbn* was added to the *Gm·(t)-p³-itn*. Supporting such a relative chronology is the depiction of the king's growing family: in *Gm·(t)-p³-itn* only the first daughter is shown (Pl. 4.15), albeit sporadically, whereas by the time *Ḥwt-bnbn* was ready for decoration, a second daughter would occasionally be depicted with her older sister. Just before the abandonment of Thebes in the fifth year a third daughter had made her appearance, and very rarely a trio of little princesses is shown following their mother.

The Four Sun-Temples

A detailed examination of the reliefs by temple indicates a number of intriguing though unexplained differences. *Tni-mnw*, for example, displayed substantial sections of wall decorated with scenes of domestic apartments, and the types of activities, such as baking bread and storing wine, that went on in them.[19] Although these scenes went on in the domestic quarters of the royal palace, this does not mean that *Tni-mnw* itself was the palace. Numerous other scenes that once adorned the same building show the king engaged in the usual offering ceremony, with the queen in attendance and the sun-disc overhead. *Rwd-mnw* likewise featured scenes of cultic import,

19. Cf. L. Daniel, *Kêmi* 21 (1971), 151ff.

though now the offering scene is carried on in a series of roofless kiosks, with which we shall become familiar in the context of *Gm·(t)-p³-itn*. Also displayed on the walls of *Rwd-mnw* were lengthy scenes showing the king and his court riding out to visit open-air installations comprising row upon row of ten-foot-tall offering stands, each laden with offerings of fowl, bread, and wine (Fig. 4). On the other walls, row upon row of domestic servants advanced, each with a container of foodstuffs on his head, and each intoning a benedictory phrase: "O thou Neferkheprure, thou beautiful child of the Sun-disc! May the Sun-disc favor thee!" (Pl. 4.9).

One of the surprises (and as we shall see, there were many), that a close study of the *talatat* produced was the ubiquitous presence of military attendants with the king. Especially in *Rwd-mnw*, armed troops surround Amenophis IV when he leaves his palace, run behind his chariot as he proceeds down the avenue, or bow low, their swords reversed and their spears to the ground, as he enters the temple (Pl. 2.1). There are Egyptian spearmen and shocktroops, auxiliaries from Syria and Nubia, feather-wearing Libyans with throw-sticks, and everywhere the regimental sergeant majors with the standards of their companies. Paramilitary units also abound. One sees the "police" with their billy clubs, bowing low as the royal entourage passes by, and always standing discreetly behind the ladies of the court are the "overseers of the king's harem." Also present are the "agents of the harem ladies," and they, too, are occasionally armed with sticks. Interestingly, when foreign potentates are presented to His Majesty to make their salaams, the military standard-bearers are always close at hand (Fig. 5; Pl. 3.4).

The purpose of *Rwd-mnw* and *Tni-mnw* eludes us, though it is a fair guess that it was cultic in some manner. No inscriptions have so far been matched that might make their function explicit, nor, as we shall see, have their sites been yet identified.

Such is not the case with the largest of the four, the *Gm·(t)-p³-itn* temple, both whose purpose and location have now been discovered; but as this subject will be dealt with in detail in Chapter 7, we will postpone discussion at this point.

Of the four temples, only the *Ḥwt-bnbn* enjoys a connection with the paraphernalia of the earlier solar cult at Heliopolis. The *bnbn*-stone, variously depicted as a cone, pyramidion, or stepped object, had been sacred to the sun god Re from time immemorial. Its shape recalls the profile of pyramids of the 3rd Dynasty and later, almost 1,200 years before Amenophis IV's time, mortuary monuments which themselves showed the inspiration of the

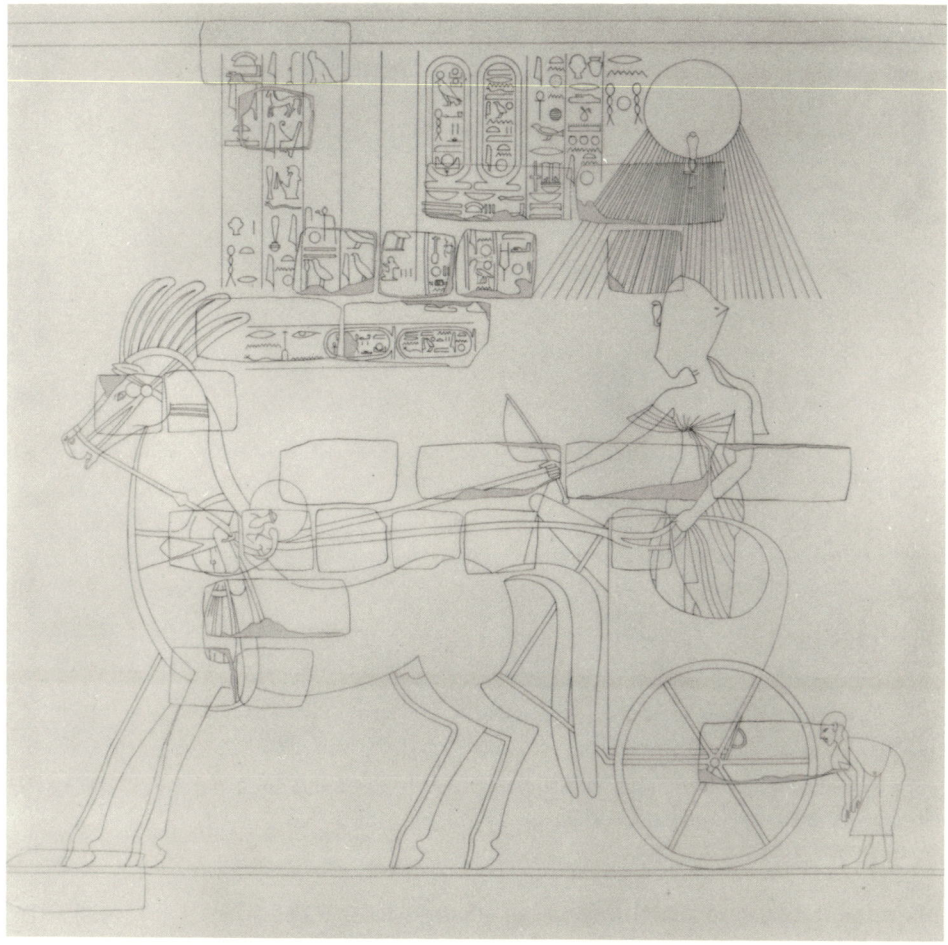

4. Facsmile of chariot scene from Rwd-mnw *(A. Shaheen). The king in blue crown and with riding whip stands in his chariot, about to move off to an unspecified destination. The text reads: "Appearance in glory [. . . on (his) char]iot, by His Majesty like the Sun-disc in [the midst of heaven], brightening the Two Lands. . . ." Behind the horses's plumed heads is a band of text that seems to name them: "its (the team's) beautiful name (is) 'Made by the (Sun-disc).'"*

Heliopolitan cult. Though its precise origin had long since been lost, in historic times the *bnbn* was attributed to the actualization of the primeval hill, the first solid ground to emerge from the primeval ocean, on which the sun god had effected his acts of creation. That Amenophis IV should, in the light of his well-attested aversion to polytheistic symbolism in mythology, have permitted this icon to a naive account of creation to find a

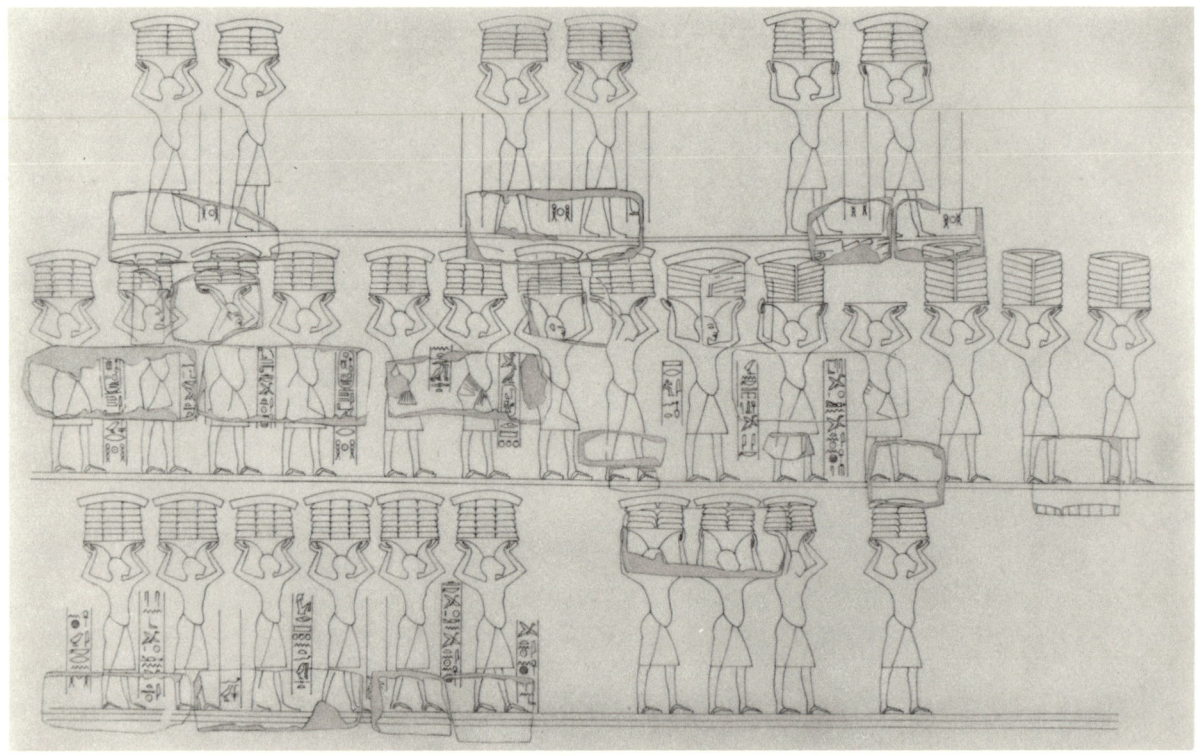

4.9. *Rows of servants, seen in echelon, carry trestles laden with flat bread. The scene (TS 5410) depicts the preparation for one of the feasts of the* sd-*festival.*

prominent place in his thinking, is strange to say the least. Obviously the *bnbn* did not conjure up for the king the objectionable connections with mythology that we might have expected.

But when we examine the spelling of the name *Ḥwt-bnbn* in the hieroglyphic script used in the *talatat*, a peculiarity immediately stands out: the determinative★ sign does not show the expected picture of a pyramidion or a stepped object. Instead the word displays the unique determinative of a single obelisk! Now, the word for "obelisk" is not *bnbn*, nor is it etymologically related to *bnbn*. Moreover, obelisks were almost always erected in pairs, not singly. But at Thebes, as we noted at the commencement of the present chapter, Thutmose IV, Amenophis IV's grandfather, had set up a single obelisk on the east side of Karnak, perfectly centered on the main east-west axis of the temple. Significantly, the god to whom the object was dedicated was Re-Harakhty, the very form of the sun god whom Amenophis

74

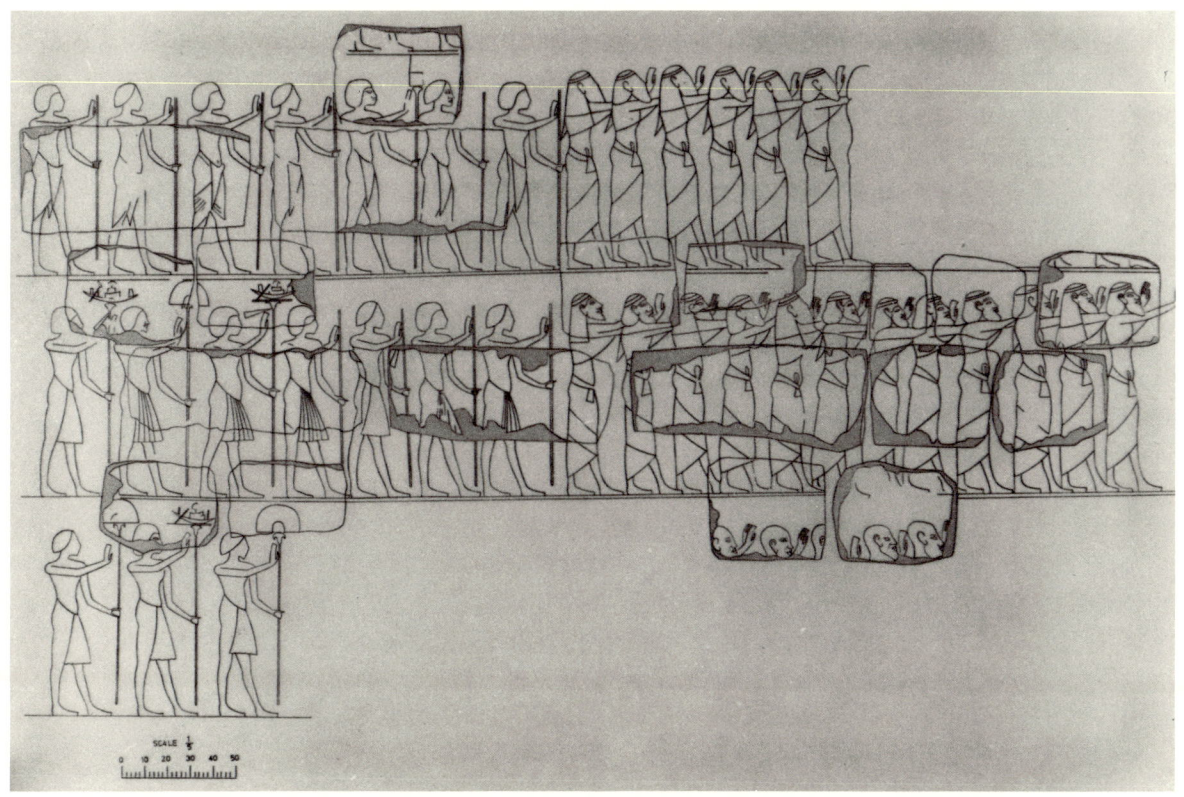

5. Facsimile of foreign dignitaries, greeting the king (TS 4917, A. Shaheen). Two rows of Amorite princes are depicted, with typical clubbed hair, filets, and wrap-around gowns, each with his arm raised in adoration of pharaoh. The bald heads in the lowest preserved register may represent Hittites. Note the Egyptian company commanders, each with the standard of his company, in close attendance on the foreigners.

had espoused! Could it possibly be that the structure known as *Ḥwt-bnbn* had been built with the single obelisk as its focus and raison d'être?

Ḥwt-bnbn displays other curious features. Although the ground plan of the building remains unknown, many of the interior walls must have been slender, for we find numerous *talatat* of this provenience decorated with relief on opposite faces. This would mean that the walls to which they belonged were only fifty-two centimeters thick. Again, matching and painstaking study have revealed that doors within the structure were built in the form of tall, graceful pylons, with the usual "broken cornice" at the top (Fig. 6). Another architectural element that may have formed part (a façade?)

75

6. *Reconstruction of an interior gateway in the* Ḥwt-bnbn *(R. Aicher)*

76

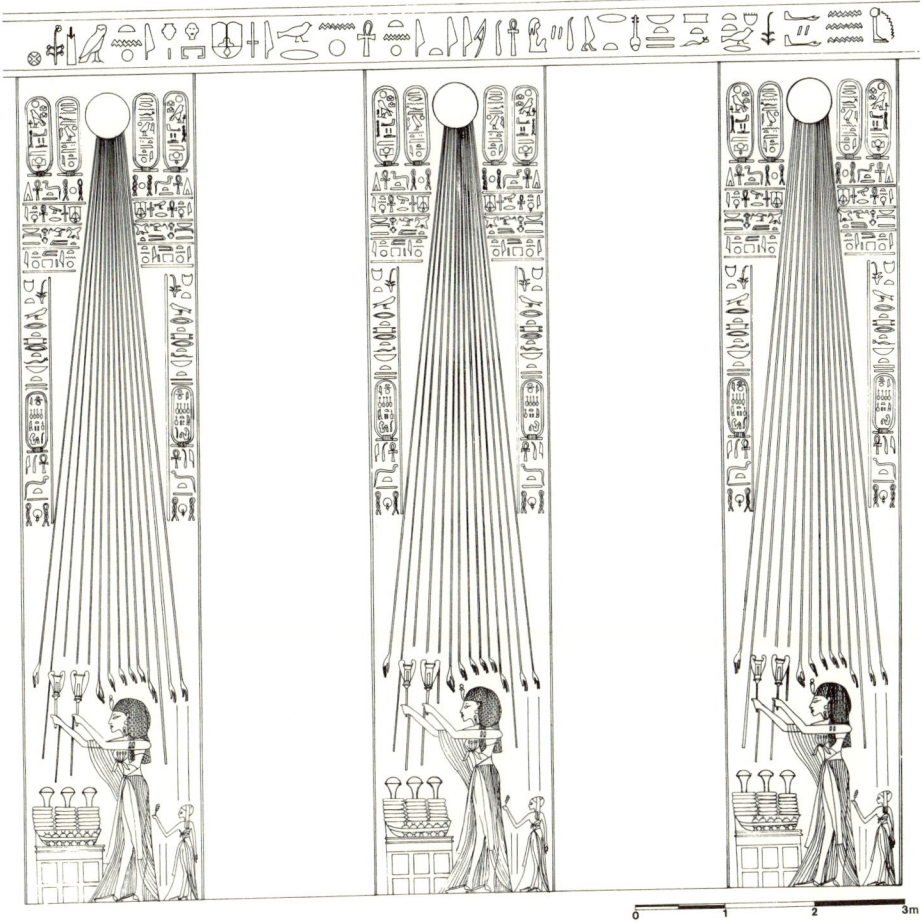

7. *Reconstruction of part of the "Nefertity Colonnade." Many talatat comprising a series of pillars were recovered by Chevrier in the core of the second pylon. It was possible to reconstruct, in part, twelve of the piers, but the many remaining blocks clearly from similar pillar construction argue the presence of many more. The scene on each "long" side shows Nefertity and Meretaten offering to the Sun-disc identified as "residing in Gm·(t)-p³-itn"; on the other three sides similar scenes are repeated in four superimposed panels. The architrave texts are restored from the fragmentary architraves extracted from the ninth pylon and presumed to come originally from this colonnade. The text reads "she pure of hands, great king's wife whom he loves, Lady of the Two Lands, Nefertity, may she live! beloved of the great living Sun-disc who is in jubilee, residing in the House of the Sun-disc in Southern Heliopolis." Other fragments of the same architraves also mention the king.*

of the *Ḥwt-bnbn*, though the texts mention only the *Gm·(t)-pꜣ-itn*, is the colonnade (?) of square piers. Due entirely to the painstaking work of Mme. Asmahan Shoukry, one of our staff, the true nature and dimensions of these piers became evident. Approximately twelve piers have been matched to date, each about 9.5 meters high, but additional blocks and fragments may attest to the existence originally of three times that number. Though when first matched the colonnade seemed to lack architraves, these have since been identified in the filling of the 9th pylon, removed years ago by Ramadan Saad (see Fig. 7).

One of the unexpected facts to emerge from a close examination of the *Ḥwt-bnbn*, reliefs was the identity of the celebrant of the cult: everywhere it is Nefertity, the queen of Amenophis IV, who raises the offerings to the sun-disc, both in this temple and in the colonnade just described (Pl. 4.9). Amenophis IV is nowhere depicted in the decoration of these structures! Who was this lady who could dominate the repertoire the artists were obliged to work with, to the exclusion of her illustrious husband?

The Royal Family in the Talatat

No text known at present specifies the parentage of Nefertity. The name itself, meaning literally "the beautiful one is come" is an Egyptian birthname, probably indicative of the festival of some female divinity; there is no reason, therefore, simply on the basis of the meaning of the name to postulate a foreign origin for the woman. That she had an Egyptian wet-nurse, and one of noble rank, militates strongly in favor of the contention that she was born in Egypt within the circle of the court. She might possibly have been a cousin of Amenophis IV, but even this is conjecture.[20]

Of more interest is the unexpectedly prominent role Nefertity plays in the Theban period of the reign (Pls. 4.10–15). Not only is she alone portrayed in the *Ḥwt-bnbn*, but also, when the sum total of attested scenes from the *talatat* are tallied, we find that Nefertity appears nearly twice as often as her husband the king! Art motifs devised originally for and inspired by the pharaoh are carefully translated into a female idiom: Nefertity wields the club or sword in the head-smiting scene, and captive females (alternating blonds and blacks to represent the two ends of the empire) kneel around

20. K. C. Seele, *JNES* 14 (1955), 169f.

her throne dais (frontpiece). A surprisingly large number of the ceremonial acts Amenophis IV is obliged to perform are shared by the queen, although she cannot, of course, take over the jubilee for her own benefit. Very often she accompanies her husband and is depicted, slightly smaller in stature, standing behind him, shaking the sacred sistrum. At some unknown point in the reign, but well before the 5th year, the monarch conferred on his wife a new title, which henceforth appears with her name, *nfr-nfrw-itn*, "exquisite beauty of the sun-disc."

It is hard to avoid the conclusion that this high profile which Nefertity enjoyed in the first five years of the reign is evidence of her political importance. But beyond this simple statement of suspicion it is folly to proceed. We must admit we know nothing about her at his point, and it is therefore idle to speculate about the nature of her power.

Other ladies at court are equally mysterious. We see in most reliefs well-dressed women, accompanied by harem officials, who constitute what in ancient Egyptian parlance are called "the king's ornaments," but none is ever named in the reliefs. It is a good guess that this crowd contained sisters, cousins, nieces of the king, as well as the wives and daughters of his grandees. One lady who does emerge clearly from this nameless crowd of beauties is the queen mother Tiy. Although we cannot identify her in the reliefs, the Amarna letters prove she was still residing at court, and still being courted by foreign potentates.

About Amenophis's own family the *talatat* reliefs for once yield hard and unequivocal evidence. In even the earliest reliefs Nefertity is very often accompanied by a little daughter who follows behind her, clad like her mother and shaking the sistrum (Pl. 4.10). The stereotyped caption text never changes: she is identified as "the king's bodily daughter whom he loves, Meretaten, born of the great king's wife Nefertity, may she live." If Meretaten was already a toddler in the second year of the reign, when the *talatat* structures began to arise, she can scarcely have been born later than the earliest months of her father's occupancy of the throne. The second daughter, however, puts in an appearance much later. As noted above, it is in the decoration of the *Ḥwt-bnbn*, possibly no earlier than the fourth year of the reign, that we first see two daughters toddling behind the queen. These are identified in the columns of text above their heads as Meretaten and Meketaten. Only three times are three daughters seen in the reliefs at Thebes, and this must mean that Ankhesenpaaten, the next in order of birth, was born about year 4. All three, and in fact all subsequent offspring, are iden-

4.10–4.15. Nefertity. Nefertity as she appears in the offering scenes in the talatat reliefs. Two types of headdress are depicted, the long blue wig topped by the modius and feathers (4.10, 4.11, and 4.15) and the short "Nubian" wig (4.12, 4.13). Her costume, a sheer pleated linen gown drawn in and tied beneath the breasts, never varies in such scenes. Behind her stands her eldest daughter, identified in most examples by the stereotyped caption "king's bodily daughter whom he loves. Meretaten, born of the great king's wife whom he loves, mistress of the Two Lands, Nefertity may she live!" Only in 4.10 does a variant occur, which is susceptible of the rendering "king's-wife, king's daughter . . ."; but it could also be translated "daughter of the king's wife. . . ." The elaborate offering table in the artist's facsimile (4.15) piled high with edibles and equipped with a small statuette of the queen holding a conical loaf, is provided with a band of text identifying recipient and celebrant: "the great living Sun-disc, Lord of heaven and earth, who is in jubilee, who resides in the Mansion of the benben-stone in Gm·(t)-p³-itn; the king's wife Nefertity, may she live!"

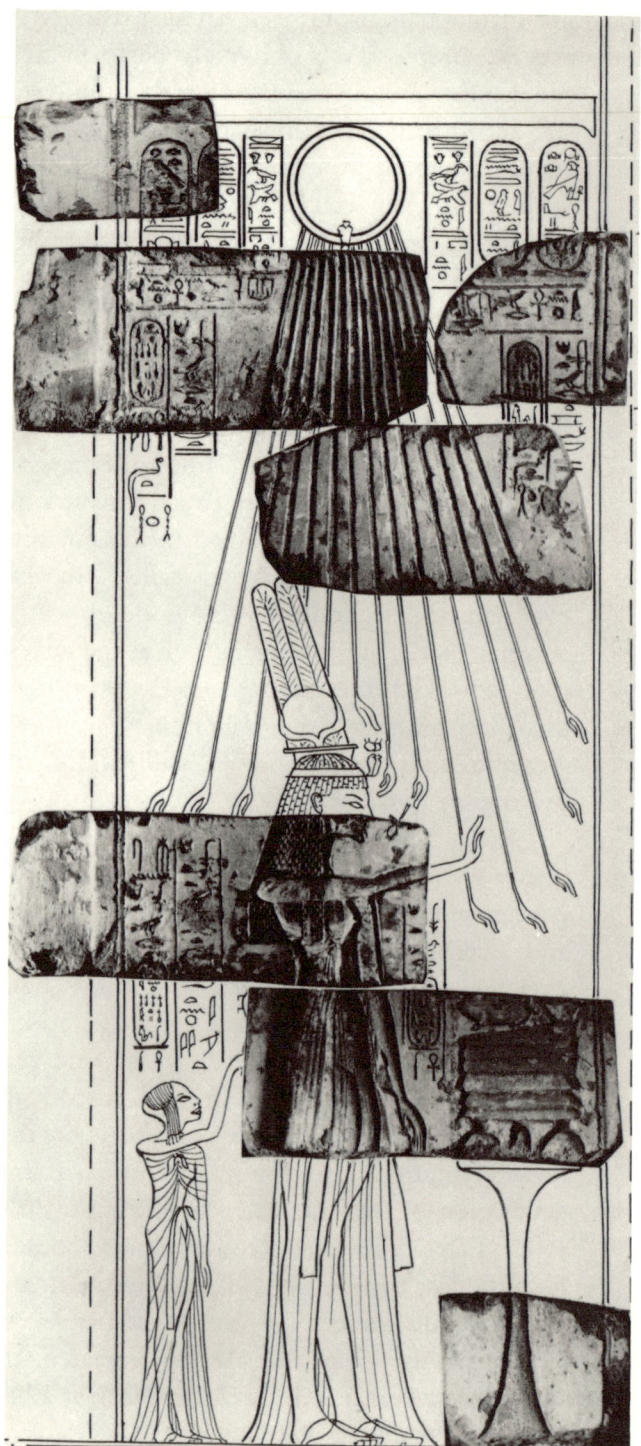

4.10

4.11

4.12

4.13

4.14

4.15

tified in the captions as "king's bodily daughters . . . born of the great king's wife Nefertity," which would seem to put their parentage beyond doubt. But if, as the medical consensus would have it, Amenophis IV suffered from some ailment resulting in eunuchoidism, is it possible that he could have sired any children? Again, in view of the predilection of the age to show only daughters in the royal entourage, how much faith should one place in the implication of the reliefs that the royal family numbered no sons in its ranks? These are questions to which we shall return in Chapters 8 and 11; it is sufficient at this point simply to adumbrate the general thrust of our suspicions.

The Provenience of the Talatat

The matching of blocks into ever-growing scenes continued uninterrupted for nearly a decade from 1966. Between 15 and 20 percent of the 45,000 blocks were matched, and although the total may seem small, it must be remembered that the constant repetition of motifs made completion of every scene unnecessary. Soon, for example, it became possible to reconstruct offering scenes or processional scenes in every detail and to the proper scale simply by the evidence of one or two component pieces. The project therefore increasingly fell back on reconstructing by line drawing scenes of which we already had matched photographic collages.

By 1975 the era of short returns had set in. We had a good idea of the total repertoire of artistic decoration of the temples but matches were fewer, apart from the occasional major discovery that two whole collages fitted together. Unanswered questions remained, especially about points of construction. What percentage of the total did the 45,000 blocks represent? Was much of the masonry of Amenophis IV's temples still eluding us within standing pylons, or beneath the ground? How high were the walls of these temples and what types of coping or dado had been used at the top and bottom of the walls? We already knew that some of the wall surfaces must have been of great height, for we had succeeded in matching some large figures of the king and queen, the tallest of which approached thirteen meters. Again, although the reliefs that decorated the walls were fairly well known to us, we had no idea on what lines the walls ran: it was essential to recover the ground plans of the buildings whose walls we were reconstructing, almost out of thin air! But in order to say anything about the layout of Amenophis's temples to the sun-disc, their original sites had to be identified.

Although in 1975 we knew of no site of a sun-disc temple at Karnak, we were not wholly lacking in clues. Despite the poor records that had been kept during the early years of the program to recover *talatat*, it was possible by a little detective work to discover the provenience of many of the blocks. For example, blocks originally from *Rwd-mnw* came almost exclusively from either the lowest courses of the ninth pylon core or from the area of the Luxor temple. The middle courses of the ninth pylon yielded *talatat* decorated with scenes from *Tni-mnw*, while the upper parts of the same pylon contained *Gm·(t)-p³-itn* material. The prime source for the latter, however, was the second pylon, whence came over 80 percent of blocks from this the largest of the sun-disc temples. *Talatat* from the *Ḥwt-bnbn* came only from the second pylon and the foundations of the hypostyle hall, while the scattering of several hundred blocks in the late shrines of north Karnak likewise represented *Ḥwt-bnbn* or *Gm·(t)-p³-itn*.

A spatial separation was therefore in evidence in the secondary placement of the *talatat*: *Rwd-mnw* and *Tni-mnw* are represented on the south of Karnak, while *Gm·(t)-p³-itn* and *Ḥwt-bnbn* are confined to the north. Can this have anything to do with the locations of the original shrines? Is it only coincidence that the phrases *Rwd-mnw* "sturdy are the monuments . . ." and *Tni-mnw*, "exalted are the monuments . . ." enter into the names of other buildings, both earlier and later, in the general vicinity of the tenth pylon?

A more exciting, and ultimately more rewarding clue was provided by chance discovery in 1925. In that year a ditch was excavated encircling the Karnak ruins in order to provide better drainage for a rising water table. In the course of digging that portion of the conduit that lay due east of the eastern gate of Karnak, erected c. 350 B.C. by pharaoh Nectanebo, a line of fallen colossi of Amenophis IV was unearthed. Inspector Chevrier, newly arrived in Luxor as the Antiquités representative, was given the task of exploring further this important find. From 1926 until he retired from the Service over a quarter-century later, scarcely a year went by in which Chevrier did not devote some of his time and budget to continuing the diggings in "East Karnak," as it has come to be known (Fig. 8). Chevrier found that the row of colossi continued in an east-west line for nearly 200 meters. Many were represented only by fragments, and all had been pushed over to the north and now lay on their faces. Behind them to the south ran a line of worn stumps of sandstone masonry, interpreted at the time as pedestals, at

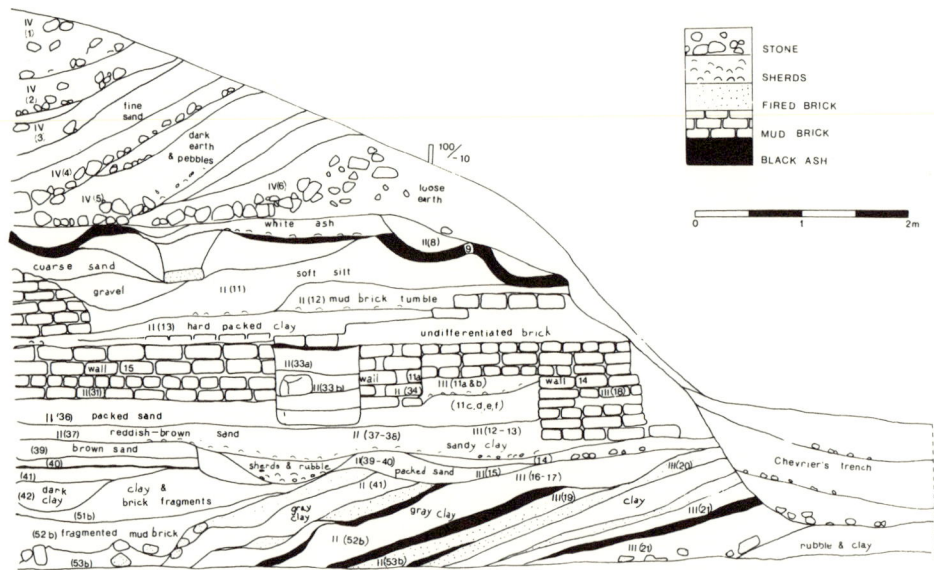

8. *Cross-section through quadrant BB, facing east. The surface at the bottom represents the open court of the* Gm·(t)-p³-itn *temple, onto which at the moment of the final destruction of the temple fell the charred temenos wall (II, 41, 52b, 53b; III, 16, 17, 19, 20, 21). Further debris fell to the north, and was added to over the centuries as the area was used as a garbage dump (II, 42, 51b, 52b, 53b). At last, at the close of the 8th century B.C. the site was leveled up (I, 37–38; III, 12, 13, 14, 15) and houses were built (wall 11a, 14, 15; see Chapter 5). These were twice rebuilt, once in the middle of the 6th century, and again around 400 B.C.; but before the coming of Alexander the Great (331 B.C.) the area had been abandoned (II, 11, 12, 13), wind-blown ash was allowed to accumulate (II, 8, 9). This remained the surface until 1925 when Chevrier dug his huge trench (right), flinging the earth to the north to form his own dump over the rest of the site (IV, 1–6).*

two-meter intervals; and behind these again, at a distance of two meters, the foundation courses of what appeared to be a wall. Fallen statues, "pedestals," and wall approached to within about seventy-nine meters of the Nectanebo gate, and then described a right angle toward the north. Soon, however, as Chevrier's workmen tried to trace the complex to the north, the remains grew ever more meager until, within ten meters, they had petered out entirely. Desperately Chevrier tried to detect some traces on this western side of whatever construction it was that he had stumbled on, but it was no use, for the destruction seemed complete. His last frantic attempts, made in the early Fifties with the use of a narrow gauge railway, can still be seen today in the gigantic hole his men dug about ninety meters due north of the turning described above. On the west he had more success, but soon found that the remains were covered by the modern village.

What was it that Chevrier had found? It seemed clearly a building of some sort, adorned with a colonnade fronted by standing colossal statues of Amenophis IV. But no decorated or inscribed blocks are reported by Chevrier, and he passed from the scene still uncertain as to what he had discovered. Guesses continued to be made, along with fantastic estimates about the structure's dimensions.

In 1975 it had become clear that the matching of *talatat* had proceeded to the limit of its usefulness. Unless some new evidence was brought to bear on the problem, preferably involving information on the ground plans of the temples, we could have no hope of establishing the sequence of scenes along walls. Excavation was called for, but it had to include the most up-to-date methods: Chevrier's work, it was felt, though valuable to a limited degree, had destroyed far more evidence than it had uncovered. There was no sense in digging madly through superimposed and underlying levels, with no records being kept, just to find a temple. Here was an opportunity to apply a meticulous methodology to a site to "milk" it of every scrap of evidence on a wide variety of problems: the history of the site as a whole, its ecology and industries, the diet of the people, the chemistry of the soil, the faunal population of the area, and its cereal production. Where better to start than the sole area where material from Amenophis IV's time had been found *in situ*, namely the undulating terrain of East Karnak?

In early 1975 a concession was obtained from the Egyptian government to excavate the sector known as East Karnak. The contract delineated the area as bounded on the north by the northeast angle of the Karnak enclosure, on the south by the *temenos* of Mut, on the east by the Cairo-Luxor railway line, and on the west by the wall of the Karnak enclosure. This irregular tract is enormous: about 800 meters by 250 meters. How in the world could we do justice to it?

CHAPTER FIVE

The Excavation of East Karnak

The vast terrain of East Karnak owes its present desolate aspect to events of the late 4th century B.C. It was not, indeed, always a bleak prospect that greeted the viewer's gaze when he looked east from the Karnak complex. When, in c. 712 B.C., Thebes came under the suzerainty of those puritanical black kings of the Sudan, known to history as the 25th Dynasty, the site experienced a revival of prosperity and an increase in its population. The little cluster of chapels northeast of the main temple of Amun, which had evinced the growing interest of the 22nd and 23rd Dynasties★ in the abandoned land to the east, were embellished with additions, and shrines of the Divine Worshippers of Amun began to grow up around them. Taharqa★ added a portico to the old Upper Gate of Ramesses II, and simultaneously the houses of the people began to spread eastward over the site of Amenophis IV's structure that Chevrier was later to find (Fig. 8). The site had been used as a garbage dump for nearly six centuries, and so had to be evened up by

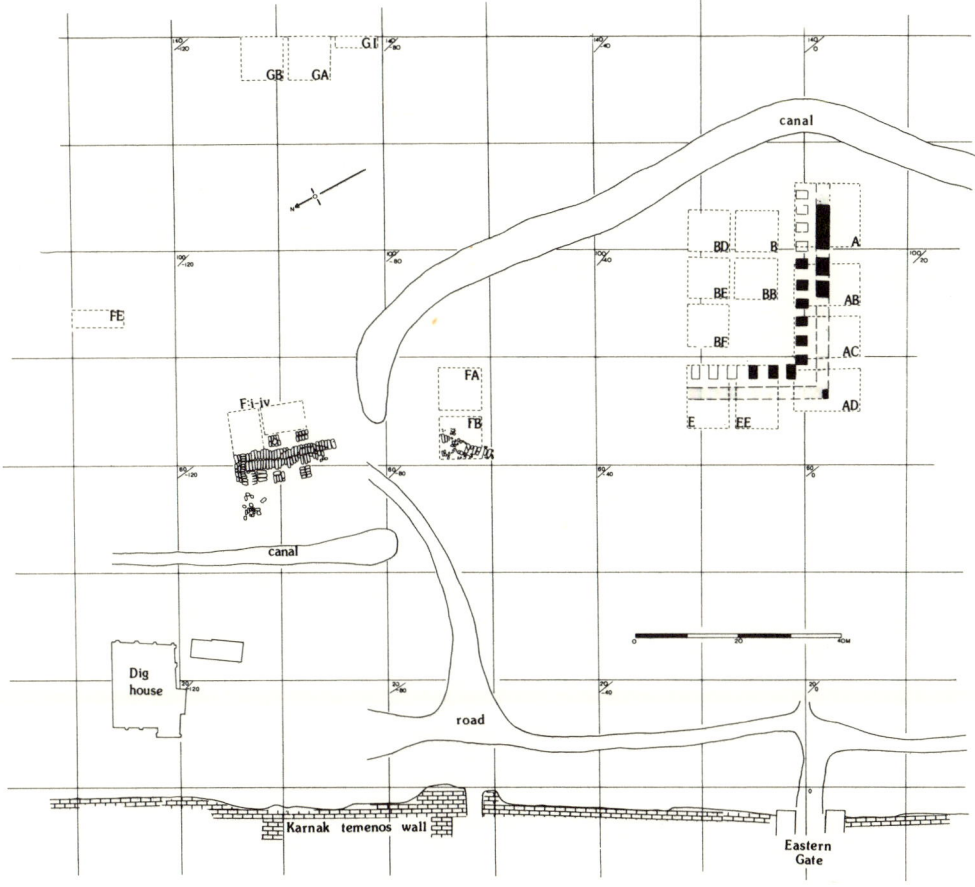

9. Plan of excavation in East Karnak (grid squares 20m. on a side). The quadrants are lettered in bold type. Those of A, B, and E series (upper right-hand corner) are exposed to the level of phase N (14th century B.C.), viz. that of the Gm·(t)-p³-itn temple, showing south and west colonnades. The F series (center left) is exposed at phase B (4th century B.C.).

the deposit of artificial fill. An axial street was run eastward, continuing the Karnak axis, and an enclosure wall was thrown up, creating a sort of "satellite" community. Despite the Assyrian invasion, in the course of which, in 663 B.C., the Assyrian king Ashurbanipal reached Thebes and sacked it, this new eastern quarter prospered. By the mid-6th century the houses had been rebuilt, and now showed signs of overcrowding. Pottery kilns dotted the street on the south; the kitchens of scribes' or priests' houses opened on the north. Even the overthrow of the 26th Dynasty did not appreciably alter

87

5.1. Modern view of East Karnak, facing north. The temenos *wall of the Amun enclosure is on the left, the drainage canal in the center, and the site of* Gm·(t)-p³-itn *beyond the trees on the right.*

conditions in East Karnak: the settlement continued through the 5th century under Persian rule in essentially the same way as before. Only with the coming of independence under Amurtaeus (28th Dynasty) in 406 B.C. is a modification in evidence. The old houses are destroyed, but in their place rise new and larger ones, and overcrowding seems no longer a problem. The end of the 4th century, however, witnessed the settlement's ultimate fate. The second Persian invasion under Artaxerxes III (343 B.C.) and the coming of Greek hegemony with the advent of Alexander the Great and his political heir in North Africa, Ptolemy Lagus, spelled doom for Thebes "the southern city." The houses were mostly abandoned, their furniture salvaged, and their collapsing rooms used as refuse pits. Here and there squatters persisted in some old houses, but the suppression of the Theban rebellion in 186 B.C. must have driven away even these. By the first century B.C.

East Karnak was a desolation, and the center of the town had shifted south to Luxor where it has remained ever since.

Today the land east of the Nectanebo gate in the eastern *temenos* wall sweeps away in a haphazard series of mounds and depressions, intersected by donkey paths (Pl. 5.1). A straggling village called Nag el-Fokkani, "the upper hamlet" (an echo of Ramesses II's "upper gate"), encroaches on the eastern fringe of the ancient site and is hemmed in on the east by the railway tracks. For over a century the excavators and Antiquities inspectors of Karnak used the area as a convenient dump in their clearing operations within the enclosure of the temple of Amun, and the resultant debris, 3.5 meters in depth, which caps a pentagonal area 100 by 150 meters outside the Nectanebo gate, only increases the aspect of desolation. Goats feed on the camel thorn and scrub; donkeys plod over paths leading to the village; at night snakes abound and mangy dogs bark, and everywhere the ground is dusty and stony. Only in November through February is the weather supportable. By *hamseen*★ season in March and April, the wind often whips the dust into towering dust devils, and the concomitant mugginess in the atmosphere can make living conditions thoroughly unpleasant.

The Search For the Temple of the Heretic

On such a day as this our search began.[1] Throughout the late spring and summer of 1975 our small party of excavators toiled to excavate a single, eight-by-twelve-meter quadrant, cut back on the south side of the huge trench dug by Chevrier in an effort to recover the statues of Amenophis IV. The late dump was removed in about ten days, but immediately beneath, the virgin strata yielded late 4th century B.C. material. Excavation eventually revealed nondescript domestic walls and seven superimposed floor-surfaces belonging to three major building phases from c. 700-300 B.C. This was not primarily what the expedition had set out to find, and the remains were not historically or culturally very important. But archaeology cannot play favorites, and one must be as meticulous an analyst as one can be at all times; one must never say this is not what I want, and abandon the site. Consequently, as more and more of this late settlement come to light as we

1. On the excavations, see in particular D. B. Redford, *JARCE* 14 (1977), 9ff; *Scientific American* 239, no. 6 (Dec. 1978), 136ff.; *Expedition* 21, no. 2 (1979), 54ff.; *ROM Archaeological Newsletter* no. 179 (Apr. 1980); *JSSEA Journal* 11, no. 4 (Aug. 1981), 243ff.

opened new quadrants and squares in 1977 and after, we began a careful study of every aspect of ancient domestic life our modern techniques would permit from the four centuries in question.

It soon became apparent that, although East Karnak had not been the most affluent quarter of ancient Thebes, the inhabitants had enjoyed a reasonable standard of living. Some fine vessels would have adorned their cupboards and some attractive figurines their cabinets. Ubiquitous were animal-dolls made of clay and the crude female "fertility" figures; occasionally a cultic vessel with the face of Hathor★ modeled on the outside would turn up. One curious feature that puzzled us for a time was the relatively high proportion among osteological samples of bovid bones. At first we thought the reason was the faulty sampling technique used in the first season, but even after refining our method, ox and cow bones continued to be in the majority. Did the inhabitants of ancient Thebes enjoy a diet richer in beef than elsewhere in the general vicinity? But the answer was obvious. Thebes in the c. 7th–6th B.C., as it had for 1,000 years, constituted a network of major temples: Amun and Montu on the north, Khonsu and Mut on the south, were serviced by hundreds of priests daily. Central to any ancient Egyptian temple organization was the daily offering, placed before the god on all his altars, and this inevitably included, *inter alia*, the beef offering. One medium-sized temple in Middle Egypt, that of the ram-god Arsaphes,★ offered one whole bull each day of the year; we may well imagine the much larger Theban complex demanding many more. Naturally, the haunches and cuts of meat, once placed on the offering tables before the gods, were not allowed to sit there and rot; the practical Egyptians removed them, after the deity had had his fill, and they became the rations of all the members of the temple community, priest and layman alike. If the inhabitants of East Karnak ate more meat in antiquity than they do today, it is because the temples were a "going concern" in those days.

The levels below the earliest of the three building phases showed evidence of a quite different type of occupation. For, prior to 700 B.C., East Karnak had been used as a garbage dump, which had had to be leveled up before houses could be built over it. Fortunately, the date when the dump was begun and the point in time when it ceased to be used were clear.

Throughout the levels following the 7th century B.C., we had already encountered, built into house walls at random, bricks of good quality that had been *fired*. This fact alone is of some moment, in view of the almost exclusive ancient preference for sun-dried mud-brick in domestic architecture. Scholars, moreover, had long been wedded to an untested hypothesis that baked brick was characteristic of only the Roman period in Egypt. Another surprise, however, lay in store: many of these bricks had been stamped before firing with the name and title of the contemporary potentate under whom they had been manufactured. Ninety-nine percent of several score which have been recovered bore a double oval stamp with the inscription, "the High Priest of Amun, Menkheperre." This is a well-known figure in Egyptian history, a famous scion of a family of high priests, which had held the pontificate, and ipso facto temporal power, in Upper Egypt after the demise of the New Kingdom, c. 1070 B.C. Menkheperre had held the office from c. 1020-1000 B.C., and his major accomplishment at Thebes seems to have been the construction of an enclosure wall around the north side of the Temple of Amun. In a fortunately surviving stele from the east gate of Ramesses II, Menkheperre says he "made for him (i.e., Amun) a very great wall on the north of Karnak . . . for the purpose of concealing the temple of his father Amunre and ridding (it) of hoi polloi, after he had found it cluttered with the houses of the common people which had been implanted in the courts of the house of Amun. . . ."[2] Where precisely this wall ran is as yet uncertain, but scattered bricks stamped "Menkheperre" were long ago found in the northwest corner of Karnak. Now our find of hundreds of similarly stamped bricks in East Karnak reopens the question. The best guess would appear to postulate a wall running roughly along the line of the present north *temenos* wall, but turning south to enclose the "high gate" of Ramesses II. If, as seems most likely, our bricks emanate from this wall, they must have been taken at a time when it was falling into delapidation; and since the aforesaid dump contains examples of Menkheperre bricks in its upper levels, it is certain that it must have been in a ruinous state already in the 8th century B.C.

The beginning of the dump is also not difficult to ascertain. The lower levels show late New Kingdom, or Ramesside, pottery. Some jar handles, stamped with the name of the institution to whom they belonged, display the identification "The Mansion (i.e., mortuary temple) of Menmare Sety Merenptah." This must mean that the area came into use as a dump at the beginning of the 19th Dynasty, c. 1300 B.C., and continued as such for six centuries.

2. P. Barquet, *Le Temple d'Amon-rê à Karnak* (Cairo, 1962).

As our excavation in A-quadrant continued in this dump, we sensed that the levels, which toward the top had been roughly horizontal, were beginning to decline sharply to the north. Some prominent declivity running east-west must have existed here at the close of the 18th Dynasty. Only later were we to realize the significant fact that this trench (as it turned out to be) was aligned on the central axis of the Karnak Temple to the west!

Our 1975 season terminated in September with few traces having been yet found of the period of Amenophis IV. True, from time to time in the upper levels reused fragments of *talatat* had come to light, but these could have been carried to the site from elsewhere. It was clear, however, that the depth of unexcavated occupational stratification was still great in A-quadrant, and we determined to pursue excavation in this area until the water table blocked any further descent, no matter whether we were ultimately thwarted in our expectation of a *talatat*-structure.

In January of 1976 the work in East Karnak resumed; in the interim a house had been built for the expedition. Now at last the ground began to yield a bounty. Everywhere in the southern half of A-quadrant, immediately beneath the dump, piles of broken *talatat* appeared, approaching in places a depth of c. fifty centimeters (cf. Pl. 5.2). To the north, as presaged by the incline of the overlying dump, the rubble declined into an east-west trench, which was c. three meters wide at the top. On the extreme north of the quadrant a most curious but enlightening feature emerged: four equidistant and rectangular beds of sandstone chips, c. 1.80 by 2 meters in dimension, running parallel to the trench in an east-west direction. These could only be, and in fact later proved to be, the foundations of the rough "bases" that Chevrier had uncovered in the late Twenties and that he had understood to be pedestals for the colossi he had found lying in front of each. In A-quadrant the blocks themselves had been stolen; but the beds of chips were sufficient to indicate their erstwhile presence.

Clearly, this composite of features offered tantalizing prospects of identification, and throughout the first two weeks of January hopes were high. The *talatat* rubble pointed to the period of Amenophis IV, since he alone had initiated and carried through construction in this size of masonry, but how could our conjecture be finally proven? Without a doubt the rubble represented one of the sun-disc temples that Horemheb had destroyed and used the blocks as fill for one of his Karnak constructions, but could we identify it by name? The sinking feeling assailed us that perhaps all facing

5.2. Piers of the south colonnade (quadrant AB), facing north. Immediately behind the piers, excavation has begun to reveal the foundations of the wall. A tumble of broken sandstone blocks in the foundation trench is coming to light.

blocks that had once borne relief had been removed, and that not even a fragment of decoration remained amidst the rubble to provide the much-needed clue. Happily, we were wrong. Shortly after the uncovering of the first patch of these shattered stones, the workmen came running with the news that one of the pieces was a *hajar maktub* ("inscribed block"). It was a header, with traces of men's legs moving past a column. The same day another fragment came to light showing the head of a man with the finial of a pole across his shoulder. The suspicion that both pieces came from a scene depicting a royal palanquin with its bearers was confirmed when a beautiful well-preserved block with bearers and poles was uncovered (Pl. 5.3). And then the inscribed pieces began to come thick and fast. A preserved header showed bowing priests with their sacred standards and the name of the sun-disc, while another showed the bent knees of the palanquin bearers caught in the act of letting their precious burden down. Courtiers bowing, Nubians adoring, pharaoh offering, the sun-disc beaming—often only the merest fragments of these themes remained, but to our amazement and joy

93

5.3. Talatat fragments recovered in the A and AB quadrants showing palanquin bearers conveying the king to the temple (probably part of the great progress of TS 235, now known to have stood in A).

our familiarity with these stereotypes made them instantly recognizable. Over 100 inscribed pieces were eventually to be registered from A-quadrant, and very few escaped identification!

And what was the temple from which they had all come? The answer was crystal clear. Almost all fragments could be fitted in or accommodated in a type of scene long known to us from our matching of blocks in the earlier years of the project, and that was the processional scene, showing the king being carried in his palanquin from palace to temple. It is confined to the repertoire of scenes depicting the jubilee and, as such, is known solely from the *Gm·(t)-p³-itn* temple. Confirmation soon came: a header showing the white crown, recovered from the center of A-quadrant, bore the fragmentary inscription "[the great Disc . . .] residing in *Gm·(t)-p³-itn*." The problem was solved; we had found our temple!

94

CHAPTER SIX

East Karnak before Amenophis IV

When Amenophis IV ascended the throne, his city of Thebes, the "Southern City," or the "Upper Egyptian Heliopolis," as it was variously called, already had a long and distinguished history. The spatial limits of the settlement had ebbed and flowed over the centuries, but in the mid-18th Dynasty most of the houses appear to have been strung out along the river bank. The site that Amenophis chose for the $Gm \cdot (t)$-p^3-itn lay east of the great Amun temple, and here, in the first year of his reign, lay a vast tract of vacant land, abandoned for over two centuries. Why had such prime land been deserted?

One of the unexpected problems we have encountered in the excavations in East Karnak is a water table substantially higher than it was in antiquity.[1] This is alleged to be, and probably is, the result of the Aswan High Dam,

---

1. *SSEA Journal* 11, no. 4, 247ff.

which has reduced the effects of the annual inundation but has maintained the level of water in the Nile valley north of Aswan at a constant height. In Karnak there is fluctuation in the water table, due in part to the opening and closing of local irrigation ditches. The maximum difference, however, is only about seventy-five centimeters, and never exceeds a meter, at least in our experience of five years' digging.

In spite of the waterlogged condition of the lowest levels, we have been able to recover what may be the earliest phase of occupation in East Karnak. The lowest strata, to a point 1.30 meters above the water table, belong to the Middle Kingdom. In our initial quadrant, A, in early 1976, we unearthed a small mud-brick house with thin walls, some only the width of a brick. Though the area had been heavily pitted in later times, there was no mistaking the date of the pottery the house contained: it was the plum-red or brown burnished ware usually labeled in the broad designation "Middle Kingdom" by most ceramic experts in Egyptology. The house showed two stages of construction, and beneath it were walls of earlier structures, the whole sequence possibly representing the passage of several centuries. Though we have yet to excavate them, we have ascertained that house walls of similar Middle Kingdom date underlie the entire site at least as far north as the dig house (i.e., the northeast corner of the present Karnak *temenos*); and the IFAO★ excavations by Helen and Jean Jacquet have revealed them at a similar level on the north side of Karnak as well. It is nearly a decade since M. Jean Lauffray, sometime director of CFE, found the remains of similar Middle Kingdom houses inside the Karnak enclosure, about 160 meters due west of the area we are currently excavating. Finally, in 1971–1972 I unearthed, just above water table in the forecourt of Osiris Heqa Djet★ within the northeast angle of the Karnak *temenos*, houses and silos of the exact same date.

The distinct impression given by this evidence is of a very large Middle Kingdom city, extending 200 to 300 meters both east and north of the present Akh-menu★ (built by Thutmose III on the site of the older Middle Kingdom *temenos* wall of the Amun Temple), and encompassing many areas not to be covered again by private houses until Kushite-Saite times. One must eliminate in any imaginative reconstruction any restricting *temenos* walls, such as those built later by Ramesses II or Nectanebo I: apparently residential building extended in all directions, and with little evidence of town planning. For what we are seeing in the Middle Kingdom level at Karnak is the high-water mark of a city as yet a glorified provincial town. Thanks to the wars of unification waged by Montuhotep I, the inconsequential hamlets on the Theban plain found themselves suddenly transformed into a royal residence and erstwhile capital. Even so, while the 11th Dynasty held sway, the addition of a note of monumentality was a favor bestowed only on the west bank. The one major structure worthy of gracing a royal residence on the west bank was Montuhotep's podium-tomb at Deir el-Bahri★ with its surrounding colonnades and its tree-lined forecourt. On the east bank there were temples, but these were small affairs whose origins antedated the triumph of Thebes: that of Montu, the falcon-headed, north of Karnak; Mut the "Mother" to the south; Amun the "Hidden," presumably on the site of the present Karnak. It is quite likely that a few of the Old Kingdom monarchs deigned to donate some small memorials to these country shrines, but Thebes nonetheless remained for the pyramid-pharaohs of the 3rd millennium B.C. a remote backwoods.

All this changed for the city on the east bank with the coming to power of the 12th Dynasty (c. 1990 B.C.). In spite of the founder's brilliant decision to move his capital to a new city some thirty to forty miles south of Memphis, it was his son and successor Senwosret I who placed Thebes forever in his debt by constructing a new temple to Amun (under his "solar" designation "Amun-Re") called the "Thrones of the Two Lands." In the sanctuary of this temple, "the Most Select of Places," Senwosret I built a great alabaster altar, and adorned the approaches with subsidiary buildings of which one beautiful wayside chapel of alabaster has been recovered and reconstructed. To the south the house of the high priest was built. On the mud-brick *temenos* wall on the east side a painted scene showed the king enthroned on a dais, receiving his court, and an accompanying hieroglyphic record, dated to his 9th year, recorded (in all probability) the audience at which the announcement was made of the king's intent to build the temple. Thutmose III tore down this wall five centuries later to clear the ground for his festival hall, but remained faithful to his ancestor's memory by doing a copy of the ancient scene in stone on the south external wall of Hatshepsut's block of rooms. Senwosret I's temple no longer exists, but it was probably coextensive with the later temple of Thutmose I (late 16th century B.C.). If this is so, then the structure was a rectangular one, preceded by a mud-brick pylon that gave on to an open court surrounded by Osiride statues of the king (Thutmose I's rebuilding would simply have redone the structure in stone, but not changed the design).

One important point emerges about the relationship between Senwosret

I's new temple and the surrounding town. All the houses in the latter, whether in east, north, or central Karnak, are laid out with an orientation toward the points of the compass; this must represent the original orientation of the primitive settlements in the area, dating back to Old Kingdom times. The temple of Amun Senwosret built, however, is constructed not on the same orientation at all, but is so aligned that its longer axis (local east-west) lines up with some lost structure (temple? palace?) in Drah abu'l naga★ across the river to the west; while the southern end of a north-south axis, close to Mut, lines up with the causeway of Montuhotpe's tomb at Deir el-Bahri. The new alignments of Thebes' monumental pretension may well be symbolic, but they also prove that Senwosret I's Temple of Amun is the latecomer in a town already in existence and not ready to change its layout to accommodate the temple.

Although excavation may not fully reveal the answer, there is a little evidence now to ascertain how far east the Middle Kingdom city extended. When we continued our excavations in 1977 by the addition of quadrant AB to the *west* of A we encountered at the Middle Kingdom level a massive mud-brick wall over six meters thick, running (true) north-south. The house we had excavated in the previous season lay *east* of this wall. Since a wall of this magnitude could only have been an enclosure wall of some sort, the thought immediately springs to mind that it may be the eastern wall of the city. If so, the house in A-quadrant would have been outside the enclosed area. Whatever truth resides in this postulate, quadrant G, about seventy meters east-northeast of A, revealed nothing of the Middle Kingdom. The last meter above water in G reveals layer after layer of tightly packed New Kingdom sherds, suggesting that, at this point at least, the Middle Kingdom surface had declined rather sharply.

The ultimate fate of the Middle Kingdom city is fairly clear, though not the reason. The house in A had been demolished by fire, and the stumps of the walls had lain open to the air for a considerable time. The layer of ash in the rooms had been windblown, and was piled deeper in the corners than in the center. Gradually sand had been blown in to conceal the worn-down ruins from sight. No further occupation is attested for centuries: the inhabitants, or those who had survived, evidently went elsewhere.

Our textual evidence from the times should further elucidate the archaeological evidence, but does it?[2] There is no evidence whatsoever of any

2. See J. von Beckerath, *Untersuchungen zur politischen Geschichte der zweiten Zwischen-* *zeit in Ägypten* (Gluckstadt, 1965).

decline in the prosperity of the Thebaid while the 12th Dynasty held sway. In fact, down to the end of the reign of the second king of the 13th Dynasty the archaeological and textual record agrees in excluding the possibility of a serious political disturbance in the south. Thereafter the picture changes. Eleven kings succeeded each other in rapid succession, the total of their reigns amounting to not more than ten years. Such a sequence of ephemeral heads of state usually signals a breakdown in central authority, resulting in a weakening of law and order, if not a lapse into outright anarchy. Around 1740 B.C. order was restored by Sobkhotpe II and his three strong successors on the throne; but the restoration of good times was brief. Three short-lived nonentities occupied the throne for approximately three years, one with the unlikely name of Emramesha^c ("Army general"), a second with the plebeian name of Sutekh ("Seth"). Four strong kings, Sobekhotpe III, Neferhotpe I, Si-Hathor, and Sobekhotpe IV, once again restored prosperity from c. 1749 to 1725; but, while their monuments are found all over Egypt, theirs was not a true *risorgimento*. Following 1725 a slow decline set in. After half a dozen reigns the occupants of the throne leave fewer and fewer traces until we are felt with the Turin Canon* alone, our one true king-list. There remain only the names, all too fragmentary for assured restoration after 1682.

It is a lawless age, which throws up warlike saber-rattlers, faceless names, and childish simpletons. There is, for example, the famine stele of Sekhemre Se^{c}onkhtowy Neferhotpe, who, appropriately enough for the occasion, took the added cartouche (in a pleasing flash of originality) "Ikhernofret," lit. "He who comes bearing good things." ". . . Beloved of Amun, who enters into his city with sustenance preceding him, [united] with holidays, a mighty king beloved of his army, good Horus who brings offerings and gives life to his city which had fallen into need; leader of mighty Thebes, the Good God, beloved of Re, son of Amun King-of the-Gods, protecting his city when it had 'gone under'; defending it from (?) the foreigners [who had . . .] to it, the foreign lands which had rebelled being terror-struck by his father Amun; overthrowing the [recalcitrant?] who had rebelled against him."[3] Through its rather pompous and high-flown jargon, one can get a glimpse of Thebes, stricken by famine, beset by restless bands of Nubians(?), and saved by a perhaps desperate intervention of an otherwise ephemeral king.

3. W. Helck, *Historisch-biographische Text*   no. 62 (corrected from personal copy). *der 2. Zwischenzeit* (Wiesbaden, 1975), 45f.,

But there is also jingoism and nonsense. An unpublished stele of a certain king Montuhotpe acquaints us with the former. Montuhotpe is "a Horus beloved in by his army. . . . I am a king . . . who repulses all foreign lands, and rescues his city from [want(?). . . .] One like Sekhmet★ in the year of pestilence. . . . This Thebes [is] my city, the mistress of the entire land, the victorious town."[4] Thebes in need of rescue, foreign lands a threat, victory by means of fierce bellicosity, Thebes victorious and at the head of the entire land—these are themes that at one and the same time evoke the mighty traditions of the 12th Dynasty and the utter bankruptcy of the 13th.

The final scene we might entitle "Thebes underwater and the ruler at play." Sobekhotpe VIII has left a crude stele in the Karnak temple, the family shrine, that reads as follows: "Live the son of Re, Sobekhotpe, beloved of the Great Flood, given life forever. Regnal year 4, 4th month of shōmu,★ day 5 of the epagomenal days★ under the Majesty of this god—may he live forever! His Majesty proceeded to the broad hall of this temple [Karnak] to see the Great Inundation. When His Majesty came to the broad hall of this temple it was full of water. Then His Majesty waded in it. . . ."[5] A broken-down irrigation system and a ruler who singles out for commemoration from the res gestae of his reign nought but a "splash party"—the end is close at hand. It may well be that the archaeological evidence of the violent destruction of the Middle Kingdom city finds corroboration and explanation in the "time of troubles" vaguely hinted at in the texts examined above.

Sometime early in the 17th century B.C. (c. 1670 B.C.) Egypt was invaded by West Semitic-speaking peoples, who quickly subverted the Delta and Middle Egypt as far as Cusae. The leaders of the invaders, called by the Egyptians $ḥḳ^3w$ $ḫ^3swt$ "foreign rulers," a term later garbled into "Hyksos," provided the country with the 15th Dynasty, comprising a line of six kings who ruled the country for a little over a century. The center of power had shifted to the Delta and the fate of half of Egypt lay in foreign hands; an impoverished Thebaid, as the result of geography rather than Theban effort, maintained a sort of freedom far to the south.

Between the destruction of the Middle Kingdom city in the late 18th century B.C. (?) and the early 14th, the vast reaches of East Karnak were regarded as unsuitable for human habitation. Cursory observation over seventy-five years ago prompted several Egyptologists, on the basis of sherd

4. Author's personal collection.
5. Helck, *Historisch-biographische Text.*, 46, no. 63.

material alone, to opine that the area had been used as a burial ground by the "Pan-grave People." These latter, Nubian warrior groups who had entered the employ of the Theban kings of the 16th and 17th Dynasties in their incipient war against the foreign Hyksos conquerors of the Delta, are well known from their cemeteries, which range from Aswan to Asyut. Their seminomadic southern origins are eloquently attested by their pottery, the appearance of bovid bones in their burials, and their weapons. To date we have not recovered any intact pan-graves, although one 17th-century burial was inadvertently uncovered by local children.

CHAPTER SEVEN

The *Gm·(t)-p³-itn*

Insofar as the excavations have shed light on the matter, the *Gm·(t)-p³-itn* temple was a simple but vast rectangle, about 130 by 200 (?) meters, oriented toward the east. It consisted of an open court, possibly divided by lateral walls and gates, around the periphery of which ran a roofed colonnade of square piers. The latter reached a height in excess of seven meters, with a correspondingly greater height for the roof, and against each pier was set a colossos of the king facing into the court (Figs. 10, 11; Pl. 4.2). The statues were gaily painted, and depicted the king in that eccentric and grotesque manner characteristic of his early years. Although there is some variation, in that part of the court where preservation is best (i.e., the southwest corner) the colossi seem to alternate in wearing the double-feather headdress of the air god Shu,★ and the double crown symbolic of the rule of Upper and Lower Egypt. The costume (not an innovation with Amenophis IV, but depicted by him ad nauseam) is the shin–length kilt of sheer linen, starched,

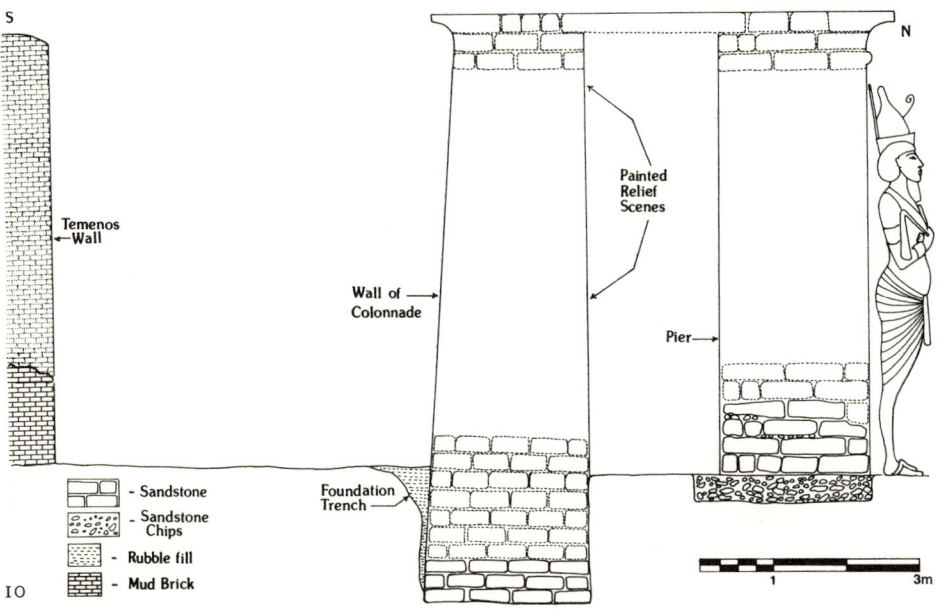

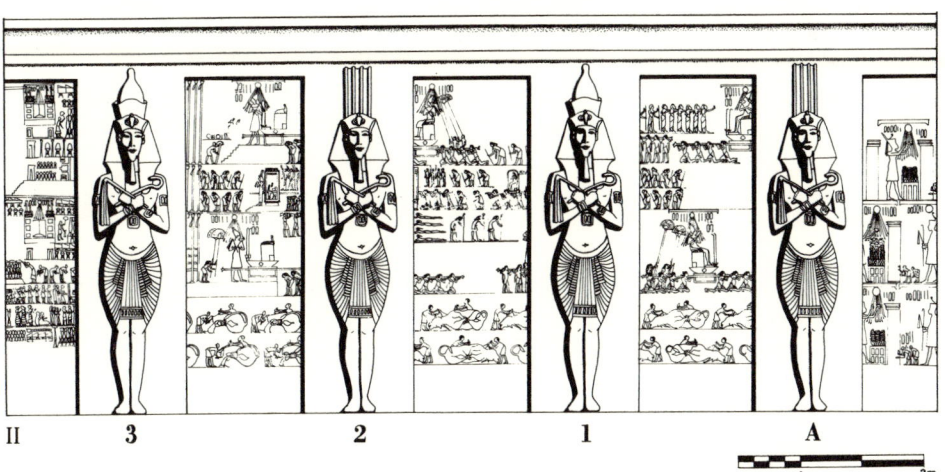

10. *Section through the south colonnade of* Gm(t)-p³-itn, *facing west. Surviving masonry, brickwork, and earth are shown in solid line, restored in broken line. Small statues and steles are known to have been set up in the colonnade.*

11. *Elevation of the south colonnade of* Gm·(t)-p³-itn *facing south in the reach of quadrants A and AB. The colossi are designated according to Chevrier's original numbering scheme. The back wall of the colonnade is shown decorated with a facsimile of TS 238 which we now know to have stood here. Additions not attested in the matching, but proven to have been present by fragments recovered in the excavations are 1) the palace on the left; 2) the dado of bull-slaughtering; 3) the adoring foreigners.*

7.1. Matching of talatat *(TS 28) recovered from the ninth pylon, originally from* Rwd-mnw. *The king wears a white bag-wig, as in Pl. 7.6 below, and a flowing gown whose pleats are discernible on the extended arm. The flesh tone is a beautiful reddish-brown.*

pleated, and brought round the hips and fastened below the navel (Pl. 7.1). Most of the statues show the kilt carved in the stone, but one shows a naked torso without genitalia! As one may well imagine, this curious exemplar of the sculptor's art has occasioned no end of sober reflection among humorless colleagues. Is this really Nefertity? Is Amenophis depicted as hermaphroditic? Was it an expression of a deep theological doctrine? For my own part, I can imagine that this image might have been clothed with some sort of applied garment. In any case, it need not be pointed out how ill-advised it is to read profound meaning into such a flimsy piece of evidence.

104

The Architecture

The piers of the colonnade were composed of rather coarse sandstone, probably faced with a veneer of finer stone of some sort. Each measured about 1.80 by 2.00 meters, and the piers were spaced at two-meter intervals. Almost everywhere along the south side the piers had been robbed out right down to the underlying beds of chips; only nine piers at the southwest corner (six on the south, three on the west) showed any stones remaining.

The temple wall on the south formed the back of the colonnade behind the piers, the interval of approximately two meters forming a roofed ambulatory. The wall itself, of which we found in quadrants A and AB three courses still remaining in the foundation trench, was 2.10 meters wide at the base. Courses consisted of four rows of headers, alternating with a core of three rows of headers faced on either side by stretchers. This produced exactly what the rule of thumb derived from trial and error in the matching had predicted, that is, alternating courses of headers and stretchers in the wall face. In all quadrants the wall was robbed out well below the contemporary ground level, but fortunately, the southwest corner had survived to a couple of courses above ground level, and the torus roll was intact (Pls. 7.3–5). The section through the wall thus provided (Pl. 7.5) showed a slight but pronounced batter on the outer face. The inner face, of course, on which the reliefs had been carved, had no batter, as we had long ago deduced in our photographic matching of the blocks.

Around the entire perimeter of the temple, at a distance of five meters outside the stone wall just described, ran a *temenos* wall of sun-dried mudbrick (Fig. 9). Excavation has not yet revealed the thickness of the wall, but in places its remains have survived to a respectable height, archaeologically speaking, of one meter or more. As in many *temenos* walls of later date, the courses of bricks when viewed horizontally undulate at regular intervals of three meters. This is because the damp course at the bottom of the foundation trench alternated (at this interval) between bricks placed on end with bricks laid flat. The remainder of the foundation was packed with hastily laid bricks and rubble, but this simple arrangement of the lowest course affected the lie of all the subsequent courses well above the ground level.

If, as all the evidence indicates, the temple was oriented toward the east, we should expect a gate and perhaps a monumental approach on the western side. Here all remains have been badly robbed out. Where one might expect the jamb of the gate, or towers of a pylon, nought remains but a deep hole

7.2

7.3

7.2 (above, left) Remains of piers along the south colonnade of the temple. A colossal Osiride statue of the king, like the one pictured in Pl. 4.2 and Fig. 11 at one time stood against each of these piers, facing right (north) into the open court of the temple.

7.3 (above, right) The southwest corner of the temple in quadrant AD facing north, surrounded by the shattered talatat from the destruction of the temple.

7.4 (opposite, left) The southwest corner of the temple facing east. The remains of the vertical torus-roll, a common device used on the exterior of a right angle in Egyptian architecture, is the feature that betrayed the nature of the in situ remains. Note the pattern of block-laying.

7.5 (opposite, right) Section through the southwest corner, facing south. Note the depth of the foundations, as well as the irregular laying of the talatat at the corner. The exterior face of the wall inclines inward at the expected angle of 3°.

7.4 7.5

with one large granite block on its side. North of the putative east-west axis of the structure two irregular quadrants were sunk in an area formerly cleared by Chevrier. Here two lines of rectangular beds of chips, each 1.80 by 1.25 meters, ran in an east-west line, flanked on the south by a *talatat*-wall, 1.60 meters thick, running in the same direction (Fig. 12). The presence of this unexpected structure introduces an anomaly into the symmetry of the temple on its northern side, and we are somewhat perplexed. Are these piers and wall part of a subsidiary aperture of some sort, or are we dealing with a separate building that intrudes into the western side of $Gm \cdot (t)$-p^3-itn? (Pl. 7.6)

The northern wall, and therefore an exact computation of the temple's width, have eluded us thus far. In 1976 a magnetometer survey was undertaken in various parts of East Karnak that had already been selected for

107

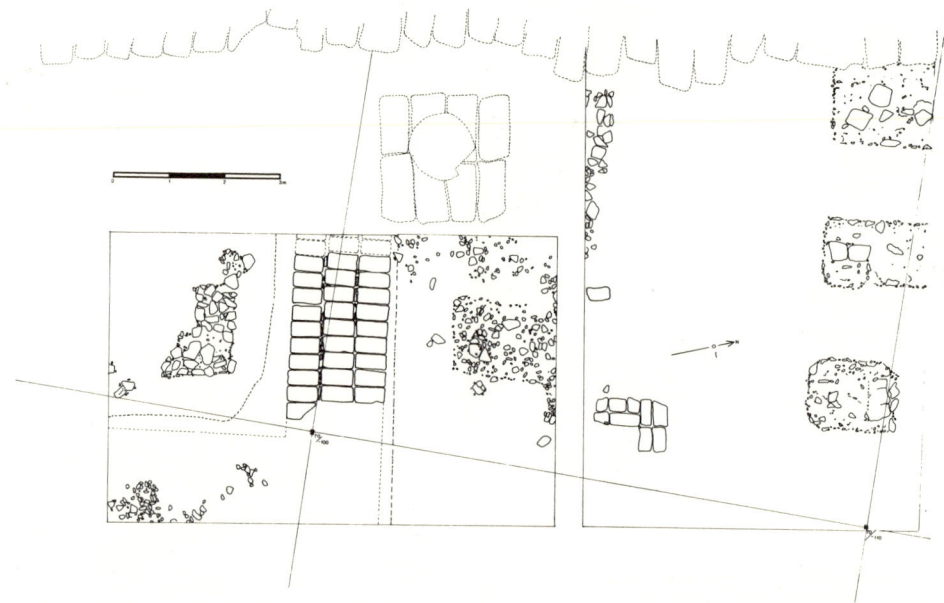

12. Area F, phase N. the partly preserved talatat *wall (left) and the two rows of pier-bases probably constitute part of the western approach to the* Gm·(t)-p³-itn. *Near here were found the fragmentary inscriptions pictured in Pls. 4.5 and 7.17. The structure indicated by the broken lines at the top belongs to the 4th century B.C. and stands at a higher level.*

excavation. One of the aims was, through a sequence of readings running north-south, to try to intersect the north wall, which would at once, we felt, be identifiable as a distinct anomaly. At a point approximately ninety meters north of the south wall such an anomaly was detected, but it was not as clear as we had hoped. Unfortunately, as we discovered when digging commenced in this area in 1979, the magnetometer had picked up the substantial house walls of the Saite period (7th-6th century B.C.); at the much lower 18th-Dynasty level nothing at all was found.

Consequently, a new sector was set aside for probing, almost as far to the north as our concession allowed. We opted for a "gas-pipe" trench,★ three by ten meters in dimension, running north-south at the 70/-130 meter grid-peg. The trench was to be driven north from a very large depression, partly water-filled, which represented the last desperate excavation of Henri Chevrier in 1951–1952, just before he retired from the Service. Chevrier during these seasons had made one final attempt on a grand scale to find

7.6. Talatat *recovered in 1978 from Area F on the slopes of the drainage canal, close to the point where probably the eastern gate of* Gm·(t)-p³-itn *was located. The face of the king and his bag wig are in evidence on the left. He appears to be leaning forward slightly, and his shoulder partly overlaps his neck, as though he were engaged in arranging or handling objects at a lower level than himself.*

the north side of the temple. A narrow gauge railway was installed and earth was removed by the wagonload. Nevertheless, Chevrier was disappointed in his quest: no evidence that he could appreciate was uncovered (though one suspects a harvest of information might have been reaped). Our trench, labeled FE, proceeded down to the 18th-Dynasty level in two seasons, and by late June, 1980, we had reached a surface of shattered sandstone *talatat*—drafted edges were clearly visible—that resembled markedly the destruction level encountered four years earlier on the south side. It looked very much as though the north wall was about to be revealed!

Other signs were propitious as well. Three statue fragments came to light, and one, although itself rather small, could only have formed part of the chest of a colossus. Again, the presence of three blocks originally part of a vertical *torus roll*, but not *in situ*, suggested that a corner (undoubtedly the northwest) was not far away. Symmetry demanded that the arrangement of the south colonnade, with its piers, reliefs, and colossal statues, be repeated on the north; this evidence from FE was in perfect accord.

Again, we were to be frustrated. The level of shattered sandstone was scarcely fifteen centimeters thick, the stone having disintegrated to a sort of moist grit: the outlines of blocks proved to be "ghosts" and we felt cheated of possible inscribed fragments. No foundation trench and no pier bases were in evidence, although it is clear that we are not far away. A chilling thought we have tried to put out of our minds: what if Chevrier, in his frantic digging, inadvertently destroyed the corner?

The Relief Decoration

The pile of shattered *talatat*, representing the phase of the temple's destruction, was not confined to A quadrant (see above, p. 100), but was found to run in a swath behind, i.e., south of, the southern colonnade down to the southwest corner. Nor did it stop here, but continued along the west side of the temple as well (Pls. 7.7–9). In fact, wherever *talatat* walls had run, there we were sure to find the pile of sandstone fragments. And everywhere in this wide-ranging debris, pieces decorated with relief from the walls would inevitably turn up. To date over 350 have emerged, though all are not immediately recognizable.

It became clear at an early stage in our work that the precise location of a decorated fragment in the swath of debris was of the utmost importance. Since fragments lay just where they had fallen from a particular spot on a stretch of wall, and had not been moved afterwards, they would provide, if they could be identified, a clue as to the particular scene used to decorate that specific section of wall. The prospect of putting together whole sequences of hitherto unrelated reliefs along a stretch of the colonnade at once arose in our minds; we began carefully to note the position of all decorated pieces, no matter how small. By the close of the 1978 season we were in a position to reconstruct a forty meter stretch of wall along the south side, east of the southwest corner, and a twenty meter stretch along the west side. Chart 1 locates the major identified fragments in terms of their quadrant and their distance along the colonnade from the corner, and identifies the scene-type from which they come.

There are numerous clues here as to the nature of the scenes and their sequence. The large vertical cartouches attested by fragments close to the corner, for example, confirm a suspicion long entertained because of the matching of blocks during the "office"-period of the Project. At that time we had become familiar with a type of block, occupying the inner angle of a corner, on which the carved traces consisted of large hieroglyphs. Matching of such blocks revealed long vertical columns of the cartouches and epithets of the sun god, clearly providing a vertical border at the end of a wall.

The presence of bowing courtiers and a fragment of their speech likewise conjured up parallels. We have only a few attested speeches that have emerged from the matching, and all are in the mouth of the king. The kind of adulatory response, however, on the part of the assembled court is a well-known element in Egyptian relief-scenes in which pharaoh, at a "royal sitting," makes a speech outlining a proposal. For such a speech to be included in the ceremonies depicted in the $Gm\cdot(t)-p^3-itn$ would not at all be out of place.

But the most interesting revelation of the excavated fragments is the ubiquity of the scene of the jubilee procession (Pl. 7.11). This had long proved to be the most common scene-type to be identified in our matching, but until the excavations we did not know how it had been used nor why it was so frequent. The motif varies only slightly, involving a series of vignettes that trace the sequence of movement. The king and queen are shown leaving the palace and entering their ceremonial carrying chairs, while chamberlains prostrate themselves (Pl. 7.12). The bearers then lift their burdens, the sunshade bearers fall in and elevate their large fans, and the assembled courtiers bow low (Pl. 7.13). The cortege now moves off from the palace and its progress is depicted in the lower registers of the wall. Unfortunately no scene reconstituted thus far has contained those parts showing the arrival at the temple (those blocks seem always to be missing; cf. Pl. 7.11); but there could be no doubt that, as at Amarna, the procession arrived at a pylon and was greeted by priests (Fig. 14). The temple enclosure itself is well-represented in the matched scenes (Fig. 15). It is usually within a double circumvallation, one wall (sinusoidal?) being depicted as a wavy line. Postern gates occasionally interrupt the continuity of the lines. Sometimes a large, monumental pylon with flag staffs and fluttering pennants fronts the whole. Within the enclosure, schematically thus defined, numerous small-scale registers show the king moving about among a host of small, roofless kiosks. He is accompanied by three dignitaries: the high priest of the sun, the chief lector priest, and the high priest of Neferkheprure Waʿenre (i.e., the king himself). The return from the temple to the palace occupies the registers immediately above those showing the outward procession; so that the same palace and temple depictions suffice for outward-bound and homeward progresses, and act as limits left and right to a "unit" of relief scene.

The fragments recovered from excavation clearly show that such a scene occupied the wall of the colonnade in the sector of our quadrant A. One should note especially the evidence between the 8–32-meter mark, which indicates the presence of a sinusoidal wall and pylon. This must be the approach to the temple, a hypothesis that seems confirmed by the presence of

7.7. Recovering the Destruction Level of the Temple. Encountering the first tumble of talatat in trench III of E quadrant, Dec. 1977.

adoring foreigners and attendant priests in the same general area. As one might expect, 32 to 36 meters from the corner brings us upon fragments showing the palanquin, both on the ground and being carried, and its bearers. Here we must be in the vicinity of that part of the scene depicting movement to and from the temple. Presumably the kneeling bearers at c. 37 meters signal the end of the journey and the reentry of the king into his palace. The entire progress, then, from palace to temple, would have occupied about seven meters of space along the wall; and it is of considerable significance that the largest relief scene matched to date, viz. TS 235, which is a marvelously detailed depiction of the processional, measures c. 7.5 meters from palace façade to the front of the temple! One fragment unearthed in

7.8 (above) E quadrant (facing east) as finally cleared down to phase L (the destruction level) of the Gm·(t)-p³-itn temple (Summer 1978). In the background are the emplacement beds for the piers of the west colonnade.

7.9 Removing talatat in quadrant EE, May 1979.

CHART 1 DISTRIBUTION ALONG THE SOUTH SIDE

Meters from Corner	Scenes Attested	Quadrant
1–4	—large vertical cartouches of the sun-disc —bowing courtiers	AD I
4–8	—nondescript fragments	AD II
8–13	—fragments of an inscription (note phrase: "they said . . .") —sun-disc with rays —traces of sinusoidal wall	AC I
13–18	—traces of sinusoidal wall —doorway —ornamental chests in palace setting —king offering in temple context —courtiers bowing	AC II
20–24	—bulls being thrown and slaughtered by butchers (many fragments) (Pl. 7.10) —bowing courtiers —sun-discs with rays	AB I
24–28	—king, (→) and offering table —bouquets —royal cartouches —king with priests —pylon of temple	AB II
28–32	—traces of sinusoidal wall —chief lector priest —Nubians with arms raised in adoration (→) (Pl. 3.5) —priests bowing with standards (→)	A I

CHART 1 CONTINUED

Meters from Corner	Scenes Attested	Quadrant
	—palanquin bearers (← →), carrying the king in his jubilee palanquin (Pl. 5.3)	
32–36	—courtiers bowing (Fig. 13) —king in white crown ascending his jubilee palanquin —king in jubilee costume	A II-III
36–40	—palanquin bearers (← →), some kneeling —king offering in temple —priests in attendance —door (of temple?)	A III-IV

A III, in fact, showing the king's white crown, seems to be the completion of part of TS 235; and if this is the case, this very scene whose blocks were found reused in the ninth pylon will have been located along the south colonnade at c. 29–37 meters from the corner.[1] The part of TS 235 showing the palace would then probably have been shown at the 37–38-meter point; but at 38–40 meters, at the eastern limit of our excavations in A-area, the fragments attest the presence of yet another temple representation and the ceremonies that went on there. This must be the western extremity of another "processional" scene, which would have stretched along the colonnade further to the east (where the drainage ditch now lies). Again to the west, while the fragments from 20 to 26 meters from the corner betray scenes of the temple ritual, and must therefore belong to the TS 235 unit, those found between the 15 and 18-meter marks attest the presence of the palace again. Between 8 and 14 meters the sinusoidal circumvallation once more signals the presence of the temple complex, so that between the 8 and 20-meter points yet another "processional" scene must have occurred.

1. For TS 235, see Smith and Redford, *The Akhenaten Temple Project* 1: end papers.

7.10. Talatat *fragments recovered in A and AB quadrants, showing a bull in the process of being thrown preparatory to trussing and slaughtering.*

The evidence we have passed in review is unanimous, therefore, in its support for the contention that the south wall of the temple was decorated in a series of "relief units" that took the jubilee processional as its theme. Remains of three such units can be identified, which in sum cover an expanse of wall stretching at least fifty meters from the corner. Each shows the temple and palace, and the activity that went on in each, as the extremities to the unit, separated by registers devoted to the procession itself. We should by no means consider each example of the motif identical with those lying contiguous to it. Thus the unit closest to the corner seems to have involved a lengthy speech placed in the mouths of bowing courtiers, though whether stationed in palace, temple, or along the route we cannot tell. The next example of the motif to the east was accompanied by scenes of butchers engaged in slaughtering. We know from other sources that the jubilee was a time for the king to fete the people in sumptuous banquets at which beef dishes figured prominently; and depictions of butchers and trussed bulls in the abattoir abound in the blocks we have matched. Often an especially fat animal will be shown being force-fed, while a gang of exuberant servants drags it along on a cart or sledge: it has been sedentary so long that it cannot walk and its hooves have curled up! Frequently the slaughtering scenes occupy a lower position on the wall, as a sort of horizontal border along the bottom of a scene; this is how we feel they were used in the wall in the range of AB-quadrant.

Since the south colonnade was robbed out well below ground level, it is difficult to ascertain whether postern gates pierced the wall at any points. In certain quadrants (e.g., A III–IV, and all of AC) the number of decorated fragments diminishes suddenly and dramatically when compared with the areas on either side, and this may well betray the presence of an aperture and therefore less wall space for decoration. In A III–IV a deep pit filled with rough limestone blocks intersects the line of the colonnade, as if destined to support a heavy superstructure, and fragments of statuary (one carrying a stele) found in A III, such as might have been set near a gate, support the postulate of some kind of opening here.

The swath of fractured *talatat*, which yielded such revealing evidence in the four quadrants from A to AD, continued undiminished in quadrants E and EE on the west side of the temple. Chevrier's trench had removed all the blocks from the southwest corner northward for 10 meters, but from that point (i.e., the width of E and EE and their balk) the destruction level was unearthed intact.

Of the 120-odd fragments recovered, Chart 2 provides evidence on the distribution of motifs. The content of the reliefs in this sector is, if anything, easier to identify than that in the A-area. Once again, interestingly enough, we are dealing with the jubilee processional, but here there is a more even representation of detail. The domestic touches in the palace fragments recovered from c. 14–15 meters, although well-known in the matched scenes, are absent from A-area due to chance, one suspects (Fig. 16). Palace scenes usually show both king and queen seated facing each other across a table piled high with food, while servants bustle about with wine jars. An orchestra, consisting partly of blindfolded musicians from Asia, entertains the royal couple; presently king and queen will appear in the "window of appearances" and greet the courtiers assembled below in the palace yard. Traces of the palanquin and its bearers between 14 and 18 meters demonstrate the presence of the expected procession to and from the temple; while the latter is represented by most if not all the pieces emanating from E quadrant (i.e., 18 to 27 meters).

The temple scenes, however, appeared to have differed slightly from those depicted along the adjacent south side. No scenes of the king and his

7.11 The Jubilee Processional (L. Greener). The king in white crown is born along on his basket palanquin, to be followed by the queen in her chair and the "royal children" (stand-ins playing a role, rather than blood offspring) in their hooped palanquins. The artist has caught the moment when the day's ceremonies are ended and the cortege has set out once more for the royal palace. A joyous crowd waits to cheer the royal family while in the background priests and courtiers libate toward the procession in a veritable forest of offering tables. The musicians in the lower left have for once appeared out of doors; usually their functions are fulfilled in the dining hall.

priestly cortege offering in the roofless shrines seem to be present here, but a fragment with a courtier pouring libation into a basin thrusts us into the context of a well-attested motif in the repertoire of *Gm·(t)-p³-itn* decoration. The king, offering at a large offering table, is confronted by a series of other tables, shown in smaller scale, behind which courtiers are standing. Each

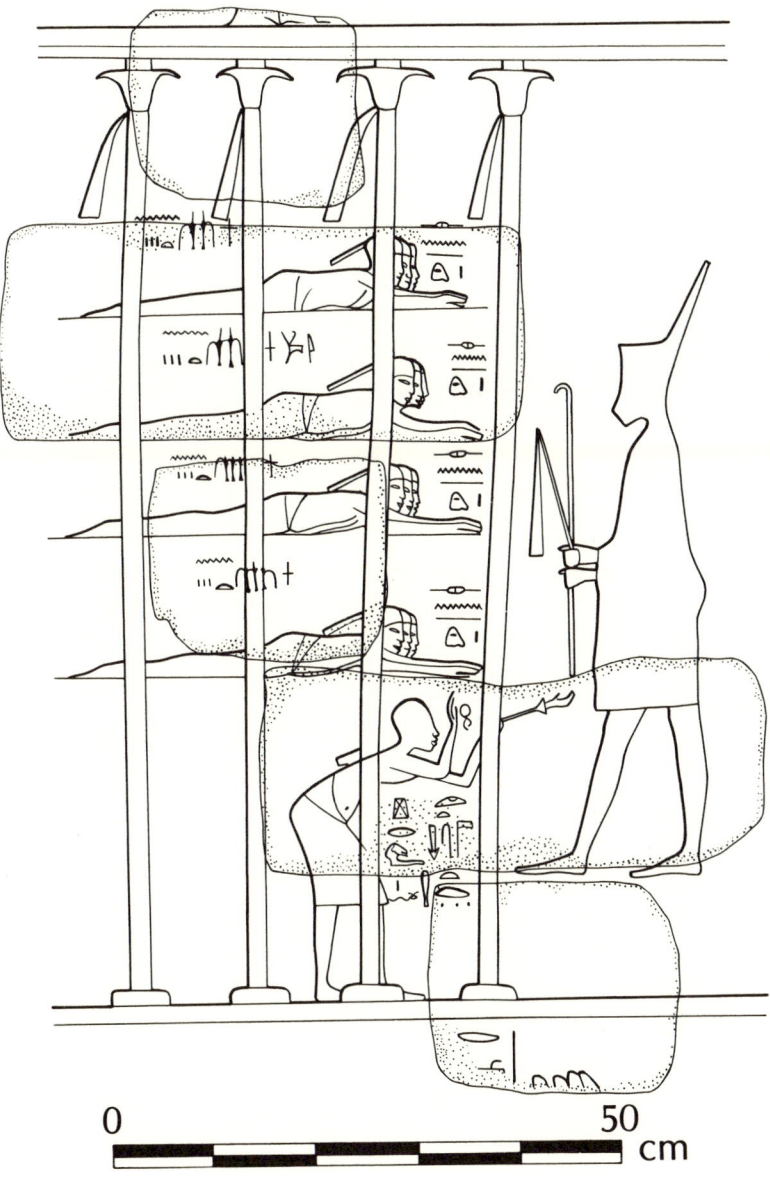

7.12 Part of a matched cultic scene of blocks from the Gm·(t)-p³-itn, *showing the king (on the right), about to proceed out of his palace through a colonnade and into his waiting palanquin. In front of him, backing away down the steps is the high priest of the sun, burning incense before his lord; while the prostrate figures in the colonnade are accompanied by the text "kissing the earth by the chamberlains"; from one of the royal progresses from palace to temple (R. Aicher).*

0   50 cm

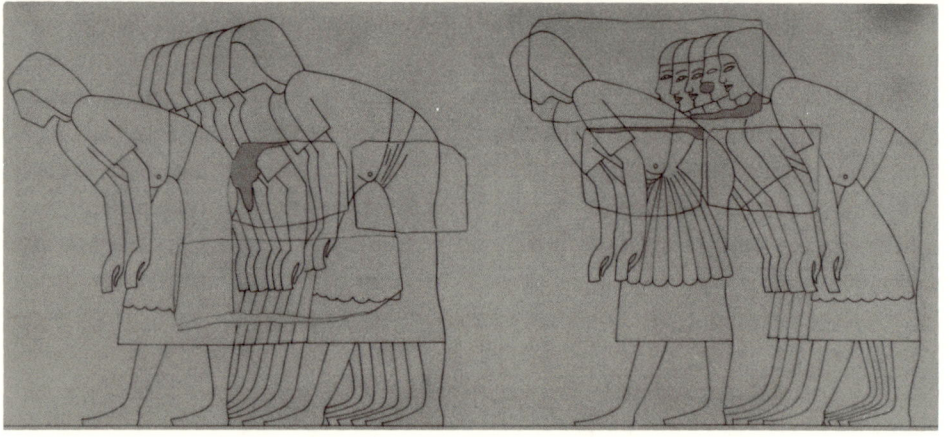

7.13 (above) Matched scene (TS 5521) showing the bearers of the queen's sedan chair, seen in part at the left. (The walking sphinx forms the arm of her chair). The head between the last two men in the row is that of a sunshade carrier. As there are five men shouldering the pole at the rear, and since they are paralleled on the other side by an equal number, we may estimate the total complement of bearers at twenty.

13. (below) Facsimile of bowing courtiers (TS 5594; A. Shaheen). Rows of civil servants, with characteristic flounced sporans, bow before the king, each group led by a supervisor.

14. (opposite, above) Facsimile of the party of priests (god's-fathers) greeting the king upon his arrival at the temple with sweet-smelling bouquets (R. Aicher).

15. (opposite, below) Facsimile of palace and temple (K. Bard). This collage of blocks, originally from the north wall of Gm·(t)-p³-itn, shows the point of join between two "processional scenes." On the right is the temple, with its many small kiosks among which the king is moving. On the left is the palace, with servants and wine jars. Both complexes are surrounded by "wavy" lines, possibly depicting sinusoidal walling systems.

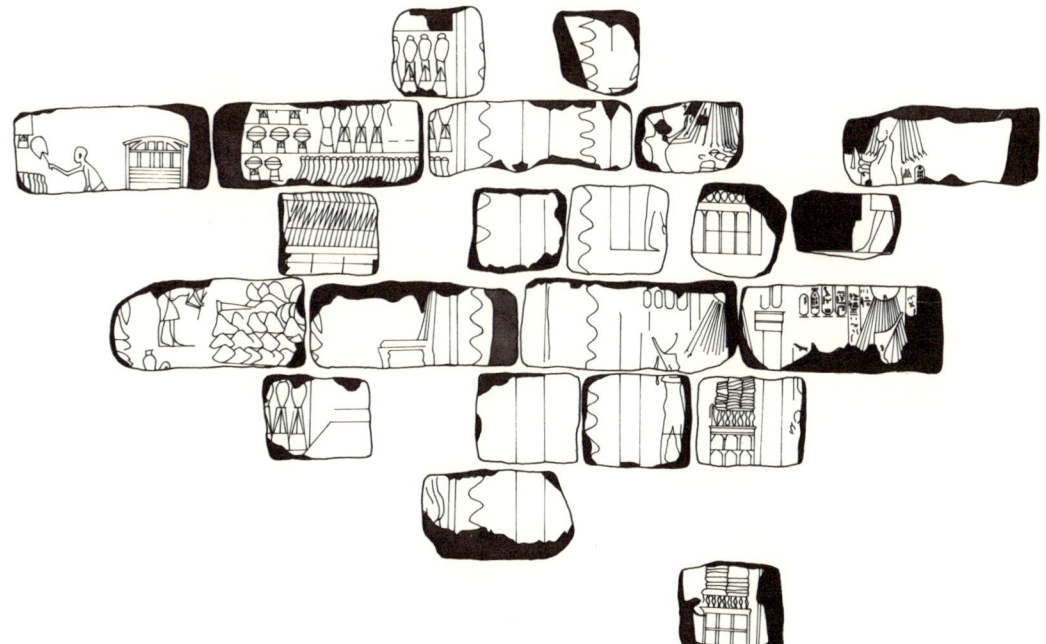

121

CHART 2 DISTRIBUTION ALONG THE WEST SIDE

Meters from Corner	Scenes Attested	Quadrant
11-14	—large hieroglyphs, some from cartouches of sun-disc —servants with trestles	EE IV-III
14-18	—king at table (→) —servants and wine jars —standing and bowing courtiers —palanquin and bearers (→)	EE II-I
18-23	—palanquin bearers, lowering palanquin (Pl. 7.14) —priests with sacred standards (Pl. 7.15) —doors on kiosk —soldiers and attendants	E IV-III
23-27	—priests with sacred standards (cf. Pl. 7.16) —attendant figures (→) —courtier pouring libation (→)	E II-I

man elevates a censer to the king and/or with the other hand, pours a libation. Above his head a brief hieroglyphic text records a stock, adulatory benediction, which runs something like this: "May the Sun-disc favor thee, may he cause thee to be healthy, O thou ruler Neferkheprure . . . !" This dedication of the offerings must have preceded a feast on a grand scale, and as we said earlier such manifestations of the king's bounty are typical of the jubilee. It is within the realm of possibility that the feasting evidenced in the palace at 13–15 meters is connected with this consecration of the massive offering.

The Sd-Festival in Egypt

Virtually the whole of the relief decoration adduced by the recovered fragments of the $Gm·(t)-p^3-itn$ takes as its theme the jubilee of the king, in Egyp-

7.14 (above) Talatat *from the excavations in E-quadrant in 1978, showing the heads of palanquin bearers and the front of the large basket palanquin which bears the king; from a scene showing a royal progress from palace to temple.*

7.15 (left) Talatat *from the excavations in E quadrant in 1978, showing a bowing priest shouldering a sacred standard; the two hieroglyphs above his head identify him as "prophet"; from a scene showing the king's entry into the temple (cf. Pl. 7.16).*

7.16 (right) Talatat *from the second pylon showing part of a row of bowing priests shouldering sacred standards, in procession in front of the king. The text identifies the whole as coming from the Gm·(t)–p³-itn; from a processional scene showing the king's entry into the temple (cf. Pl. 7.15).*

123

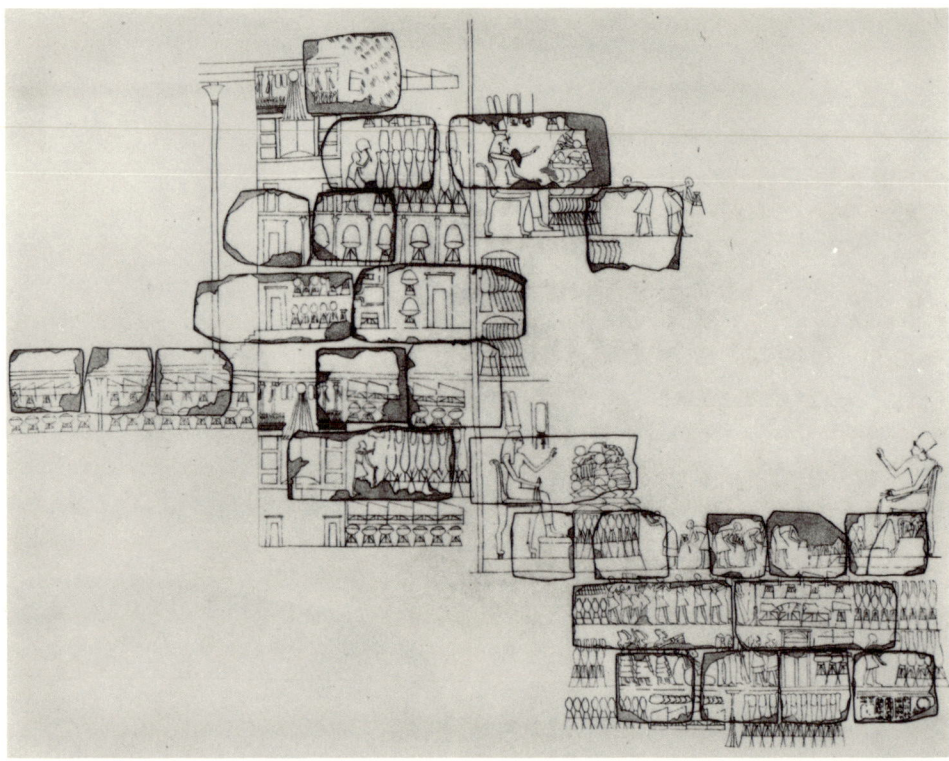

16. Facsimile of palace scene (A. Shaheen). The scene divides horizontally in the center into two nearly identical depictions of the palace, the lower representing the feasting prior to the departure for the temple, the upper the feasting after the return. To the left in each is shown the "window of appearance" and a storage area for wine, beer, and food. A servant is busy with a fan cooling the liquid and driving off flies. To the right is the large dining hall with king and queen at separate tables, and a platoon of servants bustling about. At the bottom an orchestra entertains.

tian the "*sd*-festival." What was this rite that so dominated the capital in the early years of the new reign? Why was Amenophis IV so captivated by the prospect of such a celebration?[2]

The first question is a trifle easier to answer than the second. The *sd*-festival was a very ancient ritual, attested already in the 1st Dynasty (31st-

2. Literature on the *sd*-festival is voluminous. See in particular J. J. Clère, *RdE* 20 (1968), 51ff.; H. Frankfort, *Kingship and the Gods* (Chicago, 1949); E. Hornung, *Geschichte als Fest* (Basel, 1966); E. Hornung and E. Staehelin, *Studien zum Sedfest* (Basel and Geneva, 1974); W. Helck, *ZÄS* 93 (1966), 74ff.; W. K. Simpson, *JARCE* 2 (1964), 59ff.; E. Uphill, *JNES* 22 (1963), 123ff.; *idem, JNES* 24 (1965), 365ff.

30th century B.C.) and with roots in prehistoric times, which sought to reaffirm the king's reign and responsibility to rule Egypt. Some evidence suggests an early connection with an especially high Nile flood, and therefore the fertility resulting in an especially good harvest, but whether this be so or not, the sd-festival constituted an act of rejuvenation on the part of pharaoh, and involved the prominent use of coronation imagery. Although the exact point in the reign for its celebration might vary, the sd was most often performed in the 30th year of a reign.

Throughout Egyptian history allusions to the jubilee, both in art and literature, abound, but a precise order of service is yet to be found. Four great compendia of descriptive reliefs have survived, scattered over 2,000 years of history: those from Abu Gurob of King Ne-woserre (c. 2400 B.C.); the reliefs of Amenophis III from the Theban Khonsu temple and elsewhere (c. 1400 B.C.); the present collection of *talatat* scenes from the *Gm·(t)-p³-itn* temple (the most detailed of the four); and the representation of Osorkon II's festival at Bubastis (c. 840 B.C.). None of these collections is complete, and the sequence of the fragments remains subject to debate. The principal acts of the ritual, however, changed little throughout the course of Egyptian history, and could we but recover a complete format we could assume its validity from the 1st Dynasty to Ptolemaic times. The present attempt to recover the detail and sequence of the scenes along the walls of *Gm·(t)-p³-itn* proffers precisely the hope of the eventual reconstruction of the order of service for the sd-festival, which would then assist the study of the Abu Gurob and Bubastite reliefs. Even at this early stage in our research, the other three collections appear much abbreviated and schematized, thus increasing even more the value of the reconstructed decoration of the *Gm·(t)-p³-itn* temple.

The sd-festival basically comprised a conclave of gods and grandees from all over the kingdom. Summoned well in advance of the celebration—some performances are known to have allowed lead time of as much as one year—the invited guests both mortal and divine were convened in a great complex of buildings erected for the occasion at Memphis. (Occasionally the venue might vary, depending on the whereabouts of the royal residence.) Upon arrival the cult images of the gods were housed in groups of shrines built for the purpose in, or sometimes on either side of, an open court known as "the court of the great ones." The shrines were of two varieties, spatially separated: one was a mock-up of the "house of the flame," the edicule of the tutelary deity of Lower Egypt, Edjo; the other an imitation of "the great house," the shrine of Nekhbit, patron goddess of Upper Egypt. Divine visitors were assigned temporary quarters according to the part of the country they hailed from. A canopied dais was also to be found in the vicinity of this court, and pursuant to the twofold symbolism of the festival, it contained two thrones back to back. With the inclusion of other buildings destined for rites connected with the dual nature of the kingdom, and a racecourse symbolic of the extent of the king's domain, the complex took on the character of a microcosm of Egypt itself.

The various *sd*-festival installations having been dedicated and purified by a torchlight procession, the sacred drama opened with a procession of the gods and their standards, the deputations and the king's court, and the king himself riding in his palanquin attended by fan-bearers. This procession, excluding the gods (who thenceforth took their places in the shrines assigned to them), was to be repeated many times over on successive days, as the king visited in turn all the shrines in the "court of the great ones." In each shrine he offered to its deity, and won acceptance of his continued rule. Naturally his accouterments suited the gods whom he was visiting: for those from Upper Egypt he wore the white crown, while for the deities of the Delta he donned the red crown.

A key act in the jubilee was the reenactment of the coronation. Having achieved acceptance by the gods, the king would mount the dais and be crowned, once with the white crown on one throne, then with the red on the other. There followed a parade of officials and deputations—including ten "chiefs" from Upper Egypt and ten from Lower Egypt—to the throne to offer allegiance to the newly crowned king. So central was this coronation to the proceedings that the double-edicule on the dais became the hieroglyphic sign meaning "jubilee."

At some point in the ceremony the king would run a ritual race around the sides of a rectangular open space. In his hand he held a document called in the texts "the Secret of the Two Partners" (i.e., Horus and Seth) or "the Will of my Father." As he ran he would chant "I have run holding the Secret of the Two Partners, viz. the will which my father has given me before Geb.★ I have passed through the land and touched its four sides; I run through it as I desire." The symbolism seems clear: the racecourse is Egypt, the "secret" or "will" is the king's right to continue ruling. By running through the entire land with the document in his hand, the king takes possession of his inheritance and reaffirms his right to rule over Egypt. Again, like the

126

double-edicule, the image of the king in full stride became, in art, a potent abbreviation of the entire ceremony, and even impinged on other rites which in origin had nothing to do with the *sd*-festival.

Concluding ceremonies were brief. There was the ritual shooting of arrows to the points of the compass, and the singing of hymns. The participants once again paraded in all their glory. The atmosphere was charged with hilarity and rejoicing.

A good deal of fresh light can now and in the future be shed on the details of this festival. In particular the repertoire of scenes we have uncovered decorating the south colonnade reflects the visits made by the king to the shrines of the gods in the "court of the great ones." Two blocks from the second pylon bear a fragmentary text referring to "the appearance [in the temple(?)] by the king on the throne, [in order to] perform the ritual during the 'days of the Red-crown.'" A parallel text refers to the "Going forth by [His Majesty] to [. . .]. His Majesty's appearance at the 'Great House' (*pr wr*) [. . .] during the days [of the White-crown]." The two texts thus constitute an allusion to the procedure of offering in the Upper and Lower Egyptian shrines in order to acquire the sanction of the gods of the entire land. This strongly implies that the visits to the individual shrines was a drawn-out affair occupying several days, and would have involved not one, but many processionals to the temple and recessionals to the palace. This is the reason why so many examples of the motif are present in the *talatat* scenes, and why four are already attested for those stretches of wall converging on the south-west corner. It may even transpire that, once the entire perimeter wall has been exposed, we can make an accurate estimate of how many "days" were devoted to each crown by simply counting the number of repetitions of the scene; for one processional unit will probably correspond to the rites of one full day.

Egyptian architects and planners were obsessed with symmetrical layouts. In particular, iconography peculiar to one of the two halves of the country would find its place on the appropriate wall: Upper Egyptian motifs on south walls, Lower Egyptian on the north walls. Just as expected, in the scenes we have exposed in the south colonnade the king consistently wears the tall white hat of Upper Egypt, and these must be the "days of the White-crown" we see unfolding before us. The "days of the Red-crown" would then have been the subject matter of the reliefs on the opposite colonnade, along the north wall (Pl. 7.17).

7.17 Talatat *from the second pylon, originally from the north wall of* Gm·(t)-p³-itn. *King in red crown elevates jars, within the context of the* sd-*festival. Note the defacement of the king's features.*

It would seem that at the end of each day, after the cortege had come back to the palace, a great banquet took place. The king and queen dined in a great hall inside, and the courtiers, officers, and servants feasted outside in the temple yard. The "window of appearance," a kind of second-story balcony (Fig. 17), overlooked the yard, and while the feasters were gorging themselves the king and queen might favor them with an appearance. Then the cheers would resound and arms would be raised in adoration, while the chorus would spontaneously arise, "Many are the things the Sun-disc is able to give, to the slaking of his heart's desire!" Back inside the proceedings were more decorous. While servants bustled about with trays of food, or broke open the wine jars, the royal couple were entertained by an all-female orchestra, playing harp, lute, double-pipe, and percussion instruments. Sometimes they would be joined by a group of Asiatic musicians in tall conical caps and blindfolds, symbolic perhaps of the fact that blindness and excellence in music often went hand in hand. Their curious feminine robes may possibly mark them as transvestites, and parallels can be adduced from the sphere of Akkadian culture, but precisely where they came from remains a mystery. Their accouterments point either to North Syria or central Mesopotamia (Pl. 7.11).

17. Isometric projection of the "window of appearance" (L. Greener). The tall pillars support a light canopy before the window; in the center are the pillars of the dining hall behind.

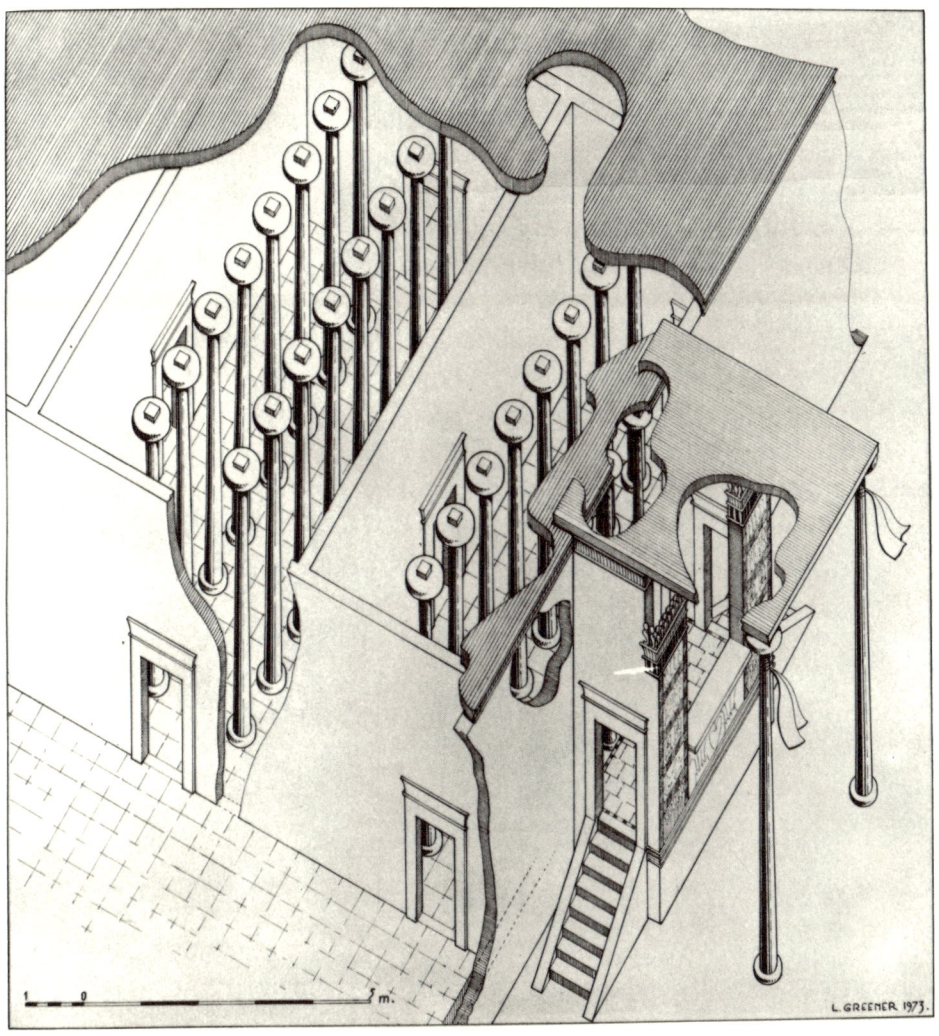

The location of this palace, the starting point for each day's procession, remains unknown. It could not have been far from the *Gm·(t)-p³-itn* temple, as the procession was made on foot and chariots dispensed with. Now, the *Gm·(t)-p³-itn* as revealed by excavation lies north of, but flush with, the central east–west axis of Karnak, a location that cries out for some balancing structure *south* of the axis. The drainage canal in this area has revealed some column bases (which protrude from the bank about thirty meters south of the south colonnade), and the palace scenes have abundantly testified to the presence of numerous columns in the construction of that building. Admittedly this is slim evidence, but could the palace be the structure required by the expected symmetry?

Some episodes in the *sd*-festival are as yet poorly represented in the *talatat*. The ceremonial race, for example, is not reflected. Only one or two blocks depict, as at Bubastis, the "king's peasants" running between the hoof-shaped boundary stones. The scene of the king enthroned on his dais, receiving dignitaries, seems also not to have survived, and I know of no representation of the shooting of arrows.

Frequently a curious ambivalence manifests itself in Amenophis IV's reaction to the presence of the "gods" in the ceremony. In the "court of the great ones," for example, the individual shrines are shown standing, as if to receive the divine visitors, but in all the same god is depicted as residing: the many-armed sun-disc beams down through the open roof of each shrine upon the king within! The offering of the *šbt*-object (food offering) upon the great dais is omitted, but the king mounts the steps all the same to the accompaniment of music and the chorus of "king's-children." The priests shoulder the divine standards, emblematic of individual deities, and designated in a caption as "the gods upon their standards," but elsewhere they play no part. The king apparently felt no aversion to the scorpion-goddess Selkit, whose image is carried in procession by her priest (Pl. 7.18); and the hymn to Hathor was allowed to stand, suitably edited to eliminate polytheistic overtones. But the great gods are conspicuous by their absence. No mention is made of Amun, Ptah, Thoth, or the gods of the Osirian cycle.

The Personnel of the Court and Sun-Cult

As we have seen, Amenophis IV was aping his father Amenophis III not only in the format of his jubilee, but also in the details and extent of the

7.18. Matched scene (TS 5517) showing a procession of priests carrying sacred para-
phernalia. In the upper register two priests carry sacred standards (cf. Pls. 7.15, 7.16) away
from a kiosk containing an offering table, toward another edicule with closed doors, the sides
of which are decorated with rearing uraeus serpents. In the lower register a row of priests
carry door-hinges and the holy image of the goddess Selkit, the scorpion.

relief representations devoted to the subject. In one significant way, as we
have attempted to show, the two sets of depictions differed, that is, in the
absence of most of the gods from the scenes of Amenophis IV; but there is
another startling contrast as well.

In the reliefs of the festival with which Amenophis III decorated his mortuary temple on the west bank, and which are known to us in fragments only, the major participants in the ceremonies, the courtiers and priests, are mentioned both by name and title. We are thus made to feel that we are onlookers at a living, historic event, celebrated by familiar people such as Amenophis son of Hapu, Ramose, and others. In Amenophis IV's reliefs, on the other hand, no one is named except the members of the royal family. Titles abound, but they enlighten us as to function alone; we are left to guess whether this celebrant is Meryre or that one the god's father Ay or that one Parennefer. Admittedly this was the norm—it is Amenophis III's reliefs that are aberrant—nonetheless it removes Amenophis IV's jubilee into a timeless, almost unreal, realm.

The following list of caption texts is intended to convey the importance placed on function rather than identity in the reliefs. Most are tiresomely repeated whenever the action in question is depicted and they have the effect of making one somewhat irritable.

1. (Beside the bearers of the queen's sedan chair) "Carrying the great king's wife in the following of His Majesty at the performance of the rites of the *sd*-festival."
2. (Over the priest with censer who backs away in front of the walking king) "Burning incense before His Majesty" (Pl. 7.12).
3. (Above forms prostrating themselves as the king leaves the palace) "Kissing the earth by the chamberlains."
4. (Over the king?) "Resting in the temple [in (?)] the House of the Sun-disc. . . . Giving instructions [to (?) . . .]."
5. (Above the vizier) "Making jubilation four times. The Mayor of the City and Vizier."
6. (Before king with an offering tray) "Elevating the offerings to (the Sun-disc) by king Amenophis."
7. (Above the king, walking) "Coming in peace to the House of the Sun-disc in Southern Heliopolis★ . . . all lands [being under his feet,] to perform all that is pleasing to the Sun-disc."
8. (Context unclear) "Induction of [the king] in Southern Heliopolis into the House of the Sun-disc."
9. (Over a courtier censing and performing libations before the king) "Receive fine, proper, and pure stuffs for thy spirit, O thou [child of the Sun-disc]!"

The repetitive captions are ubiquitous with the king and queen. The former, to give him his full titulary, appears as "Horus, Mighty Bull: tall of feathers; the Two Ladies' (man): great of kingship in Karnak; Horus-of-Gold: he with uplifted diadems in Southern Heliopolis; king of Upper and Lower Egypt, living on Truth, Lord of the Two Lands, Neferkheprure Waʿenre, Son of Re, living on Truth, Amenophis the Divine, Ruler of Thebes, with a long lifetime." The queen's epithets make her sound like a

7.19 Titulary of Nefertity from Karnak. The text reads: "Heiress, Great of Favor, Mistress of Sweetness, beloved one, Mistress of Upper and Lower Egypt, Great King's Wife, whom he loves, Lady of the Two Lands, Nefertity".

133

veritable bundle of charm: "heiress, great of favor, possessed of charm, exuding happiness," "mistress of Upper and Lower Egypt, beautiful and fair in the Two Feathers, soothing the king's heart in his house, soft-spoken in all," "at the sound of whose voice people rejoice," "the great king's wife whom he loves, lady of the Two Lands, Nefertity" (Pl. 7.19).[3]

Below the rank of king's daughter names disappear. Harem ladies attend in droves, all of ostensibly lofty station, for they accompany the queen and never bow; but we are left to guess which are sisters, cousins, or aunts of the king. We see the priests with their standards, the god's-fathers★ proffering bouquets, the vizier, the chief lector-priest, and the courtiers, and we are *sure* we are looking upon the likeness of the vizier Ramose, or the lector-priest Meryet. But no names confirm our suspicions.

The Regulations for the Sun Temple

Amenophis IV was more careful to record the instructions that were to govern the operation of his new shrines. On steles or on the wall itself, near the entrance to his temples, the official prescriptions for the daily offerings to the sun god were inscribed for all to see.[4] One such stele has been recovered from the 9th pylon, but in the *talatat*-reliefs they are depicted five or six times. A representative text reads as follows (TS 256): "[The god's offering which His Majesty laid down for his father] (the Sun-disc) as an offering menu for every day on the [altar] of Re which is in (space left blank!): *bit*-bread, at a baker's ratio★ of forty, [x] loaves; *pisn*-loaves, at a baker's ratio of forty, eighty-seven loaves; [jugs of beer, at a brewing ratio of twenty, thirty-three jugs; . . . to]tal of the various (types of) bread of the god's offering, 265; pigeons, two; incense, [one] *hin*-jar; vegetables, one bundle; vegetables, four bunches; milk, [x] jugs . . ." and so forth. Much larger quantities are indicated in surviving offering-lists for the daily menu of the solar temple at Memphis.

Offering prescriptions for other shrines are preserved as well. Thus for the otherwise unknown structure "The House of Him that Rejoices in the Horizon of the Sun-disc" we have the following: "[God's offering which His Majesty laid down for his father] (the Sun-disc) [residing in 'the House of Him that Rejoices in the Horizon of the Sun-disc' in Southern Heliopolis,

3. On queen's titles, see M. Gitton, *BIFAO* 78 (1978), 389ff.

4. R. Saad, *JEA* 57 (1971), 70ff.; W. Helck, *JEA* 59 (1973), 95ff.

the First Great (Place) of Re: [*bit*-bread . . .]; jugs of beer, sixteen; pigeons, eight [. . .]; that which the first god's-father of the House of the Sun-disc gave [*bit*-bread (?) . . . jugs of beer (?) . . .]; pigeons, eight; bouquets, four; bunches (of vegetables), seven; milk, three (?) bowls; [. . .]."

It is not at all strange to find one of the chief priests obliged to supply part of the offering. The food income of the temples was usually provided for by placing a tax, or impost quota, upon certain towns, estates, units of production, and the principal officers of the realm. This was to be paid yearly in perpetuity, no matter what changes occurred in the personnel of the institutions in question. We have already heard Parennefer gloat that, probably by the diversion of the income of other temple estates, the wealth of the temple of the Sun-disc was increasing phenomenally. What he is talking about is probably the impost quotas now established for the new temples. One text (TS 8842) alludes to the "[bread and beer] comprising the impost quotas of every year destined for the House of the Sun-disc" and goes on in a broken context to imply that the high priest of the sun was somehow responsible for it. A very colorful scene showing fat cattle being led to the stalls of the temple specifies the number of cows and oxen exacted as an impost from the officials of the realm. Our blocks mention this cattle tax (usually between five and ten animals per official) imposed on the mayors of about half a dozen Upper Egyptian towns. But a new and more complete text recovered by the CFE, and shortly to be published by M. Claude Traunecker, lists in remarkable detail the benevolences expected from the dignitaries and townships all over Egypt, listed in geographical order. Probably specifically for the *sd*-festival, commodites were expected to be contributed by the middle and lower ranks of the bureaucracy. The list includes the first god's-father of the temple, the controller of Sais, the accountant of livestock, the overseer of Nile mouths, the overseer of the treasury of the House of the Sun-disc, the scribe of the granary, the livestock-overseer of sheep of the [Western] River, the chief of the beekeepers of the Southern District, the livestock-overseer of goats . . . in the Southern District, the chief of the beekeepers of the Western River.

A number of *talatat*, mainly from the 2nd pylon, yield an insight of sorts into the riches of the new Theban temples. In broken contexts they seem to list the assets of the establishment: "[chattels] of the House of the Sun-disc who [. . .] 6,800 persons [. . .] their [du]es (?) for every [year . . .] introduced into the House of the Sun-disc (there follows a list of cloth) 3,622 persons, [. . . x] herdsmen [. . .] the chief [. . .] of the [. . .]. 1,049 persons

[. . .] their [du]es (?) for every [year . . .] introduced into the House of the Sun-disc (there follows a reference to silver)." Elsewhere the totals seem staggering: 400,000 of an unspecified commodity, 22,000 great white loaves, 260 plus storage jars (of wine), and so forth. It is quite likely that here we have the provisions assembled for the jubilee.

The sheer mass of foodstuffs brought together by the state to be bestowed upon the people at the jubilee as the king's largesse, helps us better to appreciate the atmosphere of hilarity and fervent loyalty with which the plebes anticipated the festival. No better means could be imagined to bring the nation together and to remind its citizens of the political system to which they owed their all. Such a festival was one of the few occasions in the course of their relatively short lives when peasant, laborer, and artisan would enjoy a square meal. No wonder hands are lifted in adoration to the "window of appearance," and the royal courts resound to the chorus of thousands of voices raised in a paeon of praise! To serve pharaoh meant that one would eat!

CHAPTER EIGHT

"The Horizon of the Sun-disc"

Sometime in the 5th year of his reign, the heretic pharaoh moved the court from Thebes to a new capital in Middle Egypt. Though the change seems to be sudden, it was in fact premeditated. It proved to be the major watershed in the Amarna period. At this point then, let us take stock of the earliest, "Theban" phase of this unusual reign, before moving on toward the denouement of the drama.

General Character of the "Theban" Years

The jubilee, of course, must have been for contemporaries the single most important event of these years. One cannot help but suspect that the three gala celebrations of his father's last decade influenced the young Amenophis IV in his choice of format and venue. Most of the specific ceremonies and

137

texts used by Amenophis III turn up, suitably purged of polytheistic overtones, in the jubilee of his son; and in this connection it should not be forgotten that Amenophis III claimed to have discovered an old order of service for the *sd*-festival in the archives.[1] Amenophis IV undoubtedly followed his father's revised text for the festival. It remains a problem, however, as to why he chose the second anniversary of his accession as the calendrical pivot for his celebration.

The prominence enjoyed by Nefertity at Thebes is perhaps the major discovery of the current research into the Amarna Period. The evidence, so far entirely from the field of art, has been interpreted by us as reflecting a cultic and political importance, but at the present time beyond this it is impossible to go. Was Nefertity a native of Thebes? Was she a domineering woman? Were many of the king's revolutionary ideas originally hers? Was someone other than Amenophis the father of her daughters? These questions need not all be answered in the affirmative, but they help to chart the course of present speculation. The problem is that the nature of the evidence is so entirely unexpected. Who would have believed, for example, that the "Mansion of the benben-stone" had been wholly given over to the use of the queen? The insinuation of Nefertity into such bellicose motifs as head-smiting scenes seems clear enough in its general intent; but if she were so politically dominant, why is she never mentioned in the diplomatic correspondence of her husband? At Amarna we shall shortly witness a gradual decline in her fortunes, but she remains in the picture at least until the death of her husband and probably beyond.

Amenophis IV's innovations strike us, as they probably did his contemporaries, with a bewildering suddenness. It is presumed that a good many of the forms he espoused were of Heliopolitan inspiration: the simple open layout adopted for his sun-temples, for example, is allegedly derived from a Heliopolitan original. All this may be the case, but at present no one can say with certainty. We know too little about Heliopolis—the site has not been and cannot be adequately excavated—to be confident in tracing elements of the new cult back to forms at home there.

We can never expect the artistic evidence to reveal how the people reacted to the initial shock of finding old temples closed and new ones open, decorated withal in a new and garish style. Nowhere in the happy faces of the courtiers, priests, and laity surrounding the king in the reliefs is there a

1. *Urk.* IV, 1862.

shadow of censure. The army is everywhere; disloyalty is nowhere in evidence. In all probability this is an accurate reading of the pictorial evidence: the new cult, and especially the jubilee, involved such an outlay of the king's wealth in the form of food and presents to the masses that any dismay must at first been tempered with gratitude. Nevertheless, there was some sort of grumbling to be heard. In a later text in which he swears never to leave his newfound home in Middle Egypt, Amenophis IV alludes cryptically to the "evil words" his father and grandfather were obliged to listen to, and which even he in his time had heard. Nowhere, of course, are we likely to come upon elucidation of these dark hints, but they may well reflect general criticism of the monarch's acts.

Whether opposition was threatening or ineffectual, overt or concealed, the king's next move proved sudden and irrevocable: he and his court abandoned the "Southern City." Thebes had not been the only city to benefit from embellishments in the new style to the cult: Heliopolis had received a new sun-temple, "(Amenophis is) the Exalter of the Disc,"[2] and Memphis was the site of one of the newfangled shrines as well.[3] Far away in Nubia a *Gm-itn* began to arise, and possibly Sam-Behdet in the north of the Delta boasted a sun-temple too. But to none of these sites did the king proceed. His choice was one that, he says, the sun-disc itself made for him, which the king may have discovered on some unrecorded progress down river. It is described by the king as the Sun-disc's "seat of the First Occasion (i.e., the first moment of creation), which he had made for himself that he might rest in it." The place was a large, windswept plain, seven miles long and about three miles wide, on the east bank of the Nile in the Hare Township of Middle Egypt. Apart from a vague but intriguing resemblance, when seen from the river, to a large hieroglyph for "horizon,"[4] the desolate site has little to recommend it. The rugged cliffs recede from the Nile leaving a deep sandy bay, waterless and extremely hot, with only the thinnest band of cultivable land along the river. It lay close to the route leading to the alabaster quarries of Hatnub, and 1,000 years before the nobles of the township had carved their tombs in the cliffs overlooking the northern end of the plain. Apart from the remains of a village or two of earlier date, this "horizon of the Sun-disc" (as the king called it) was a virgin site; even the

2. Amenophis IV certainly built at Heliopolis: cf. H. S. K. Bakry, *CdE* 47 (1972), 55ff; L. Habachi, *Beitrage zur ägyptischen Bauforschung und Altertumskunde* 12 (1971), 35ff.

3. B. Löhr, *SAK* 2 (1975), 139ff.
4. C. Aldred, *JEA* 62 (1976), 184.

8.1. Text from a representation of an offering table in Gm·(t)-pꜣ-itn. The prenomen and nomen of the king on the left are flanked by the name of Nefertity on the right. Note "Akhen[aten]" carved over the earlier "[Amenophis], the divine, ruler of Thebes." At a later date someone took exception to the epithet in the prenomen wꜥ-n-rꜥ, lit. "unique one of Re," and carefully effaced the glyphs for "unique one" leaving the sun-disc undamaged!

mighty city of Hermopolis, home of Thoth the god of wisdom, just across the river to the west, exercised no cultural influence on the area.

Though his intent may have crystallized in his 4th year, Amenophis IV appears to have made no move until his 5th. Then planners, surveyors, and builders appeared at the chosen site, and work began at a feverish pace.

But the king was not quite finished with Thebes. Before departing, and almost by way of a Parthian shot, he unfurled his true iconoclastic colors.

8.2. Fragment of an alabaster offering table, excavated in 1979 in the area of the western gate of the temple. As in Pl. 8.1, the two cartouches of the king are grouped with that of Nefertity. The nomen of the king has been carefully abrased, and the name "Akhenaten" carved in as a replacement.

Amun was declared anathema. The king changed his name from "Amenophis, the Divine, the Ruler of Thebes" to Akhenaten, which means something like "He who is useful to the Sun-disc," or perhaps "Glorified Spirit of the Sun-disc." Everywhere at Thebes and other cities, in the sun-temples he had built, workmen laid coats of gypsum plaster over the second of the royal cartouches and recut the new name over the old (Pls. 8.1-2). Undoubtedly it was at the same time that hatchetmen were dispatched to range throughout the temples of the land to desecrate the name "Amun" wherever it appeared on walls, steles, tombs, or objets d'art. Amun's congeners Mut, Osiris, and others suffered too, but to a lesser extent. So widespread and

141

thorough was this program of erasure, in fact, that today investigators can often date a piece as pre- or post-Amarna by examining the hieroglyphs for "Amun." It cannot be proven, but it seems likely that it was at this time that the temple estates, which had for half a decade suffered the diminution of their revenue, were now formally closed. By year 6 revenue from Amun's domain was being diverted to the House of the Disc in the new city. Work also stopped on the Theban sun-temples. The courts of *Gm·(t)-p³-itn*, which had once received the cheering crowds at the *sd*-festival, were now to remain silent and abandoned for twelve years. All efforts were now concentrated on building the new "dream city" of Akhetaten, the "Horizon of the Disc."[5]

The Building of Akhetaten

Sometime during the 5th year, Amenophis IV, or Akhenaten as we shall now call him, arrived at the construction site with his court. No building was as yet complete, and most were probably but a marked layout on the ground; but the king was impatient to live with his father, the sun-disc, in his own special city, and was willing to put up with temporary quarters. The royal family for the rest of that year, and well into the 6th year, made do with a prefabricated dwelling, probably tentlike, which is called "tent (*imw psšt*) of apartments(?)" in the texts.[6]

The first thing to do was to demarcate the site. Akhenaten clearly envisaged a somewhat wider bailiwick for his father the sun than the narrow confines of the eastern bank, even though this was the spot destined for the city itself. Fourteen boundary steles were carved in rock, extending in a great arc across the Nile and the Bahr Yussef to the western desert edge and back again, thus defining the bounds of a "greater" Akhetaten. Each stele was elaborately carved with the king's formal proclamation of the founding of the city and a beautiful vignette showing the royal family worshipping the sun god.

Sometime early in April, 1370 B.C., when the construction site that was to become the new city was already pleasantly warm, the king "[appeared] on the great chariot of electrum like the Sun-disc when he shines on his

5. That the changes in the royal name came about while the king was still in Thebes is suggested by the fact that three examples of the new name, which are *original* and not cut over an earlier "Amenophis," have been found in the *talatat*. The Amun Temple is last heard of in year 6.

6. *Urk*. IV, 1981.

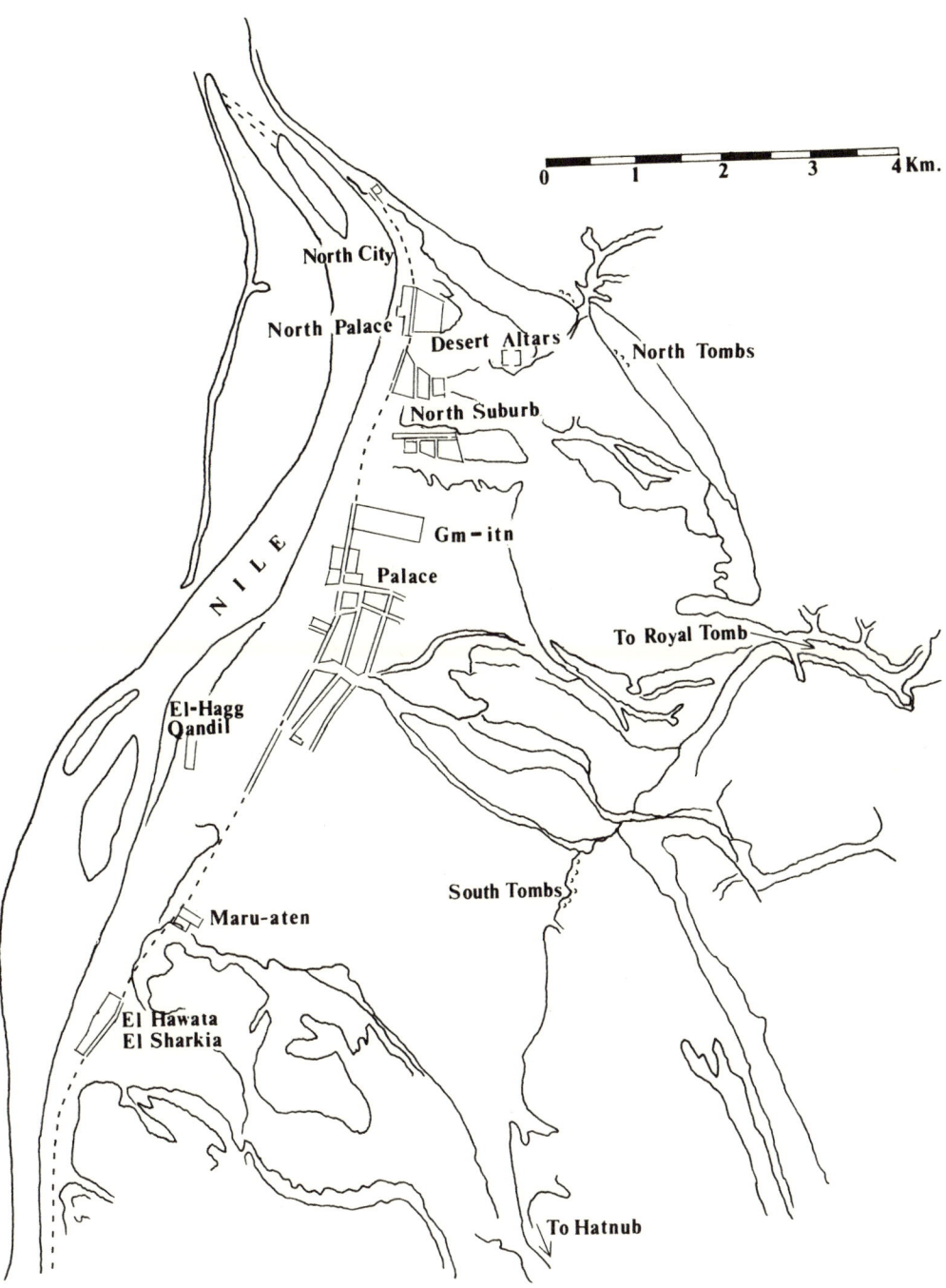

18. Plan of Akhetaten

143

horizon and fills the earth with his love. . . . The land was jubilant and every heart rejoiced when they saw him (the king) making the great hecatomb to his father (the Sun-disc) of bread, beer, long- and shorthorned cattle, wild game, fowl, wine, fruit, incense, libations, and all fine vegetables. . . ."[7] The king had often at Thebes lavished this sort of offering on the sun god; he was fond of expressing his devotion in this manner. But this occasion was special. Following the offering

> His Majesty [said]: "Bring me the royal courtiers, the great ones of the palace, the army officers, [. . . and the] entire [entourage(?)]"; and they were quickly ushered in to him. Then they were on their bellies before him, kissing the earth in his presence. Said His Majesty to them: "See [Akhetaten], which the Sun-disc wishes to have built [for] himself as a memorial in [his] own name. Now it was the Sun-disc, my father that [made the proposal (lit. witnessed)] concerning Akhetaten; no official proposed it, nor [any man in] the entire land. . . . And my father has conversed with me:[1] It shall belong to me as a horizon of the Disc for ever and ever!"[8]

The king proceeds to give a thumbnail sketch of his plans for the site and of the buildings he wishes to erect: the House of the Sun-disc, the Mansion of the Sun-disc, a Sunshade for the queen, a House of Rejoicing, royal apartments for himself and others for the queen, and a necropolis.

Nine days later, on "the day of the founding of Akhetaten for the living Sun-disc,"[9] the king was back again, making the rounds of the boundary steles on his chariot. At each he raised his hand to heaven and solemnly asseverated that he would never encroach on land beyond these boundaries, nor move to another site. The hegira had been made official: Egypt now had a new capital, a new pivotal center of government.[10]

As in all the construction undertaken during his reign, the buildings Akhenaten threw up were hastily designed and assembled. A modern engineer, asked to cast a judgment on the $Gm\cdot(t)-p^3-itn$ temple in East Karnak, could scarcely opine that it was anything but jerry-built; a like opinion would

7. Ibid.
8. *Urk.* IV, 1969.
9. *Urk.* IV, 1983.
10. On Akhetaten, see Sir W.M.F. Petrie, *Tell el-Amarna* (London, 1894); J.D.S. Pendelbury, B. Gunn, H. Frankfort, H. W. Fairman et al., *The City of Akhenaten*, 3 vols (London, 1923–1951); J.D.S. Pendlebury, *Tell el-Amarna* (London, 1935); J. Samson, *Amarna, City of Akhenaten and Nefertiti* (London, 1972).

undoubtedly be tendered on the construction at the new city. Sandstone was still used, in roughly cut blocks slightly smaller than the Karnak *talatat*, but extensive use was also made of mud-brick for cores, and limestone now came into general employment as the external veneer in which to cut reliefs. Commonly used, as at Thebes, were columns and piers. The former turn up both in lotiform and palm-trunk varieties, utilizing both wood and stone as material. Painted scenes now occur in some profusion on interior and exterior walls, and also as decoration on plastered floors. Walls and floors were also adorned with faience tiles, a practice that may have also originated in the "Theban years" of the reign. Certainly of Theban origin are the many "pylon gateways" with "broken" cornice, which we have seen to be a hallmark of the *Ḥwt-bnbn* at Karnak.

With no prior occupation at the site, the king was free to design his city as he and his father the Sun-disc willed. The whole was to be strung out along a north-south thoroughfare (dubbed by moderns "the Royal Road") over eight kilometers long, which extended from El Hawata el-Sharkia in the south to the "north city" beneath the cliffs of the Old Kingdom tombs. Three "boroughs" were eventually laid out to provide nuclei for domestic and administrative buildings: a central city with the palace, temples, and storehouses, and northern and southern satellite towns. To the west of the Royal Road, and probably occupying all the ground down to the river, were the magnificent and extensive apartments of one of the largest palaces ever to be built in the Middle East.[11] Most of this structure, including the approaches from the river, is buried under present cultivation, though excavations could conceivably be conducted in the future. A major portion of the part of the palace so far excavated centered upon a large open court, surrounded on at least two sides by statues of the king, larger than life-size. Those on the south were standing in much the same attitude as those at Karnak, and behind them was a colonnade carved with relief scenes, again similar to the same feature in the Theban *Gm·(t)-pȝ-itn*.

The king's private apartments seem to have lain on the east side of the avenue, directly across from the palace. Sometime after year 9 it was decided to make the latter communicate with the apartments by means of a "bridge" with piers of mud-brick, but there is no reason to believe that the king ever

---

11. Some have denied that this structure was a palace and proposed instead that a cultic function was paramount. This is, however, most unlikely. The apartments had a clearly domestic intent, whether for royal family or for the hosts of dependents whom the king supported.

showed himself from a "window of appearances" on the bridge. Relief scenes indicate that the window was set into the palace façade, as at Thebes, and overlooked the palace yard (Fig. 16).

To the south of the palace, on the same side of the avenue, stood the *Ḥwt-itn*, "Mansion of the Sun-disc," the best-preserved of the meager ruins still visible at the site. The *Ḥwt-itn*, interestingly enough, has roughly the same dimensions, 127 by 200 meters, as we have estimated for the *Gm·(t)-p³-itn* at Karnak; and the arrangement of courts end to end, separated by cross-walls and pylon gates, may prove to be another feature held in common by the two buildings. But here the comparison ends. So far as is known, the new structure lacked colossi and colonnades, but had added external buttresses to the circumference, a feature not (so far) attested by Karnak. In the third and easternmost court of the *Ḥwt-itn* lay a sanctuary, independently constructed, fronted by a prostyle porch. The precise function of this building is not yet known: that it was a sort of "chapel royal" is a flight of fancy. Far more likely, in view of name and orientation—in line with the wadi containing the royal tomb—is Professor N. B. Millet's view that it was to serve as the king's mortuary temple.

On the northern side of the central quarter, and also east of the avenue, lay the largest temple of all, "the House of the Sun-disc." This consisted of a vast rectangular walled enclosure measuring 760 by 290 meters, within which lay several independent temples. In succession from the west end, the ingress to the whole, these were "the House of Rejoicing (or the Rejoicer)," a sort of hypostyle that gave on to the *Gm-itn*, a series of six diminishing courts, open to the sky, and the *Ḥwt-bnbn* at the eastern end, associated with a slaughterhouse. Like most of the cultic installations, both here and at Thebes, all courts were open to the sky so that the sun might shine on all the rites directed toward him. Offering tables groaning beneath the bounty bestowed by the sun were everywhere. The continuity of time and the constancy of the calendar depended wholly on the tireless regularity of the Sun-disc, and as if to commemorate the calendric continuum, 365 offering tables flanked *Gm-itn* on one side and 365 on the other.[12] Though the *Ḥwt-bnbn* recalls Thebes, the sacred stone at Akhetaten assumed a new shape. Gone was the obelisk that had lent itself as determinative to the name at Thebes, and in its place appeared a round-topped stele on a dais. The

12. A. Badawy, *ZÄS* 87 (1962), 79ff.

146

schematized scenes of this temple in the private tombs show a blind orchestra with singers in attendance near the stele.

The change in the *bnbn* is only another of the enigmas of the Amarna Age. Why did the shape of the round-topped stele sit better with the king than the stately outline of the slender obelisk? Whatever the answer, the excavators of the "House of the Sun-disc" found, at the point where the tomb-scenes indicated the presence of the *bnbn*, fragments of quartzite strewn over the ground. The same stone is the material out of which was hewn a tall, round-topped stele discovered long since at Heliopolis, and on which Akhenaten and his family are shown prostrating themselves in the presence of the sun.[13] Such a posture is seldom adopted by the king, and its rarity argues a very special purpose. Could the Heliopolitan stele be the sacred *bnbn*-stone, used at the sun-city as a focal point for the cult?

Within the precinct of the "House of Rejoicing," built against the *temenos* wall, stood a number of small chapels and "sunshades." These originally belonged to the queen, and perhaps other female (?) members of the royal family, but were later appropriated by Akhenaten's daughters. Thanks to the German excavations at Hermopolis, whither many Amarna blocks were taken after the destruction of Akhetaten, we can now describe something of the decoration of these chapels and perhaps of the "House of the Sun-disc" in general.[14] Akhenaten's predilection for the offering to the sun as the main theme of decoration had not abated since Theban days: as at Karnak so at Akhetaten, the scene in which Akhenaten, Nefertity, and one daughter officiate before the altar seems to predominate. There were, of course, by now four daughters with two others on the way; but the early prototype, which showed only one little toddler behind her mother, still dominated the sculptors' fancy. A good deal of wall space was also given to depictions of royal apartments and storehouses, which must have functioned as accompanying detail to scenes of royal activity. The palace façade and its columned courts look remarkably similar to what we have become familiar with at Karnak: gates, columns, the "window of appearance," stairs, and furniture show no significant modifications when compared with their antecedents at Thebes. Large chariot scenes continue to grace long walls, as

13. L. Habachi, *Beiträge zur Ägyptischen Bauforschung und Altertumskunde* 12 (1971), 42, fig. 20.

14. G. Roeder, *Amarna-Reliefs aus Her-* *mopolis* (Hildesheim, 1969); R. Hanke, *Amarna-Reliefs aus Hermopolis* (Hildesheim, 1978).

they had in the *Rwd-mnw* at Thebes, and artists still delight in carving quantities of foodstuffs everywhere—on altars, tables, and in storerooms.

One series of reliefs, conspicuous by their absence, are those depicting the *sd*-festival. There is no evidence that at Amarna additional jubilees were celebrated, and nothing comparable to the endless wall reliefs devoted to the subject at Thebes has as yet turned up at Akhetaten.

Subsidiary buildings soon packed all available space in the central city. Long storehouses flanked the two large temples, and priests' houses lay close at hand in the choicest locations. Government offices and the archives, and barracks for the police and soldiery stood due east of the king's house. It was in the ruins of the archives building that in the winter of 1887–1888 a peasant woman uncovered by accident the remarkable cache of state correspondence known as the "Amarna Tablets" (see below, p. 195). Much further east a walled village was erected for the workmen engaged in the construction of the site, close to the foothills of the eastern cliffs.

To the south on both sides of the Royal Road stretched a residential area comprising the sprawling villas of the grandees of the new city. Here lay the house of the vizier Nakht, occupying over 8,000 square feet of space, with its gardens and outbuildings. Here also resided the priest Pawah and the second prophet of the king, Paynehsi. The tie with the king and the royal family in these private domains was a close and personal one: somewhere in the house a stele would be set up as an object of veneration, showing the royal couple and their children, or the grandparents, Amenophis III and Tiy. Often the tone of the icon was relaxed and intimate. Akhenaten fondles the children, or dandles his wife on his knee; his father slouches in his chair with one arm thrown around his spouse. Were these steles royal gifts, manufactured in royal workshop under a general supervision from on high, or are we to view them as expressions of how his own coterie saw the king, his wife, and offspring?

While major royal residences were undoubtedly located in the central city, there is good reason to think that the king may have preferred as his principal seat a large villa on the north side of town. At the extreme north end of the plain, where the cliffs approach the Nile, a large structure with a monumental façade lay west of the royal road, backing on the Nile. Because it extends under the present cultivation and was rather badly denuded at a later date, little can be said of the purpose or layout of this palace (for such it appears to be). Better preserved, on the other hand, is the so-called North Palace, which stood some 600 meters further south on the same side of the road. Rectangular in shape (120 by 290 meters), the North Palace was built around an open court and a garden, and contained blocks of apartments which included domestic quarters and a throne room. It also contained, however, storage rooms and stalls for cattle. The latter brings to mind the sacred Mnevis-bull, the animal consecrated to the sun at Heliopolis, whom Akhenaten also revered in his new cult, and for whom he claims to have prepared burial at the new site.

On the south of the city, close to the base of the southern cliffs, was the strange complex known as *Maru-aten*. A large, walled enclosure with gardens, pools, an artificial island, and open-air kiosks, *Maru-aten* was mistaken by the early excavators of the site for a sort of pleasure resort. Although a bucolic air surrounds the site—Amenophis III speaks of the *maru* he built for Amun as being full of gardens, vines, and pools—there seems little doubt that the basic purpose served by the installation was cultic. At a later period the temples of solar gods were equipped with a *maru*, and both the descriptive texts and the name itself (determined with an "eye") suggest a translation "viewing place." In fact it was the god's "gazebo."

Who's Who at Akhetaten

A motley though colorful throng of supporters had followed their king to the new site in the 15th township. One is struck by the marked lack of continuity between Thebes and Akhetaten: most faces are new, the "old guard" being largely absent.[15]

The king himself had modified his titulary to give even more prominence to his relationship to the sun-disc and the new city. His Horus-name now appears as "Beloved of the Sun-disc," and his Two Ladies name as "of Great Kingship in Akhetaten"; the Golden Horus appelative expresses the notion "Exalting the Name of the Sun-disc." With him, of course, was his wife, who soon bore him three more daughters: Nefer-neferu-aten minor, Nefer-neferu-re, and Satepenre. All three had probably been born by year 10, but they are rarely shown in reliefs, and may have died in childhood. Nurses are ubiquitous in the wall scenes, hovering protectingly behind their small charges. One is known to us by name; she is "the nurse of the king's daugh-

15. See especially R. Hari, *Répertoire onomastique amarnien* (Geneva, 1976).

149

ter Ankhes-en-paaten, Tia." With Akhenaten came his mother Queen Tiy, although she may not have taken up residence in Akhetaten; and with her in turn came her manager "favored by the Lord of the Two Lands, super-intendent of the royal harem, superintendent of the Treasury, major-domo in the house of the king's mother, the king's wife Tiy, Huya." The queen's sister Mut-nodjmet came along as well, and although she hovers in the background, she was to play a leading role in the post-Amarna period. Ne-fertity's major-domo Meryre (II) and other lackeys are also present.

Strangest of all was the "other" wife! Although the evidence had been available for many years, it was only comparatively recently that, through the agency of Professor Fairman of Liverpool, Queen Kiya came to be gen-erally known in the scholarly world.[16] She died before Akhenaten, and most of the memorials or the reliefs in which she was mentioned had been either usurped or smashed to pieces. To give her her full title, she was "the greatly loved wife of the King of Upper and Lower Egypt, living on Truth, Ne-ferkheprure, Waᶜenre, the beautiful child of the living Sun-disc, who shall live for ever and ever, Kiya." Unlike the epithets of Nefertity, Kiya's titulary gives pride of place to her husband; in all probability this signals a relatively low status among the female consorts of pharaoh. Nevertheless, she was important enough to appear in some reliefs, and may even have born a daughter (though this is not certain). One theory would have it that "Kiya" is simply a nickname of Nefertity herself, but this, it seems to me, founders on the marked divergence in titulary. The name has all the earmarks of a hypocorism, or pet name, and undoubtedly is a shortened form of a longer appelative. The present author has wondered whether in Kiya we have a shortened form of "Gilu-khepa" (spelled with a *k* in Egyptian transcription), the name of the Mitannian princess who, as a little girl thirty-five years before, had entered the harem of Amenophis III. There is nothing inherently improbable in this: Gilu-khepa could have been as young as thirty-eight or forty by the time of the move to Akhetaten, and could easily have won favor with the son as she had with the father.

The king's own personal staff takes a prominent place at the new resi-dence. One of the most influential, and the one destined to play a significant role in the post-Amarna period, was Ay, "the favored one of the Good God, fan-bearer on the king's right hand, true king's scribe and god's-father,

16. See W. Helck, *LdÄ* 3 (Wiesbaden, 1980), 422ff.

trusted throughout the entire land, commander of chariotry."[17] Ay's favorite title, "god's-father," has been thought by some to indicate a status of father-in-law to Akhenaten, but he is never referred to elsewhere as the father to either Nefertity or Kiya. On the other hand, his name itself and the military function he performed tie him closely to the family of Yuya, father of Queen Tiy; we are on fairly safe ground if we make him a son of Yuya and a brother of Tiy and Anen. His family connection alone would have been sufficient to catapult him into the highest circles in the land, but he is curiously absent from textual sources until we arrive at Akhetaten. Ay's wife had been Nefertity's wet-nurse, and this relationship undoubtedly helped cement his position of favor with the distaff side of the royal family.

Parennefer, "the pure-handed royal butler of His Majesty," whom we have seen at Thebes, turns up at Akhetaten as well. And there is also Tutu, "the chamberlain of the Lord of the Two Lands, and treasurer"; Khay, "the table-scribe of the Lord of the Two Lands," and Ranefer, the king's personal charioteer. Some of these magnates effect a stilted and rather old-fashioned titulary. Ahmose, the king's steward, calls himself "the seal-bearer of the King of Lower Egypt, sole friend (who follows) at the heels of the Lord of the Two Lands, praised of the Good God, whom his lord loves every day, true king's scribe whom he loves, major-domo of the house of Akhenaten, superintendent of the Porte . . . who approaches the divine limbs; greatest of the great, first of the courtiers," etc. The chamberlain and chief physician Pentu borrowed the same jargon, adding an epithet that was popular at the new city: "first servitor of the Sun-disc."

Since Akhetaten was now the seat of government, cabinet ministers and civil servants abound. We have already had occasion to mention the vizier Nakht. He was assisted by the granary overseer Ramose, who also functioned as commander of chariotry and steward of the *Ḥwt-itn*; Huy the treasurer; Apiya the chief steward assigned to Memphis; Ramose, scribe of recruits; Mahu, chief of police; Neferkhepru-hir-sekheprer, mayor of the city. Since construction work was very much in the fore in the king's thinking, engineers are also prominent. Men like Pa-aten-em-heb and Maanekhowtef, attested respectively by a tomb and a doorpost from the site, must have had a hand in the building.

---

17. Seele, *JNES* 14 (1955), 169f.; most of the individuals who follow can be found in the Amarna tombs, on which see N. de G. Davies, *The Rock Tombs of El-Amarna*, 6 vols. (London, 1903–1980).

Just as at Thebes, where the military had appeared everywhere and in large numbers around the king, so at Akhetaten platoons, marching at the double, or at ease, or bowing low, are never far from the person of the monarch; and a glance at the Amarna prosopography proves their officers enjoyed high station. The verbose and bombastic Maya held the title "general of the army of the Lord of the Two Lands," undoubtedly (he would have said) because he was "greatly trusted by his lord . . . the only competent one in the presence of the Lord of the Two Lands, who filled the ears of Horus (i.e., the king) with the truth . . . one whom the king had made great because of his fine qualities . . . the only useful one in his lord's opinion, one whom he had discerned as a good executive (lit. one who does effective things)." If ever Maya were not in charge for some reason, the king could doubtless call on the "general of the army . . . Ramose," or the battalion commander Neha(?)-em-pa-aten, or Ranefer or Ay, his chariotry commanders. Of course these were officers who had, regardless of their own military service (or lack of it) inherited a proud military tradition: their precursors in the ranks (if not a few old soldiers still living) had marched over the entire earth and conquered most of it. An air of the braggart is a necessary concomitant to participation in the military, if wars are to be won—or at least some ancients and moderns might argue.

No one need wonder at the prominence enjoyed by priests in the new regime. Shortly we shall examine the service they performed in the new cult; now it will suffice to list their names. The high priest of the sun, whom we have seen so often accompanying the king at the *sd*-festival, appears at Akhetaten with name and full titles revealed. He is "the Greatest of the Seers of the Sun-disc in Akhetaten, seal-bearer of the king of Lower Egypt, sole friend, fan-bearer on the king's right hand, Meryre." Possibly another of the priestly coterie that was nameless in the Karnak reliefs now turns up at the new city with the mask removed, namely Meraya, "the lector priest . . . and steward of the House of the Sun-disc."[18] Men like Pentu the physician or Panehsi the superintendent of cattle or the great Tutu himself, could also dub themselves "the chief servitor of the Sun-disc." And for the latter, at least, this translated into a supervisory role vis-à-vis the slaughterhouse of the temple. Officers responsible for temples in other cities of the land nonetheless resided at Akhetaten. Pawah was high priest of the sun in Heliopolis,

18. Berlin 2070.

and Maya, the general, enjoyed an administrative role in the same establishment.

Seven years after Akhenaten had come to the throne, the integrated system of politics, economics, and cult that Egypt had known for seventeen centuries had been drastically modified, if not turned upside down. True, the populace of the new city seems happy and surfeited; the new way of life had proved exciting and, so far, successful. But diverting our attention to Akhetaten may make us forget conditions elsewhere. The once-thriving administrative centers of Thebes and Memphis stood idle. Temples and government offices had been virtually shut down, and the sons of illustrious houses that had served pharaoh well suddenly found themselves bereft of function and court connection. Who caused all this? Who was this "Akhenaten"? We have postponed the attempt to answer this question long enough.

PART THREE

The Great Living Sun-disc

CHAPTER NINE

The Spiritual Milieu of Akhenaten's Reaction

Ancient Egyptian speculation about the origin and nature of the universe and Egypt's place in it strongly tended toward explaining the apparent plurality of the cosmos in terms of an underlying unity. One system, perhaps rightly dubbed "Heliopolitan," opted for Atum, the "all-inclusive," the "One," from whom (by projection and subsequent combining of substances) all the entities of the universe had come. The Memphite system exalted "Heart" (Mind) as the primal element. Heart had given existence to things by thinking, by concrete projection of willed thought. A logical continuation of this idea leads to the conclusion that Being is, and things exist, only inasmuch as Heart exists. All that exists is really only a multifarious manifestation of the underlying unity, namely Heart, or Mind. A third set of ideas, usually associated with Hermopolis, described the primal element as the infinite—infinite in size, infinite in darkness, completely fluid, and completely hidden.[1]

Of an entirely different order from these philosophical harbingers of the Pre-Socratics was the enforced worship of an abstract symbol that Akhenaten introduced. Where other cults had been syncretic, Akhenaten was exclusive. Where others had been consciously polytheistic, Akhenaten was unabashedly monotheistic. Where others were searching for what we moderns would call a First Cause, Akhenaten shows in his preserved inscriptions no interest whatsoever in imponderables. What motivated the new pharaoh to make such a radical departure from traditional thought?

Akhenaten's time and his violent reaction to it are the products of a clash between trends building up for generations in the body politic and the appearance upon the throne of an iconoclastic freak. To understand him and what he did one must examine closely 1) the phenomenon of the cult of Amun, 2) the rise of the administrative coterie, and 3) the character of the king himself.

The Cult of Amun

The single most striking feature in Egyptian religion under the early 18th Dynasty is the prominence of Amun. The kings of the period never tired of piling the booty from foreign campaigns at the feet of Amun, since they ascribed the success of their military ventures to him alone. The god's coffers bulged with wealth in quantities never experienced before in Egypt. In the leveling atmosphere bred by the war of liberation, the king could not safely lay claim to it, nor was it advisable to disperse it among members of any one class of the population, which would have created wealthy families. Best to donate it to an otherworldly figure, with men as just its custodians.

The growth of Amun's temporal possessions through conquest was supplemented by donations of livestock and real estate from Egypt proper. The practice of making such outright gifts on the part of the king was an old one, but at the inception of the 18th Dynasty there were probably additional incentives. With the reconstitution of the Nile Valley as far south as Dongola under a single regime, land ownership must have been in flux. What better

---

1. On Egyptian cosmologies and world views, one might consult *inter alia* R. Anthes, in S. N. Kramer, ed., *Mythologies of the An-* *cient World* (New York, 1961); E. Hornung, *Der Eine und die Vielen* (Darmstadt, 1973); S. Morenz, *Egyptian Religion* (Ithaca, 1973).

way to ensure efficient administration of vacant land, and deprive potential rivals of a power base, than to give substantial tracts to the god? Moreover, once the court had gravitated back to its favorite Memphite residence beginning with Tuthmosis I, some means of effectively administering the distant south had to be found. In a former age, this would have been accomplished through the agency of the nomarchs★ and the governor of the south. Now the "House of Amun" acted as a stable surrogate for the king in Upper Egypt. By the time of Amenophis III, the other great landowning institutions in the Thebaid, the mortuary temples on the west bank, were treated as subsidiaries of the estate of Amun.

Obviously, the personnel assigned the task of running Amun's house would have great responsibility, and would of necessity constitute a large organization.[2] But the size and complexity of the Amun priesthood was relatively new. In the parochial societies of the first Intermediate Period★ and the Middle Kingdom, the full-time staff of a nome god's temple was a rudimentary affair, in which the god's-prophet and lector priest appear as respected members of the community. In texts where the writer has occasion to arrange priests by order of rank, we see that the overseer of prophets stands first, and is followed variously by god's-treasurer, temple scribe, lector priest, regulator of a phyle, and lay(?) prophets,[3] or by reporter, "he who is over the mysteries," kilt-wearer(?), "overseer of the ergastulum," he who is over the broad hall," overseer of the *ku*-shrine,★ temple scribe, altar scribe, and lector priest.[4] Usually, the roster is even shorter; at Edfu, we hear of a scribe, lector priest, *wꜥb*-priest, prophets, and hour priests of the temple.[5] The staff of the Osiris temple in the Middle Kingdom comprised prophets, *wꜥb*-priests, lector priests, and scribes.[6] For the Montuhotep mortuary temple during the reign of Senwosret I, the list includes lector priests, *wꜥb*-priests, hour priests, and tenant farmers; for the Amun temple, during the same reign, the source in question lists but a prophet and hour priests.[7]

The New Kingdom at Thebes suddenly confronts us with a numerous professional priesthood. Already under Tuthmosis III, the roll in the Amun

---

2. In general on the priesthood, see S. Sauneron, *Les prêtres de l'ancienne Égypte* (Paris, 1957); H. Kees, *Das Priestertum im ägyptischen Staat* (Leiden, 1953); *idem, Die Hohenpriester des Amun von Karnak . . .* (Leiden, 1964); G. Lefebvre, *Histoire des grands prêtres d'Amun de Karnak* (Paris, 1929).

3. Cairo 20040.

4. F. Ll. Griffiths, *The Inscriptions of Siut and Deir Rifeh* (London, 1889), l. 281.

5. G. Daressy, *ASAE* 17 (1917), 243.

6. Louvre C. 50.

7. E. Naville, *The XIth Dynasty Temple at Deir el-Bahari* (London, 1907), pl. 24.

temple includes, in descending rank, prophets, god's-fathers, scribes, superintendents of the mysteries, shrine-openers, solar-priests, lector priests, assistants, w^cb-priests, mortuary priests, and a host of secular officials. By the second half of the 18th Dynasty, whole families were gaining a livelihood within the ranks of the Amun priesthood, and had been doing so for several generations.

Over the burgeoning organization, which, as time went on, became a closed community within the state, stood the First Prophet of Amun. This office, together with that of the Second Prophet, the next in order to rank, was closely controlled by the king and queen, as an inscription from the reign of Ahmose attests. The effectiveness of this control, as well as the as yet moderate-sized proportions of Amun's estate, probably explains the relative insignificance of the three earliest incumbents known to us, Khonsuemhab, Djehuty, and Min-montu. But with the reign of Hatshepsut, the situation changes.[8] The queen's reign is marked by a coterie of top officials who attained power quite probably at the behest of, and possibly the expense of, Hatshepsut herself. These officials may have felt the need to enlist the services of the organs of the state, including the cult of Amun, to justify an illegitimate, or at least unprecedented, reign. The sacerdotal titles of Hapuseneb show a twofold tendency in the religious policy of the times: first, to unite the entire temporal estate of Amun under a single authority, and second, to unite the priesthoods and estates of all Egyptian gods under the episcopal authority of the High Priest of Amun. Besides being First Prophet of Amun and first god's-father of Amun, Hapuseneb was overseer of every office of the House of Amun, overseer of the prophets of Upper and Lower Egypt, and overseer of temples. According to this newly devised system, the age-old function of overseer of priests of the gods of a nome (almost a modern "bishop") was subordinated to the authority of a new kind of "archbishop."

The two successors of Hapuseneb seem to have followed in his wake, but with the accession of Tuthmosis IV came a wholesale shake-up. One Amenemhet was evidently Tuthmosis's choice for the high priesthood. Son of a woman of lowly birth, he was still a simple priest when, at the age of fifty-four, he mourned the passing of Amenophis II. In choosing him, was Tuthmosis IV consciously asserting a royal prerogative that had been disregarded? In other words, was the king deliberately bypassing more famous

8. For Hatshepsut's reign see S. Ratié, *La reine pharaon* (Paris, 1972).

candidates of officials with "vested interests" in order to insist on his own right to appoint a "king's man"? Amenemhet was High Priest of Amun and overseer of all the prophets of Upper and Lower Egypt, but his civil offices seem to have been few. To the office of Second Prophet of Amun, Tuthmosis appointed a certain Amenophis si-se; from what lower rank is not clear. The induction ceremony takes up a good deal of space in his tomb: "He (the king) found me to be one useful to his lord / . . . I was inducted / . . . when it was brought to the attention of the king's courtiers, they were fulsome in exaltation, praising the king. 'Welcome! [. . .]' in the mouths of the priests / . . . I was advanced to the post of Second Prophet, [I was] caused [to see] the holiness of the Lord of the Gods. . . ."[9] Is there a hint here that Amenophis si-se did not theretofore belong to the priestly fraternity? Other new appointments under Tuthmosis IV include that of Tjanuna from major-domo (*3 n pr*) to superintendent of the treasury, that of Nebamun from standard-bearer on the king's flagship to chief of police, Sobekhotep to a function in the private apartments of the king's children, and possibly Neby to mayor of Tjaru.

It is unfortunate that so little is known of the occupancy of the high priesthood under the reign of Amenophis III. A Meryptah is attested from the 20th year of the reign, a [?]thotep in the tomb of Ramose, and a Ptahmose who had also at some time in his career been southern vizier. Of the three, the last seems to have been the most important, to judge at least by his titles; it would be interesting to know to what degree his power and importance made his contemporaries consider him a political threat.

The office of overseer of all the prophets of Upper and Lower Egypt was occupied by a fairly large number of men under Amenophis III. It is difficult to ascertain the reason for this. Did some incumbents die within a short time of each other? Was the office shared by more than one person at a given time? Or did the function actually change hands rapidly at the behest of the king, who perhaps was anxious to prevent an "archbishop" from becoming powerful through length of tenure? Two of the incumbents are High Priests of Amun; three have connections with the Memphite cult of Ptah. Ought one to suspect that the monarch's predilection for Ptah reflects a discreet attempt to counterbalance the power of the First Prophet of Amun? Or does the alternation between Memphite and Theban officers result from

9. N. de G. Davies and A. H. Gardiner, *The Tombs of Two Officials of Thutmosis IV* (London, 1923), pl. 13.

the simple fact that the king changed his favored place of residence at the end of the third decade of his reign from Memphis to Thebes, and in the process chose his man from *local* candidates?

Among Egyptian gods of the New Kingdom, Amun is the upstart opportunist. Clearly, this is a reflection on the theological plane of a sociological fact, that is, that through the accident of history Amun's cult—his priesthood—had become an association wherein political power-seekers could fulfill themselves. Other gods, for the most part, had distinctive characters and symbolisms, but Amun, "the hidden," was a pale god about whom, by definition, one could know little or nothing. It is hardly surprising, therefore, to find Amun's nature borrowing substantially from other cults. From the god-king he borrows the titles king of Upper and Lower Egypt, king of the gods, and sovereign of all the gods, prince of princes,[10] and assumes the guise of a great king patterned on the earthly pharaoh projected into the heavens. He is "king of heaven, risen as Harakhty-Atum whose body is unknown."[11] From the pantheistic theology usually associated with Ptah, he takes the notion of uniqueness and primacy, and becomes the primal element in the cosmos. He is "the sole god who transforms himself into an infinity of forms—every god is in him;"[12] he is "father of the fathers, infinite (in number), without peer, unique, who made all that exists, who created all that is, who linked up the limbs of the Sun-folk . . . !"[13]★ Inasmuch as he was early identified with the sun god, he naturally assumes the creative capacity and beneficence of Re. He is "the living torch which emerged from the flood," "he who created all the living and made their sustenance—strong herdsman driving his flock, their shelter / . . . every land chatters in joy at his daily rising."[14] And again, "he cleaves unto heaven, arising as the sun-disc every morning."[15] Not only is he a creator, but also a father compassionate and solicitous for his children: "The sole god without peer. He is Re who shines above, the Atum who made people, who hears the petition of him who calls on him, who rescues a man from the violent of heart . . . when he shines the people live, their hearts live and they see. (He it is) who gives breath to him who is (still) in the egg, who gives life to mankind and

10. *Urk.* IV, 494.
11. Berlin 7270.
12. I.E.S. Edwards, *JEA* 41 (1955), 100.
13. *Urk.* IV, 494f.
14. Edwards, *Hieroglyphic Texts from*

Egyptian Stelae etc. in the British Museum, Vol. 8 (London, 1939), pl. 21.
15. A Moret, *Le rituel du culte divin journalier en Égypte* (Paris, 1902), 139.

fowl, who provides the requirements of the mice in their holes, the things that creep and the things that fly likewise."[16]

That Amun's sway is not parochially confined to Egypt, but extends over the entire earth, is strongly emphasized in hymns to the god current in the 18th Dynasty. In this universalist tendency, Amun shared with Reharakhty and other solar forms, perhaps through his identificaltion with the sun, a preeminence that must surely be a spiritual ramification of the new phenomenon of world empire. "Thy two plumes rise aloft," says the devotee to Amun-re, "thou seest heaven with them, and thou lookest down upon the Nine Bows."[17]★ The sun god is "[he who con]ceived everything, lord of the whole earth, who made [that which ex]ists, sole god who lives on truth. . . ."[18] This universalism in theology, though "not strongly represented in pre-ᶜAmarnah hymns," is best exemplified by the great hymn to Amun from about the time of Amenophis II: "(O thou) who madest mankind and createdst animals . . . creator of the tree of life and herbage which nourishes cattle . . . maker of what is above and what is beneath, he brightens the two lands, ferrying across heaven in peace . . . who made the whole earth, and distinguished natures for every god. . . . Hail to thee, thou Re, lord of truth, whose shrine is hidden, lord of the gods, thou Khepry who resides in the authoritative fiat that creates the gods, thou Atum who makest mankind and distinguishest their forms, maker of life, separating one man's color from his fellow's, who hears the prayer of him who has been wronged(?), with gracious heart when called upon."[19]

A god who combined in himself not only a vast kingship on a cosmic scale, but also the universal powers of a creator and sustainer, was indeed a power to be reckoned with. And when such a deity's celestial status is mirrored sociologically by a terrestrial power exercised through a nascent, influential clergy on earth, one can perhaps excuse other lords temporal for fearing for their positions. Who was the god-king beside the mighty Amun, even though the former was of greater antiquity than the latter? Had not Amun even insinuated himself into the divine mystery of the god-king's filiation to Re by supplanting, or at best absorbing and eclipsing, Re, and obliging the earthly Horus to take the epithet "Son of Amun"?

---

16. Berlin 6910.

17. H. M. Stewart, *JEA* 46 (1960), 88.

18. *Idem, JEA* 53 (1967), pl. IV, 1.

19. S. Hassan, *Hymnes religieux du moyen empire* (Cairo, 1928), 158f. The hymn has elements that may be earlier than Amenophis II.

There were many factors in play during the 18th Dynasty that detracted from the traditional status of the Good God on earth: the strong tendency toward matriarchy, the recurring problem of the succession, the obsession with living up to an impossible ideal of physical strength, the steadily growing power of Amun, and the preponderance of a circle of important officials.

The 18th Dynasty throws up a number of examples of "cabinets" of capable, if not brilliant, officials, chosen by the discerning monarch often to his or her own partial eclipsing. The group that hovers in the background during Hatshepsut's two decades of rule constitutes a case in point; but Tuthmosis III was surrounded by a similar entourage of energetic and resourceful men, albeit not to his own detriment. And Amenophis III, as we have seen, perhaps significantly for the history of the following reign, selected a circle of top officials of outstanding ability and unequaled attainment, both in royal favor and in accomplishment.

The family of the Thutmosids, in need of imaginative and able men in the feverish task of empire-building, fostered the development of this kind of enterprising administrator. In the main, the first interest of the state lay in what we moderns would call the "secular" sphere—quarrying, construction, warfare, taxation—with the result that the typical official of the 18th Dynasty, even if he was a priest, seemed more concerned with, and better trained in, noncultic activities. The majority, as noted in Chapter 2, came to power from the ranks of the palace children, their mothers having been royal favorites or wet-nurses, and the resulting composition of the inner court in each reign must have magnified the latent rivalries and loyalties of a peer group that had been together since infancy.

Whatever may have been the exact purport of the "evil" that Akhenaten claims to have heard, there can be little doubt that he alludes to a vocal and unhesitating opposition to his projects from close at hand: "As my father (the disc) lives! If [. . .], even though it be more evil than what I heard in the 4th year, than what I heard in the [. . . year], than what [I heard in the 1st(?) year, than what my father Nebma]re [heard, or than] what Menkheperure heard. . . ."[20] Significantly, in the same boundary inscription, Akhenaten denies that it was any official that told him about the site for the new residence, avers further that it was built only for the Disc, not for any official

20. *Urk.* IV, 1975.

or for anyone else, and vehemently asserts that neither his queen nor any favored courtier shall divert his search for the Disc's "Horizon" to any other location. By the beginning of Akhenaten's reign the upper echelons of the administration must have wielded a power sufficient to arouse in a lesser scion of a once-great house a blind fear and resentment. The emotional overtones of his vow to disregard the advice of others also signals clearly his qualms about his own weakness of resolve, and a fear of the powers of persuasion of the queen and his coterie.

Akhenaten the Man

It may well have been this underlying lack of confidence in himself that led Akhenaten to reject the ancient families that had held administrative posts for generations in favor of "new men," many of them rank outsiders to the political system. One has but to examine the family trees of those who for over a century had held office in the vizierate, the treasury, or the departments of construction or food production to appreciate the sudden fall from power that occurs in each during the Amarna Period. Akhenaten simply did not know these families, and they had conversely had no opportunity under Amenophis III to become acquainted with him. Such a young king, so long sheltered and ignored, may well have lacked the ability to judge character, and therefore became vulnerable to parvenus. Many of the dramatis personae at Akhetaten appear so suddenly and disappear so quickly that it would be unfair to judge them all as opportunists, but I suspect that much of the concern in the post-Akhenaten era over the quality of officialdom stems directly from the experiences of Akhenaten's reign.

Both in ancient and modern bureaucracies the strategy of rewarding one's followers provides the lubricant that keeps the system running. We have witnessed the king's largess, beyond reasonable measure it would seem, in the gargantuan feasts at the jubilee and in the offering ceremonies of the new cult. Now, at Akhetaten, the formal distribution of rewards becomes one of the commonest royal acts.[21] There is scarcely a tomb in the necropolis at Amarna that lacks, on some wall, a depiction of the elaborate ceremony at which the collars of gold, bracelets, and other costly jewelery are bestowed

21. On the ceremony of reward in art and society, see J. Vergote, *Joseph en Égypte* (Louvain, 1959), 116ff.; D. B. Redford, *A Study of the Biblical Joseph Story* (Leiden, 1970), 208ff.

upon the lucky courtier. In the scene in the tomb of Meryre, the high priest, the king instructs his lackey to "reward the Greatest of Seers of the Sun-disc in Akhetaten, Meryre. Put gold all around his neck and gold on his feet, for he has obeyed the instruction of Pharaoh—Life, Prosperity, Health!—and has done all that was said concerning those beautiful places which Pharaoh—Life, Prosperity, Health!—has made in the Mansion of the *Bnbn* in the House of the Sun-disc in Akhetaten. . . ." To this the grateful Meryre responds with the polite formula, "Mayest thou be in health, O Wa'enre, thou beautiful child of the Sun-disc! Grant that he (*sic*) may achieve this life span—grant it ever and aye!"[22] The bestowal ceremony is an occasion of feasting and rejoicing. The entourage at Tutu's reward ceremony is typical: six Syrian chiefs led in by an Egyptian, and intoning praises to the king, four sunshade bearers who cry "O thou fair-faced one! People live at the sight of him . . . !" six dignitaries bowing and saying "O Ruler! As surely as the Sun-disc rises, many are the things that thou(?) art able to give!" six scribes writing, nine magistrates including the vizier crying "How fine are thy ways, O Neferkheprure Wa'enre'! How prosperous is he who is in thy favor, O beautiful child of the Sun-disc . . . !"[23] If the king harbored, in the deepest recesses of his being, any fear of not being liked or accepted by his contemporaries, the disbursement of the wealth amassed by his ancestors was an effective policy: the populace of Akhetaten sincerely loved him, for every day seemed a holiday.

The hypothesis set forth, in Chapter 4, that Amenophis had been kept in the background before his accession and was, therefore, largely unknown to his contemporaries is borne out by the Amarna correspondence. The letters to and from Tushratta about this time reveal that Tiy, his mother, was considered the only one who could influence him. She cautions Tushratta: "Promote your interests(?) with Napkhururiya, watch [him], and do not cease from sending pleasant delegations";[24] and in Tushratta's own letters to the young king, he is constantly reminding him that Tiy was the only one who was privy to all that passed between himself and Amenophis III. Tushratta's main complaint in these letters is that Amenophis IV has not fulfilled Tushratta's request to his father for some high-quality statuary, but instead had sent inferior, wooden statues overlaid with gold. To Tiy, Tushratta writes, "You have yourself spoken personally with me, but you have

22. Davies, *The Rock Tombs of El-Amarna*, 1: pl. 30.

23. Ibid., 6: pls. 17–18.

24. *EA* 26:20ff.

not brought the matter up before Napkhururiya,"[25] and goes on to say that if she does not do it, no one will.

If people initially treated Amenophis IV with a certain wariness born of fear of an unknown quantity, they were soon to learn that the king lacked the fear-inspiring qualities of his father. The evenhanded policy Amenophis hoped to adopt toward Egypt's dependencies, and which in a moment of foolish candor he had made known even to his least trustworthy vassal, could easily be interpreted as weakness. Perhaps from the outset it was a weakness that the king was rationalizing as fairness. At any rate, Amenophis IV soon found it impossible to enforce his will in Egypt's Levantine sphere of influence. Time and again, he would reprimand Aziru, the wily governor of Amurru, a veritable Vicar of Bray, with a vehemence that ought to have prefaced an order of arrest, only to relent and allow the villain more months of grace. When the same vassal committed the treasonable act of entertaining an envoy of an alien power while shunning pharaoh's messenger, Amenophis's only reaction was a whining complaint: "You have entertained the messenger of the king of Khatte, but my messenger you have not entertained!"[26] Of a governor who wrote incessant letters of complaint and request, he had the indiscretion to remark in an idiom corresponding to our "Not another letter from . . . ! Does he feel more responsible for the town than his colleagues?"[27] This exasperated outburst found its way into a letter to the gentleman in question, which caused him some indignation. The king's control over his Canaanite governors was so loose that they scandalously intercepted and robbed official legates from Babylon, and apparently suffered not at all for their crimes. The unfulfilled pleas for troops that are so characteristic of the Amarna Letters do not indicate the pharoah's disinterest, but rather his indecision: Akizzi of Ḳatna implies clearly that the failure of his policies toward his northern dependencies is a worry to Amenophis himself.

Part of the king's problem in dealing with the outside world lay in the fact that, in large measure, he relied upon intermediaries to communicate news and to advise him on a course of action. In the Amarna Letters, writers complain that they are being maligned and misrepresented by the king's advisors. The respect in which Aziru holds Tutu probably excelled his estimation of the king. Aziru feels as obligated to communicate the reasons

25. *EA* 26:49ff. 27. *EA* 106:13ff.
26. *EA* 161:49f.

for his actions to Tutu in letters addressed to him as to the king. In his tomb at Amarna, Tutu significantly describes one of his duties in the following terms: "As for the messengers from foreign lands, I was the one who communicated their affairs to the Palace."[28] His colleague, the much-titled Maya, was also "one to whom all matters are referred in order to present them to the Lord of the Two Lands."[29] To appreciate that this was not a normal state of affairs, one need only peruse the Boghaz Keui★ correspondence of Ramesses II, which shows him fully and directly aware of what was going on abroad. Amenophis III similarly was directly concerned with writing to his fellow great kings and his vassals alike. One cannot help but feel that Akhenaten had abnegated the responsibility of keeping in touch with the world in which he lived and had delegated that task to subordinates.

28. Davies, *The Rock Tombs of El-Amarna*, 6: pl. 19.
29. Ibid., 5: pl. 2.

CHAPTER TEN

The Object of Akhenaten's Worship

Even the casual observer will be struck first and foremost by the negative thrust of Akhenaten's reform of the cultus. He excised from the traditional religion much more than he added. The service of the gods was done away with, and their temples allowed to sit idle. In the wake of the desuetude of the cult, the myths of the gods, which provided the hypostasis of many cultic elements, simply disappeared. The sun god Akhenaten championed, of course, enjoyed no mythology; after the early months of the reign he was not even permitted an anthropomorphic depiction. No archetypal symbolism informs the artistic style that celebrates the new god, and the very few names and accouterments the sun-disc borrows are entirely from the solar cult of Re and his divine congeners. The marvelously complex world of the Beyond is banished from the minds of men. No truth can come from anyone but the king, and his truth is entirely apodictic: no gods but the sun, no processional temples, no cultic acts but the rudimentary offering, no cult

169

images, no anthropomorphisms, no myths, no concept of the ever-changing manifestation of a divine world. The Roman world might well have called Akhenaten an "atheist," for what he left to Egypt was not a "god" at all, but a disc in the heavens![1]

The Sun-Disc in Egypt before the 14th Century B.C.

The word used for the god Akhenaten worshipped, "Aten," is often left untranslated, as though it were a name; but in fact it is a common noun of some antiquity in the Egyptian lexicon, and means only "disc." We find it as early as the Old Kingdom used of circular objects such as mirrors or disclike accouterments of cult objects; probably already it was used at the same time in the expression "disc of the day" for the physical sun. This latter use gave rise to widespread derivatives in religious literature. We frequently hear of the sun god Re as one "who is in his disc," i.e., who is manifest in the physical sun-disc; and pious devotees will long for the time after death when they will ride "in the disc" together with the sun god through the heavens every day. In these cases the disc is spoken of as an entity distinct from the sun god, through which he manifests himself. A few passages associate the sun-disc with the word for "sunshine," or "sunbeams," a collocation of some significance.

Beginning sporadically in the Middle Kingdom, but much more frequently in the New Kingdom, the idiom of the new phenomenon of empire borrowed the sun-disc as a royalist and universalist symbol. The king's conquest could be said to encompass "all that the sun-disc encircles"; his deeds or sometimes his own person could be said to rival the sun's disc. Arrayed in his gleaming crowns and jewelery pharaoh could "brighten the Two Lands more than the sun-disc," and as universal ruler he could be called "the sun-disc of all lands." Through her association with the blazing daytime sun, the "Eye of Re," the uraeus serpent that adorned the king's brow whatever crown he wore, took on the attributes of the sun-disc; the disc went before the imperial army into battle.

During the early 18th Dynasty a growing interest in the cult of Re is attested by the prevalence of the hymn to the sun. Usually this text was

1. For full discussion with bibliography, see the present writer's article in *JARCE* 13 (1976); 17 (1982).

inscribed on the two sides of the entrance to the typical rock-cut tomb of the period, glossing, as it were, the figure of the deceased, depicted facing outward to greet the rising sun. By the reign of Thutmose III a type of statue had come into vogue showing a kneeling figure of the tomb owner, holding a stele on which was carved the requisite hymn to Re. Hymns vary slightly from case to case, but the jargon is largely the same:

> Hail to thee, Re at thy rising, Atum at thy beautiful setting! Thou risest and shinest upon the back of thy mother, arisen as king of the Ennead. Nut does obeisance before thee, and Ma'at embraces thee at all times. Thou crossest heaven with happy heart. . . . Re is in the day-barque, the night-barque has doomed him that attacked it. The southerners, northerners, easterners, and westerners tow thee in adoration of thee, O thou primeval one, coming into being of thyself! Sovereign, lord of what thou hast created. . . . O sole one, who came into being between heaven and earth, when earth and underworld existed not![2]

Amun had long since been identified with Re, and the compound name "Amun-Re" betokened a universal deity, a celestial king, who partook fully of all solar concepts and attributes. During the decades preceding Akhenaten one can occasionally detect a tendency to conceive of Re, or Amun-Re in terms of his physical disc, and to credit the latter with the creative and sustaining powers of Re, Atum, or Khepry. One dimly senses that this old solar icon, the visible sphere that moves across the sky daily, is graduating from the status of mere manifestation of the sun god to the rank of a deity in its own right.

Thutmose IV and Amenophis III, grandfather and father of Akhenaten, enjoyed a closer relationship with the sun-disc than their predecessors. The former, in a famous commemorative scarab, names the sun-disc as the giver of victory in battle. The high-flown diction of the court refers to the king as "the Disc in his horizon," and the royal palace as the "Mansion of the Disc." Under Amenophis III the sobriquet "Nebmare (i.e., Amenophis III) Is-the-Dazzling-Sun-Disc" was coined, and applied variously to the royal palace on the west bank at Thebes, to the royal barge, and to a company in the army. During his reign aspects of the sun god appear as the object of contemplation in the hymnic literature to a greater extent than ever before;

2. *JARCE* 13 (1976), 50.

and solar deities enjoy a greater prominence in the royal mortuary temple than had previously been the case. Finally, a great and marvelous hymn to the sun god on a stele of the architect twins Suty and Hor singles out the sun-disc as a full-fledged god, and describes him as "one who created everyone and made their life."

Akhenaten's God and His Iconography

Sometime during the first months of the reign of Amenophis III's mishappen son came the promulgation to the court of the royal pleasure to honor a new and unique deity. Why Akhenaten hit upon this god, or what private ponderings had preceded his announcement, we shall probably never know; and were it not for the lucky preservation of two blocks containing part of the speech in the fill of Horemheb's 10th pylon, we should not possess even this much knowledge. Fragmentary though the text of the speech is at present, we can still make out some tantalizing phrases that point in only one direction. The king says: "[. . .] Horus(?) [. . .]. [. . . their temples(?)] fallen to ruin, [their bodies(?)] shall / do not [. . .]. [. . . since the time of (?) the ancesto]rs; it is the wise men that [. . .]. [. . .] look, I am speaking that I might inform [you] [. . .]. [. . . the fo]rms(?) of the gods, I know [their(?)] temples [. . .]. [. . . the wri]tings of / and the inventory manual of their primeval bodies [. . .]. [. . .] they have ceased one after the other, whether of precious stones, [gold], [. . .]. [. . . who himself gave birth] to himself, and no one knows the mystery of [. . .]. [. . .] he [go]es where he pleases, and they know not [his] g[oing . . .]. [. . .] to him(?) by(?) night, but I approach [. . .]. [. . . the . . .]s which he has made, how exalted they are! [. . .] their [. . .]s as stars. Hail to thee in [thy (?)] radiance! [. . .]. [. . .] What would he be like, another of thy kind? Thou are he who [. . .]. [. . .] [to them in that(?) name of thine] [. . .]."[3]

The text yields two startling revelations: the king set on record his belief that the gods have somehow failed or "ceased" to be operative; and he describes his newly adopted god as absolutely unique and located in the heavens. On the walls of the same southern gate, from which this text must originally have come, numerous vignettes make perfectly plain that the god

3. D. B. Redford, *Bulletin of the Egyptological Seminar of New York* 3 (1981), 87ff.

in question is Reharakhty, "Re, the horizon-Horus," the great sun god of Heliopolis.

These scenes on the southern gate, as well as others from Karnak that date to the same early part of the reign (probably the first year), repeat ad nauseam the same basic scene (Pls. 4.4, 4.5). The falcon-headed man in kilt, with scepter in hand and a large sun-disc on his head, confronts the king across a table of offerings. Offerings include what is normal in the cult menu: water, wine, meat, vegetables, bread, flowers, etc. The god's epithets vary: "the august god of the primordial moment," "Harakhty the great sun-disc, the fashioner of brightness," "the living sun-disc who brightens the land with his beauty"; but the *name* of the god, with its special qualification, is constant: "Reharakhty, he who rejoices in the horizon in his name 'Light which is (in/from) the Disc.'" This epithet gives the god a traditional *name*, and qualifies it by an additional appelative that identifies him with the light which is in the sun-disc. When referring generically to his god, Akhenaten will, however, always use the term "the sun-disc."

It is important to note that already in the earliest form in which Akhenaten conceived his deity, there is a close relationship between the king and the god. In some scenes the hybrid falcon-man displays a prominent pot-belly, exactly like that of the royal figure standing opposite him! (Pl. 4.6).

The second and final stage in the development of the iconography of the new god came late in the second or early in the third regnal year, and was undoubtedly introduced coincident with the celebration of the jubilee. (Most of the buildings on whose walls the new representation of the god appears are built of *talatat*, but some large blocks in the 10th pylon decorated with the new icon prove the decoration of the older constructions was still being completed.) Now, if ever, Akhenaten's iconoclasm became fully evident. Gone is the falcon-headed man, while his sun-disc remains, enlarged, and viewed straight on (as the position of the uraei shows). Where the god's figure once was are now a series of long, straight, sticklike arms which splay down and terminate in human hands (the only concession to anthropomorphism). These either open to grasp the offering, or extend symbols of life and health to the royal celebrant. The standard name and epithet is now enclosed within two upright cartouches, of exactly the same type as those used by royalty, placed in pairs in either side of the disc, and accompanied by a new epithet, "the great, living Disc which is in jubilee, lord of heaven and earth, who resides in (temple name)" (Fig. 19).

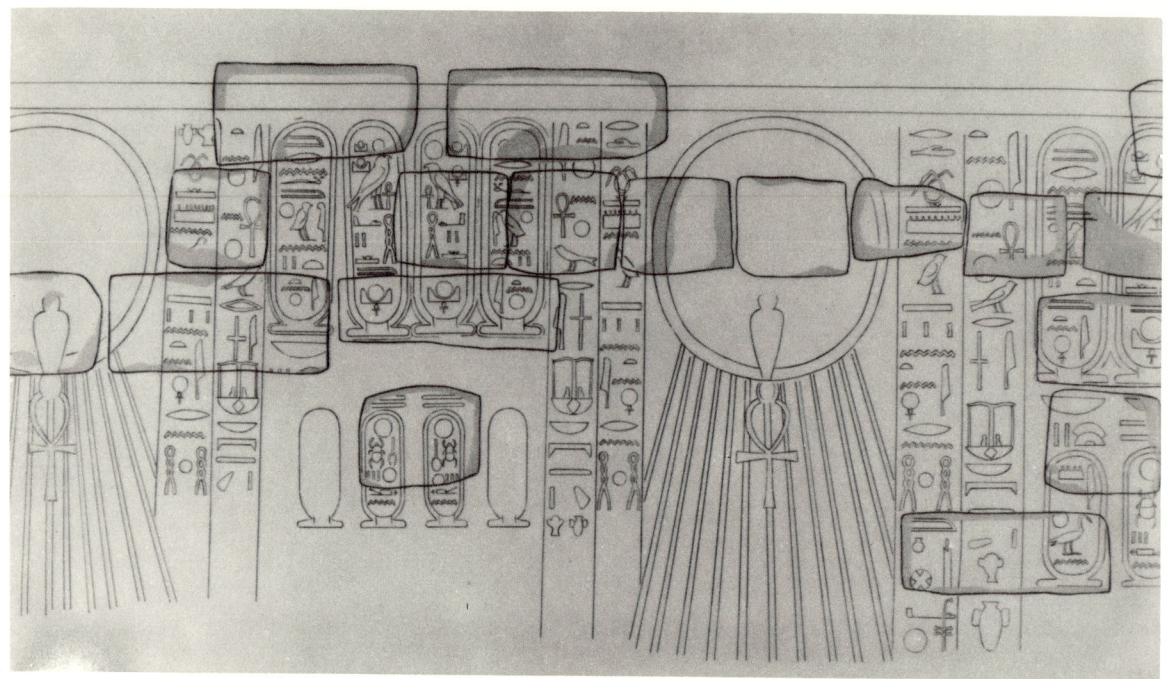

19. Facsimile of a sun-disc from Rwd–mnw (*J. Clarke*). *The Sun-disc is always shown with a rearing uraeus serpent at the bottom facing the viewer (erased in this example). Around the creature's neck an ankh-sign is suspended. The original epithet of Reharakhty is now squeezed into two cartouches, always vertical, flanked on the inward side by a new, second epithet, usually in columns. This latter reads "the great living Sun-disc, who is in jubilee, Lord of heaven and earth, residing in . . . (temple x)."*

The innovations in mode of representation evidenced here herald momentous changes in Akhenaten's thinking. Most obvious perhaps are the royal attributes that are creeping into the epithets, about which we shall have more to say below. Equally clear perhaps is the position the king is beginning to assign himself in the scheme of things. In the old type of scene in which he and the deity faced each other on either side of the rectangular frame, a balance was preserved among all the elements, human or inanimate, which went into the makeup of the vignette. Now, however, after the metamorphosis of the god and his gravitation to the top of the scene in the form of an unobtrusive disc, the king's figure remains the largest single element in the scene and, in addition, he now occupies the central position. All eyes, therefore, naturally focus upon him, and that is precisely the intent of the arrangement.

Finally, the reduction of the sun god to a nonhuman disc is but the most prominent act in a progressive move to rid concepts of the divine, and even art itself, of all anthropomorphic or theriomorphic forms. Traditional representations—or any depictions for that matter!—of the gods are no longer being carved or painted; their emblems, except for those few required for the sd-festival, are ignored. Even in the hieroglyphic script, figures of animals and humans are sometimes avoided! Only a few icons connected with the sun-cult continue to be tolerated: falcon, sphinx, baboon, bull. In all, Akhenaten was directing a strong counterblast, and doing so conciously we may be sure, against the prevailing involvement of magician and craftsman in the manufacture of the god's earthly "body," his cult-image. Pointedly the king alludes to the Disc as "the one who built himself by himself, with his [own] hands—no craftsman knows him!"

The Absolutism of the Disc

It is a curious fact that, in spite of Akhenaten's explicit exclusion of all other gods from his theological speculations, outside Thebes the gods managed somehow to survive during the first five years of the reign. If their cults had indeed been interdicted, the decree had not yet taken effect. Mortuary steles, for example, while honoring the royal cartouches and the name of Sun-disc, will offer equal devotion to Nekhbit or Osiris or Anubis. Hymns to the sun god continue to appear, not purged of their polytheistic elements, but blatantly laden with allusions to the sun-barque, Nut, and the "sea of fire." "All the gods and goddesses who are in" Memphis are invoked in the 5th year by the king's steward, who further alleges Ptah to be Akhenaten's father! In fact, it would seem that, at the outset of the reign, the degree of intensity with which the new program was pursued steadily diminished the farther one got from the royal presence.

All this changed in the fifth year. Roughly at about the same time that the king was laying firm plans for the move to the new site of Akhetaten, a drastic change overcame his cultic program. The decoration of the new temples was all but complete when the king openly broke with Amun. The "king of the gods," tolerated to this point, though his worship had probably languished through lack of priests, now witnessed the formal anathematization of his name and the closing of his temple. The program of defacement that followed was so thorough that we must postulate either a small army of hatchetmen dispatched throughout the realm, or parties of inspectors charged with seeing that local officials did the job. Everywhere, in temples, tombs, statuary, and casual inscriptions, the hieroglyphs for "Amun" and representations of the god were chiseled out; objects sacred to him were likewise defaced. People who bore names compounded with "Amun" were obliged to change them; and the king led the way by discarding the now unacceptable *Amenophis* ("Amun is satisfied") for *Akh-en-aten* ("Effective for the Sun-disc") (cf. Pls. 8.1, 8.2). Osiris and his cycle of mortuary gods suffered a like anathematization. Funerary practices might be spared, but only if purged of all polytheistic elements. Shawabtis, the little servant figurine that accompanied the dead to the next world, might be retained, but without the inscription of the chapter of the Book of the Dead containing the magic spell designed to bring the dead to life. Heart scarabs, which in the old Osirian order prevented the heart from witnessing against the deceased at the last judgment, continue to occur, but only inscribed with a simple offering formula to the Disc. The Ennead, Apophis, and the denizens of the underworld are pointedly ignored in the funerary literature; and the underworld itself is referred to simply as the place from which the deceased comes forth to view the sun. Even the script and decorative arts are purified of objectionable items such as anthropomorphic or theriomorphic signs; words tend to be written phonetically.

If any further proof is required of what the king was trying to do, let this one significant omission suffice: the plural word "gods" is never attested after year 5, and occasionally it is found erased in existing inscriptions. For Akhenaten's program, implicitly from the start, and now blatantly and universally, fostered a monotheism that would brook no divine manifestations. The Sun-disc was unique and supreme over all the universe, the only god there was. He did not change his shape or appear in other forms: he was always and only "the living Sun-disc—there is none other than he!"

The Attributes of the Sun-disc

This sole god was a supernal lord of light. The Karnak *talatat* inscriptions stress the fact that he is "uplifted" above all men, and dwell heavily on the beneficences accruing from the sunlight of the Disc. The Disc is "he who decrees life, the lord of sunbeams, maker of brightness"; he "causes everyone [to live], and people are never sated with seeing him."

At Akhetaten the major part of our knowledge about the character of the Disc comes from the great hymn inscribed in the tomb of Ay, quite likely a composition of the king himself. After Akhenaten's aversion to mythology and its symbolism had obliged him to expunge from the genre of hymns all such allusions, the only concepts that could be predicated of the deity were those of universalism, dependence of life on the sun, transcendence, creativity, cosmic regularity, and absolute power. None of this is new, and the originality of Akhenaten's poetic expression should not cloud one's mind on this score. The Disc is the creator and sustainer of the whole earth: "Thou createdst the earth when thou wert afar, namely men, cattle, all flocks, and everything on earth which moves with legs, or which is up above flying with wings. The foreign countries of Syria and Kush, and the land of Egypt, thou placest every man in his place, and makest their food. Everyone has his food, and his lifetime is reckoned; and similarly their languages are wholly separate in form. For their colors are different, for thou hast made foreign peoples different." And again, "the world came forth from thy hand, inasmuch as thou madest them." Even time is the creation of the Disc: "(Thou) creator of months and maker of days, and reckoner of hours!" His transcendence and power is extolled in the following: "Thou shinest on the eastern horizon and fillest the whole earth with thy beauty, thou art beautiful, great, dazzling, exalted above every land . . . and while thou art afar off thy beams are on earth, and thou art in every face! Thou hast made heaven afar off to shine in, in order to see everything that thou hast made from afar, shining in thy form of living Disc, arisen, resplendent, far-off!" All life depends on the Disc: "when thou shinest they live, when thou settest they die; thou thyself art lifetime, and in thee do they live. (All) eyes see thy beauty until thou settest, in order that work may be accomplished." "His sunbeams mean sight for all that he has created. One says, (there is) life (in) seeing him, but they die at not seeing him!" "Infinite life is in thee to quicken them, and the breath of life for (their) nostrils. Thy beams appear, and all nourishing plants grow in the soil, caused to grow by thy rays!" Reharakhty is "he who bestows his beauty on all mankind that they may live when he gives his beams; the land brightens at thy daily birth, in order to cause what he has created to live." As creator and sustainer, the Disc has absolute power over his creation: "the living Disc, lord of what was created and what exists!" Like an earthly king, his coming enlivens his subjects: "thy beams have brightened the earth in its entirety, every heart is happy at sight of thee, for thou art risen as their lord."[4]

In all this poetry, there is a deep-seated wonder at the beauty of the sun and its power in nature, and a firm reluctance to elaborate upon it in terms of myth. But the new concept of deity that Akhenaten produces is rather cold. His Disc created the cosmos (how we are not told; it seems not to have been of importance to the king), and keeps it going; but he seems to show no compassion on his creatures. He provides them with life and sustenance, but in a rather perfunctory way. No text tells us he hears the cry of the poor man, or succors the sick, or forgives the sinner. The reason for this as for all other conspicuous absences in the new cult is simply that a compassionate god did not serve Akhenaten's purpose.

For to Akhenaten the Sun-disc was simply the hypostasis of divine kingship, a pale reflection of his own on earth, projected heavenwards. Already with his first sd-festival, as we have seen, the unwieldy epithet of the Disc was squeezed into cartouches, as though he were a king, and qualified by the regal phrase, "given life forever and ever." Because he was absolute ruler of the universe, the sun-disc deserved the reverence due a king: everyone in the king's entourage goes about in a stooped position, or kisses the earth. Decorative creatures, such as rekhyet-birds* or snake-headed uraei are provided with hands which they raise in adoration to the Sun-disc; baboons lift paws in a similar attitude of worship.

The King and the Sun-Disc

For the doctrine of the sun-disc constituted a strong reaffirmation of divine kingship, as the role Akhenaten assigned himself proves. In the first five years the fragmentary texts from the talatat stress the paternity of the Disc and the sonship of the king: the latter is the son of the Sun-disc, the "beautiful child of the Disc" whose "beauty" was "created" by the heavenly luminary. Akhenaten has been granted the kingship by his father, and occupies his throne on earth: heaven and earth are his, his boundaries reach the limits of heaven, and all lands are beneath his feet.

4. For recent translations of the hymn, see M. Lichtheim, *Ancient Egyptian Literature*, Vol. 2: *The New Kingdom* (Berkeley, 1976), 96ff.; P. Auffret, *Hymnes d'Égypte et d'Israël* (Göttingen, 1981).

All these tenets are accentuated at Akhetaten, where no silent memories or dead rivals could interfere with the promulgation of the single theme. Akhenaten is ever the physical child of the Sun-disc, "thy son who came forth from thy body," daily reborn by the sunlight that shines upon him. Only the king truly knows the heart of "his father," and in return that loving father hearkens to his son's prayers. Akhenaten is king on earth, as his father is king in heaven. He is like his father, in fact he is his father's image on earth; and his "beauty" is that of the Sun-disc. The office of king belongs to the Sun-disc and he alone has installed Akhenaten on the throne: the king "is upon the throne of the Sun-disc that created [him]," and "thou (the Disc) hast installed him in thine office of king of Upper and Lower Egypt." The Sun-disc naturally favors his son; "he has exalted the name of no other king [who has ever been, except (that of)] thy majesty," say the courtiers of Akhenaten.

The king thus enjoyed the closest of relationships with his father. He was the Disc's image on earth, and for that reason occupied the central position in the whole system. Since he only was the one that knew his father's mind and will, he alone could interpret that will for all mankind. True teaching could come only from Akhenaten, and the texts concentrate on this "teaching" without, however, specifying its content.

The Service of the Sun-Disc

While the old priesthoods, especially that of Amun,[5] are conspicuous by their absence during the reign of the heretic, there is no lack of priests. Possibly those who formerly served other gods were now recruited for the new god. At Thebes the grades are the same: *ḥm-ntr* "god's servant," *it-ntr* "god's-father," and *wʿb* "ordinary priest." At Amarna we hear of the "Servants of the Disc in the Mansion of the Disc in Akhetaten." The celebration of the *sd*-festival required the presence of a "lector priest," but whether he read from his ritual book is doubtful in the light of Akhenaten's aversion to the traditional cult.

The hierarchy of the cult borrowed something from the organizations of Amun and Re. Like the former, the Sun-disc was served by a "First

---

5. The high priest of Amun is last heard from in year 4, when Akhenaten sent him to the diorite quarries to fetch stone: cf. D. B. Redford, *JAOS* 83 (1963), 240f.

Prophet" (high priest); but this chief pontiff was no mere mortal, but the king himself! In addition, a "Chief Seer of Re-harakhte," a title clearly derived from the sun-cult at Heliopolis, held office first at Thebes and later at Akhetaten. Probably in this officer we must see the managing head of the solar cult, but throughout the Karnak reliefs he is always subordinate to the king. He wears a kilt and head-tassel, and carries a censer or scepter and a libation vessel. His main functions appear to be two: handing the implements to the royal celebrant when he needs them, or censing before the king. As a god on earth, the pivotal figure in the running of the entire earth, Akhenaten himself was served by a priesthood, headed by a first and second "prophet of Neferkheperure Wa^{c}enre." The former appears to be a valet of the king: he is shown following the king when he performs the cultus, carrying a trestle-stool and his master's sandals.

The divine service offered to the Sun-disc is a drastic reduction of traditional practice, now that the new belief had forced the purging of all mythological symbolism. The only act retained is the essential food offering, and this is repeated ad nauseam in the reliefs. The most common term for offering is *sm3^c ^{c}3bt*, "making the great oblation," specified in one text as consisting of "oxen, shorthorns, wine, incense, all things fine and pure and all vegetables." The scene of driving, throwing, and slaughtering cattle runs in a long band along the bottom of jubilee reliefs in *Gm·(t)-p³-itn*; everywhere servants carry bread, sweetmeats, haunches of beef, wine jars, etc.

In all such scenes one theme is stressed: the bounty of the king and of his father the sun. The plenty of the land of Egypt depends upon them alone. The king is "the Nile which fills the entire land"; he is addressed as "the light (*šw*), I live through sight of thee, I am strengthened at the sound of thy voice!" The world of nature slips easily into the world of the ethical in the Egyptian's mind, and the corollary to the divine pair's omnipotence was not lost on the ancients. The king is "one who gives to whom he loves, who ordains burial for one who puts him in his heart." And from this premise follows that classic piece of advice from the mouth of the god's-father Ay, wherein we hear echoes of the same strain that resounds from Ptahhotpe or Sehtepibre-onkh to Anii: "Ho all living upon the earth, and those who shall be young men someday! I shall tell you the way of life. . . . Offer praises to the living Disc and you shall have a prosperous life; say to him 'Grant the ruler health exceedingly!' then he shall double favors for you. . . . Adore the king who is unique like the Disc, for there is none other beside him! Then he will grant you a lifetime in happiness of heart, with the sustenance he is wont to give!"[6] The kingship is central, one, indivisible, and unique. It is on earth and in heaven, solar in origin and manifestation. No one can escape its power, claims, or obligation.

6. *Urk.* IV, 1998f.; on the "Loyalist" teaching, see G. Posener, *L'enseignement loy-* *aliste* (Geneva, 1976).

PART FOUR

Sunset

CHAPTER ELEVEN

Of Politics and Foreign Affairs

We are ill-informed about the internal political history of the reign. As any formally published texts were destined for effacement after the passing of Akhenaten's regime, it is scarcely surprising that this is the case. Not even our excavations at Karnak nor the resumed British expedition to Amarna have done much to fill the void in historical sources for the reign. We can put together a chronicle of sorts listing the events we know, or suspect, took place; but we would be dishonest if we did not indicate the haphazard and often unlikely sources of our information. Wine-jar dockets and stereotyped jar labels are not the most promising texts for the historian! We have no clear idea, therefore, whether our chronicle includes the truly important events and conveys a generally accurate record, however brief, of the heretical reign.

The feverish activity of the first three years at the new site bore much fruit. By the ninth anniversary of his accession to the throne, Akhenaten could gaze forth on a city whose major buildings were built or nearing completion. Another *sd*-festival may have been celebrated about this time, though perhaps on a scale much reduced from that of the first performance at Thebes.[1] Around year 9, for some unknown reason the king decided to modify the formal, "didactic" name of the Sun-disc, which he had championed for more than a decade, and which long since had been enclosed in cartouches. Essentially the change expunged the names of "Harakhty" and "Shu" from the epithet, and made up for gaps by introducing "Re." The new, or "late" name, as it is called, was "Live Re, Ruler of the Horizon, Rejoicing in the Horizon in His Name 'Re, the Father, who has come as the Sun-disc.'"

Nefertity is still present. Wine-jar dockets of years 10 and 11 record wine of the "House of Nefer-nefru-aten," clearly a reference to the queen's estate.[2] But, as her children grew, one senses a gradual diminution of her influence.

Year 12 witnessed a magnificent reception of foreign ambassadors with tribute in a sort of durbar (to borrow a term from the British raj). Probably in the plain to the east of the city the king appeared in a kiosk, while all around flocked emissaries from Nubia, Libya, Syria, and the Hittites. Gold, silver, precious jewels, costly garments and manufactures were placed on the ground in the royal presence, while livestock milled about lowing—all constituting the expected "benevolences" due from the grandees of the empire. The king was accompanied by Nefertity and the six daughters, but this is the last time we see the family together.[3]

No earlier than the 14th year Meketaten, the second child of the royal couple, had passed away. She could have been scarcely more than eleven years of age. The mourning of the king and queen finds poignant expression in a relief scene carved in the king's tomb, albeit a curious choice of subject matter in a mortuary context.

Other members of the royal family died in rapid succession. Kiya had probably passed away before her husband (she is last mentioned with her

---

1. Admittedly this is doubtful. The Sun-disc's epithets are modified at Akhetaten to include "Lord of the *sd*-festival," but the reason for this is not known.

2. B. Gunn, *City of Akhenaten*, 1: pl. 63:169.

3. Davies, *The Rock Tombs of El-Amarna* 2: pl. 29; 3: pl. 13.

title "the favorite" in year 6).[4] The queen mother Tiy appears for the last time in year 14, when she and her son are shown in a tomb relief visiting the temple; presumably she was dead long before the end of the reign. The three youngest daughters likewise disappear from the record after year 12, and they too undoubtedly predeceased their father. It is difficult to say anything about the vicissitudes in the lives of the courtiers. Few if any of the private tombs, carved in the eastern cliffs, were in fact occupied; but it is scarcely conceivable that none of Akhenaten's entourage died during his reign.

The sudden deaths attested from about year 11 on might find an explanation in the effects of a plague which, as Professor Helck has pointed out, was ravaging the Levant at this time.[5] We hear of it first in the Amarna letters that come from the Phoenician coast. There, first in Sumur, the Egyptian headquarters for the region, and later in Byblos, the pestilence broke out, terrifying not only the inhabitants but the Egyptian officials as well. Fearful that his town might be quarantined and that he would receive no more aid, the governor of Byblos wrote frantically to Akhenaten: "they are trying to commit a felony when they report in the presence of the king 'There is a plague in the lands!' Let not the king my lord listen to the words of these men! There is no plague in the country! Things are as healthy as ever!"[6] Nevertheless, we hear talk of plague at other coastal centers with which Sumur and Byblos were in contact, and twenty years later it was raging among the Hittites. Since Egypt had closer ties with the Levantine coast than Khatte did, the likelihood is that it spread to Egypt and wreaked havoc there as well.

Unexpectedly, as the reign drew to its close, the king's eldest daughter, Meretaten, gained in power. In the final years of her father's life she continues to be referred to on wine-jar dockets and reliefs alike as "the king's (beloved) daughter." Once, in year 16, allusion is made to the "House of the Favorite," but it is a moot point as to whether this title was Meretaten's; earlier in the reign it had been Kiya's. In fact, however, there is little doubt that Meretaten had replaced many in her father's affection: the king of Babylon in a letter to Akhenaten refers to "your daughter Mayati" as "the mistress of your house.[7] Burnaburiash complains in this passage that she had sent neither

---

4. *City of Akhenaten* 2: pl. 58:16. 6. *EA* 129a:45ff.

5. Cf. Helck, *Die Beziehungen Ägyptens* 7. *EA* 11:25.
zur Vorderasien,[2] 187f.

presents nor condolences when he was ill; gifts and comforting correspondence would be expected from a king and his *consort*, not from a mere princess. Obviously Meretaten had, since we last saw her, somehow achieved this exalted station, and pursuant thereto she now appears in relief scenes cut *over* those of other royal ladies, especially Kiya, and sometimes also her mother Nefertity.

From about year 15 Meretaten is sometimes shown in statuary and relief in the company of a figure who has been taken to be a young man, her husband.[8] Occasionally his name is indicated as "Smenkhkare" ("He whom the Sprit of Re has ennobled"), to which can be added the same epithet that Nefertity had borne since year 2 or 3, Nefer-nefru-aten. The latter, in fact, seems to be of more frequent occurrence than the name itself; although, as examples are relatively few in number, such a conclusion may be dangerous. Smenkhkare certainly enjoyed as much of Akhenaten's affection as did his daughter. From the moment of his appearance in Amarna art Smenkhkare fills the role of king's co-regent: he is given a prenomen Ankh-khepru-re ("Kheprure lives"), and the epithets "beloved of Nefer-khepru-re," and "beloved of Waʿ-en-re." These names show in their formulation not only a preoccupation with the person of Akhenaten, but also a use of his names *in loco dei*; for the epithets "beloved of . . ." usually ascribe the love to a full-fledged god. Additional evidence for an intimate relationship with Akhenaten has also been adduced from minor objets d'art, some of which seem to show two kings fondling each other; but as the pieces lack texts identifying the pair, their support for the argument is less impressive than might at first appear. Stamped bricks with Smenkhkare's name, coming from a great columned hall south of the palace apartments, have suggested to some that this may have been built for his coronation; but this is at present nothing more than a guess.

The question is still debated as to whether Smenkhkare and Meretaten ever enjoyed an independent reign. In one tomb, apparently, they are shown in the accouterments of reigning royalty, rewarding the owner, and in this scene Akhenaten is nowhere to be seen.[9] Moreover wine-jar dockets mentioning an estate of Smenkhkare are dated to some king's "year 1" (the name of the reigning king is never mentioned on such dockets)[10] and a graffito from a Theban tomb, which refers in passing to a temple Smenkhkare ded-

8. On Smenkhkare and Meretaten, see R. Krauss, *Das Ende der Amarnazeit* (Hildesheim, 1976).

9. Davies, *The Rock Tombs of El-Amarna*, 2: pls. 43f.

10. Fairman, *City of Akhenaten* 3: pl. 86:35.

icated to Amun (*sic*), is ascribed to his third year.[11] Now years 1, 2, and 3 in graffiti and wine-jar dockets at Akhetaten are usually assigned to Tutankhamun, even though no unquestionable text of this man's reign can be found dated earlier than year 4. A solution might be found in assuming that Tutankhamun, upon the death of Smenkhkare in the latter's third year, simply continued his predecessor's numbering sequence for regnal years. Alternatively, Smenkhkare's three years may have been wholly, or almost wholly, coeval with the final years of Akhenaten.

That Smenkhkare, months before the end of his life, had commenced building operations for Amun at Thebes is beyond dispute. Whether he had himself removed to the old southern city is much less certain, but a discovery made in the Valley of the Kings seventy-seven years ago suggests that he was at least buried there. In 1907 an archaeological team under the auspices of the American Theodore Davis discovered a small, rock-cut tomb approached by corridor and steps near the entry to the inner valley. The interment, though sealed, had been partly ransacked, and had deteriorated through rain-seepage. The burial had been effected in haste with a minimum of equipment; what remained of the furniture, vessels, and mortuary paraphernalia mostly mentioned the names of Amenophis IV and Tiy. The investigators concluded that the burial was indeed Tiy's, and published the tomb under her name. At once, however, a problem emerged. While the mummy case had clearly been manufactured during the high Amarna Age for a court lady of royal blood, in the inscriptions which covered it all the feminine inflections placed in the mouth of the occupant had been carefully changed to the masculine! The body inside, which had been declared by an obstetrician to be a woman, proved to be that of a man when more thoroughly examined by an anatomist in Cairo. Tendencies toward femininity in some parts of the skeletal remains made a few scholars jump to the conclusion that the corpse was that of Akhenaten himself. A more recent examination in the mid-sixties, however, declared the physique to be normal for a male, and set the age at death around twenty, far too young for the heretic pharaoh, in the light of his seventeen-year reign and six daughters.[12]

The texts on the coffin might have solved the mystery but for the unfortunate fact that the name of the deceased, wherever it had occurred, was with one exception missing. The long text on the foot originally read: "Utterance by [*cartouche cut out*], deceased: 'May I breathe the sweet breath that

11. *Urk.* IV, 2024.

12. On the discovery and initial interpretation, see Sir A. Gardiner, *JEA* 43 (1957), 10ff.; R. G. Harrison, *JEA* 52 (1966), 95ff.

comes forth from thy mouth, may I see thy beauty daily; my prayer is that I might hear thy sweet, breezelike voice, and my limbs be rejuvenated in life through love of thee! Mayest thou extend me thine arms bearing thy spirit, that I may receive it and live by it. Mayest thou call on my name for eternity, and it shall never cease from thy mouth, O my [father(?), *cartouche cut out*], thou being [. . .] for ever and ever, living like the Sun-disc [. . .], the King of Upper and Lower Egypt, living on Truth, Lord of the Two Lands [*cartouche cut out*], thou beautiful child of the Sun-disc, who shall be here, living, for ever and ever [*cut out; replaced with cartouche also cut out*].'"[13]

The Amarna Age has thrown up no more tantalizing mystery than this! Who *was* in the coffin? Who *is* in the coffin? Who were the culprits and who the victims? First of all, such epithets as "living on Truth" and the "beautiful child of the Sun-disc" indicate clearly that the person addressed, whose cartouches were cut out, was Akhenaten himself. Moreover the speaker, a woman, stood in a close personal relationship to him: "father" is a restoration, but may well have been the original word, the only alternative being "brother." Again, the fact that the coffin was made for a royal lady militates strongly in favor of identifying the *speaker* (and not the addressee) as the occupant of the coffin.

Thus far most scholars would agree; but there has been no unanimity on the identity of the woman. If "father" is an appropriate restoration, then she will have been a princess; and both Meretaten and Meketaten have been suggested, though Ankesenpaaten, who would never have used an Amarna-period coffin, is a likelier candidate. If "brother" be restored, then she will have been a consort; and there have not been lacking champions of the candidacy of Nefertity herself, or the favorite Kiya.

Of more relevance to the present investigation is the identity of the man for whom the coffin was made over. Clearly the minimal changes required argue that he too enjoyed an intimate relationship with Akhenaten, and one that would not be misrepresented by burial in a woman's coffin. Although we are largely ignorant of how many cousins or nephews the king had, the evidence fortunately narrows our choice: the final section of the text cut out was replaced for the benefit of the new occupant by a patch containing "son of Re" and a cartouche. Elsewhere a fortunately surviving fragment of gold plate from the coffin yields the epithet "beloved of Wac-en-re." The con-

13. Gardiner, *JEA* 43 (1957), 10ff. For recent discussion on the coffin, see D. Schnabel, *Das Altertum* 22, no. 4 (1976), 226ff.; I. I. Perepelkin, *The Secret of the Gold Coffin* (Moscow, 1978).

clusion that the coffin was modified to accommodate the mummy of King Smenkhkare seems inescapable. Further examination of the physical remains in the sixties and early seventies produced two startling discoveries: the blood group to which both Tutankhamun and the individual belonged was the same, and when reconstructed from cranial remains, the profile of the occupant of the so-called "Tomb of Tiy" resembles Tutankhamun to a remarkable extent. That the two were brothers has now passed into the realm of accepted historical fact.

If the scenario of Akhenaten's twilight years seems to be sorting itself out, let me caution the reader to be prepared to return to a state of uncertainty. What happened to Nefertity during the final five years of her husband's *floruit*? The evidence, of course, is meager: at Akhetaten we have nothing like the abundance of source material that we benefited from at Karnak. Nefertity continues to appear in reliefs, though outshone, it would seem, by other royal favorites like Kiya and her own eldest daughter Meretaten. Nefertity still usurps kingly traits, like the blue war crown which is almost never seen on a woman; (admittedly she does not wear it often). A "House of the King's Wife" turns up with regularity on wine-jar dockets dated years 14 through 17, and the prima facie probability is that the king's wife in question is Nefertity, although Meretaten's union with Smenkhkare had conferred the title on her as well.

For the last four years of Akhenaten's reign there is an absence of evidence that might be used to date the few historical pieces still extant. One might sincerely conclude, therefore, that a principal figure had departed the scene, never to return, when in fact this is not the case. A new theory, propounded by J. R. Harris and supported by J. Samson, among others, would have it that Nefertity had made an *apparent* exit. Impressed by the fact that this alleged disappearance of the queen coincides with the appearance of the co-regent Smenkhkare, who significantly bears the same epithet as the queen, Nefer-neferu-aten, the theorists suppose the two are identical, and that Nefertity abandoned the role of king's wife for that of co-regent with her husband. The adopted function demanded titles and artistic representations almost wholly male, and involved male relationships. Chief among the latter would have been the "marriage" and the role of husband to the heiress Meretaten.[14]

14. For Harris's theory see the works listed below in "Selected Readings." For a rebuttal, see S. Tawfik, *MDIAK* 31 (1975), 159ff.

While the theory is well-reasoned and ingenious, it glosses over—and raises!—too many difficulties. The fact that Nefertity and Smenkhkare share a sobriquet in common is not significant. "Nefernefru-aten" is not a name (until it appears in Smenkhkare's cartouche) and was consistently used by Nefertity as an epithet only. "Nefernefru-aten" and the component "Nefer-neferu-" are found as elements in two of her daughters' names; and there is no difficulty in supposing it to have also been bestowed on a young male protégé of the king. There is, upon closer inspection, a slight but consistent difference in the writing of the epithet when applied to Smenkhkare, in contrast to its ubiquitous spelling when seen in Nefertity's cartouche, a variation that militates in favor of a distinction between the two individuals. Moreover, it is incorrect to assume that the name and titles of Nefertity as queen were abandoned about year 13: they turn up in the filiation of her grandchildren whose births cannot antedate the close of her husband's reign. Are we to suppose, then, that after year 13 she alternated between two sets of names? Again, what are we to make of the royal burial in the "Tomb of Tiy" in the Valley of the Kings? Even were we to deny an identification with Smenkhkare, we should still have to find a place in our historical reconstruction for a male, clearly royal, who undoubtedly reigned, was a close relative of Tutankhamun, and who bore an epithet otherwise known only from the titulary of Smenkhkare! Finally, although the matter is incapable of proof one way or the other, the appearance of a queen in art as the husband of her daughter, the latter entitled in consequence "great king's wife," seems a preposterous perversion even for the Amarna Age.

We must bring our imaginary chronicle to an end along the following lines. About year 15, or shortly thereafter, Akhenaten elevated his eldest daughter, Meretaten, to the rank of favorite and "mistress" of his house. New reliefs included the girl with her father as an adult, performing various cultic acts, and her name was insinuated in older scenes at the expense of Kiya and her own mother. At the same time Akhenaten took as his protégé and co-regent a young fourteen-year-old known later to the court as Smenkhkare. He and his seven-year-old brother Tutankhaten had probably descended from a collateral branch of the royal family—one of Akhenaten's sisters has been postulated as the mother.[15] That they were bastards of Akhenaten himself is less likely, though in the present state of our knowledge

15. D. B. Redford, *JSSEA* 9 (1979), 111ff.

this cannot be disproved. Smenkhkare, to judge by his titulary, enjoyed Akhenaten's special favor if not homoerotic attention. His union with the eldest princess and heiress Meretaten conformed to time-honored tradition in its intent to continue the royal line; but the tiny offspring who appears at the close of Akhenaten's reign (when the young couple would have been about seventeen years old) was a girl, Meretaten-minor.

A little later, perhaps while Akhenaten yet lived, the younger brother Tutankhaten was united with the third daughter, Ankhesenpaaten; on the eve of the king's death their ages must have been around nine and twelve respectively. Later still, but while Akhetaten still flourished as a city, another daughter was born, this time to Ankhesenpaaten, and named (with a curious lack of imagination) Ankhesenpaaten-minor. Nefertity survived throughout the period, and is sometimes mentioned in the filiation of the granddaughter; but she appears to have regained little of her earlier prominence.

There is no reason to question that Akhenaten died peacefully at Akhetaten in the summer of 1359 B.C., and was duly buried in the royal tomb in the far-off eastern wadi.[16] Presumably others of the family who had predeceased him had also been interred there. Where Smenkhkare died is unknown, although it may have been in Thebes. Certainly his final resting place in the Valley of the Kings was a secondary burial.

"The Victorious King, Overlord of Every Foreign Land"

War and conquest were not banished from the iconography of the "Beautiful Child of the Sun-disc." The army had never been more evident in relief art. Captives abound in heraldic motifs, around the sides of the royal dais, and beneath the "window of appearance." At the *sd*-festival the "sons of the chiefs of every foreign land" present their tribute (Pls. 3.2–3.3), while at every reward ceremony the inevitable parties of Asiatic or Nubian princes raise their hands in adoration (Pls. 3.4–3.5). Foreign potentates continue to be intimidated into sending gifts and benevolences: ships from Nubia, Syria, and Aegean Greece, whence came the beautiful Mycenaean pottery, crowded

---

16. See G. T. Martin, *The Royal Tomb of El-Amarna*, Vol. 1 (London, 1974).

the wharves at Akhetaten as they formerly had those at Memphis and Thebes.

What has been said in Chapter 9 about the temerity and uncertain resolve that show themselves in the king's character might lead us to the conclusion that his foreign policy was ineffectual. But that is only partly true. His policy toward the Nubian provinces to the south, though unoriginal, was pursued with determination and intelligence. The ancestral practice of settling the Sudan and implanting there cities of Egyptian type was carried forward; and at Kawa, near the Third Nile Cataract, a temple to the Sun-disc was founded. Akhenaten valued the fighting qualities of the Nubian contingents in his armies, and was the first pharaoh to make extensive use of them as garrison troops in his Asiatic dependencies. Conversely he saw Nubia as an admirable place of exile for recalcitrants, and thither he deported numbers of trouble-some Asiatics from the region of Damascus (see below). He even enjoyed vicarious success in the south as a warlord (although he did not accompany his forces). In July of an unspecified year, but probably after year 9, the king had apparently been informed that certain southern tribes had been stirring up trouble in the district of Akita. Though it was a hideous time of year in which to contemplate action in the hot southland, Akhenaten authorized the viceroy of Kush, one Thutmose, to move against them. A fragmentary stele from Buhen later carved by the viceroy describes the event in stereotyped phrases, and records the capture of something in excess of 145 Nubians and 361 cattle. In addition an undisclosed number of the captives were impaled upon stakes.[17]

While one may be excused for doubting whether the small dimensions of the operation justified such brutality, it nevertheless occasioned the usual adulation of pharaoh. "There are no rebels in your time," sang the viceroy, "your war cry is like a flame of fire in pursuit of all foreign lands!" A commemorative scarab struck about this time describes Akhenaten "with great war cry, possessed of a mighty reputation," and in January of his fifth year, only months before his hegira to Akhetaten, his steward Apy sent a letter to pharaoh from his post in Memphis, congratulating him on the fact that "the lands are overthrown for you through fear, he (Amun?) has placed them beneath your feet!" In the stele of Nakhtmin from early in the reign,

17. See H. S. Smith, *The Fortress of Buhen: The Inscriptions* (London, 1976), pls. 29, 75;   W. Helck, *SAK* 8 (1980), 117ff.

the king is called "Ruler of happy heart, who curbed all lands," and "the mighty king, lord of every foreign land."

The situation facing the king on his northern frontier was far more complex than the straightforward relationship with Nubian tribesmen. Notwithstanding the fact that, thanks to his father's clever diplomacy, the complexity worked initially in Egypt's favor, Akhenaten's hesitancy and lack of foresight lost him the initiative.

In particular he was largely responsible for the breakup of the Egypto-Mitannian entente, just at a time when such a rupture ill behooved either state. Shortly after Amenophis III's death, Queen Tiy had expressed in a letter to Tushratta anxiety about future relations. The tone of concern sounds strange, as Akhenaten had exchanged gifts with Tushratta and was soon to marry his daughter. But in this he was probably only acquiescing in arrangements made by his father before he died. As soon as the young king felt firmly ensconced upon his throne, he turned a cold shoulder to Mitanni: Tushratta's letters attest that he refused to send gifts or answer letters, and even kept messengers waiting at court four years before giving a reply!

"When two fall out the third rejoices," and in this case the "third" was Khatte, the great kingdom of the Hittites in Anatolia. As we have seen in Chapter 1, the Hittites by geography and historical accident had suffered at the hands of the Mitannians, and could not help but be pleased to see Tushratta discomfited. For over 100 years the Hittites had survived defeat and depression by withdrawing to the mountain fastness of Anatolia, but shortly before Akhenaten's accession their fortunes had turned with the coming to power of a new king, Suppiluliumas I. This monarch, who deserves to be ranked with the great strategists of history, lost no time in trying to widen the breach between Egypt and Mitanni. Tactfully, Suppiluliumas wrote to Akhenaten, congratulating him on his accession and sending the appropriate gifts, and others of the Hittite royal family did the same. This probably came as an agreeable surprise to Akhenaten who, throughout the Theban period of his reign, seems to have been readier to defer to Khatte than to any other country. Very soon after his accession the young pharaoh contemplated a treaty with the Hittites, and seems in fact to have eventually signed one, despite the strong advice of the king of Cyprus: "do not bind yourself to the king of Khatte . . . !"[18] What benefit Egypt would derive from a Hittite

18. *EA* 35:45f.; on Suppiluliumas and his relations with Egypt, see K. A. Kitchen, *Suppiluliuma and the Amarna Pharaohs* (Liverpool, 1961).

accord is hard to say; but for Suppiluliumas it was a godsend. He could now take on Mitanni with impunity.

Hostilities broke out—the *casus belli* was probably a boundary dispute—sometime shortly after 1370 B.C. Suppiluliumas launched an attack eastward into the Armenian highland, then suddenly turned south and descended on the broad plains of Mesopotamia. Taken by surprise, Tushratta and his court fled, abandoning his capital to the enemy. Next Suppiluliumas turned west across the Euphrates, defeating the kings of North Syria, formerly vassals of Mitanni, who dared to oppose him. Further south, on the Orontes, the king and crown prince of Kadesh tried to ambush the Hittite forces, but were themselves defeated and deported to Khatte. The expedition finally halted in the southern Lebanon, having overcome the local resistance of Damascus.

The repercussions of this single campaign can hardly be overestimated. Mitanni, as a great power, was finished; shortly Tushratta was to suffer assassination. At a single stroke a new state had thrust itself into the Levantine theater. Rumors run wild among the coastal cities subservient to Egypt: "I hear that Hittite troops are setting the countries on fire . . . and now in fact the soldiers of Khatte are being brought to take Byblos!"[19] But this proved false. In fact Suppiluliumas had carefully avoided a confrontation with any dependency of Egypt: he had not attacked the coast and had confined himself in Coele-Syria* pretty much to the Orontes valley. In his *apologia* for the attack, couched in the preamble to a treaty he later forced on Tushratta's son, he speaks only of "King Tushratta's presumptuousness," and avoids any mention of Egypt.[20]

The Hittites had stolen a march on the Egyptians. As long as Suppiluliumas refrained from overt interference in the coastal cities or districts south of the Upper Orontes, there was little Akhenaten could claim as a *casus belli*. The Hittites had, however, marched through Amurru, the northernmost of Egypt's inland dependencies. Still, we have no indication that Akhenaten resorted to any type of reprisals.

Had the Egyptians reacted with diplomatic perspicacity, the situation was far from irretrievable. The great city-states of North Syria were anything but eager to enter a new imperial relationship. Just yesterday they had been bound to Tushratta by vassal-treaties, but the Mitannian yoke had long proved easy to accept. Sharing Mitannian apprehension of these new raiders

19. *EA* 126:51ff.   20. *ANET*, 318f.

from beyond the Taurus, the North Syrian kings soon showed themselves prepared for the desperate gamble of calling in Egyptian aid. Not since the days of Thutmose III had Egypt extended its hegemony over Aleppo or Niya; and even then her control of this area had been brief. But of late the "brotherhood" of Amenophis III and Tushratta had been widely noised, and with Mitanni crippled surely Egypt would fulfil her fraternal obligation by stepping into the breach. And so three city-states bordering on the lower reaches of the Orontes, Mukish, Niya (where old pharaohs had hunted wild game), and Nukhashshe, laid plans for a rebellion, confident that Akhenaten could not fail to send assistance.

Reasoning perhaps that possession of the Syrian coast would lend strategic advantage to their venture, the three rebel kings approached the great coastal port of Ugarit, south of the mouth of the Orontes, whose king Nikmaddu had enjoyed friendly relations with Egypt and who had even married an Egyptian noblewoman. But Nikmaddu seems to have been genuinely terrified of involving himself in the insurrection. As a neutral coastal state Ugarit had put commercial enterprise above the bellicose feuding of inland Syria: Nikmaddu, therefore, returned a negative response to the invitation. The three kings, in turn, attempted to use force. The combined armies of the rebels invaded the territory of Ugarit and began to pillage and destroy border villages. By their anti-Hittite stance and their manifest leaning toward Egypt, the rebels had polarized the situation and compromised Ugarit: where could Nikmaddu turn but to the Hittites? Hastily Nikmaddu wrote to Suppiluliumas, and in a later Hittite paraphrase his appeal came out as "O Sun, the Great King, my lord! Deliver me from the power of the enemy! I am the servant of the Sun, the Great King, my lord, and the enemy of my lord's enemies. . . . These kings press us hard!"[21]

Among the rich cache of texts excavated by the French in the royal archives of Ugarit, few are of more historical importance or exert greater fascination than the subsequent Hittite correspondence and treaty. Suppiluliumas's reply was as follows:

> Although the land of Nukhashshe and the land of Mukishe are now hostile to me, do not fear them, Nikmaddu, but have confidence in yourself. Just as formerly your ancestors were friends and not enemies of Khatte, so you, Nikmaddu, be the enemy of my enemies, and the

21. C.F.A. Schaeffer, *Le Palais Royal d'Ugarit*, Vol. 4 (Paris, 1956), 17.340 (p. 49).

friend of my friends. . . . Now if all these kings launch an attack to conquer your land, Nikmaddu you are not to be afraid of them, but immediately send your messenger to me. And if you yourself, Nikmaddu, take preventive action, and with your own arms defeat the enemy . . . let no one take them out of your hands. . . .[22]

The offer extended in the letter was a most diplomatic one. Nikmaddu was invited to take the initiative and act independently, with, however, the assurance of Hittite help. Nevertheless, Nikmaddu was too timorous to take action himself. Soon his messenger was on his way to Khatte, and Hittite troops led by the crown prince descended into Syria.

The presence of the Hittites filled the rebels with dismay. They had had some success, but they despaired of victory without help. One of the rebel kings wrote to Akhenaten, pointing out that he was the descendent of one Taku, whom Thutmose III had set up as king. He further indicates that "the king of Khatte has sent me letters about a treaty," but apparently prefers to adhere to Egypt. He concludes his letter by saying ". . . and if my lord does not wish to march forth, then let him send one of his commissioners with troops and chariots."[23]

Akizzi, the king of Qatanum, though not formally in rebellion against Khatte, was strongly sympathetic to the rebel cause and became a spokesman for the northern kings. He stoutly declared himself a vassal of Egypt, and wrote Akhenaten pleading for assistance: "O my lord, just as I love the king my lord, so also do the king of Nukhashshe, the king of Niya, the king of Zinzar, and the king of Tunanat. All these kings are indeed servants of my lord!" (But there is a pressing need for military help.) "If the king my lord so desires, he marches out; but they say that the king my lord will not march out. So let my lord dispatch archers, and let them come (alone)." (The rebels do not ask for help gratis; they will pay tribute.) "Let my lord's ministers say what shall be their tribute and they shall pay it." (To give military assistance will relieve Akhenaten's anxiety too.) "O my lord, if with respect to this land a burden is to be removed from my lord's mind, then let my lord dispatch the archers, and let them come."[24]

But the cause was already lost. Even as the rebels sent off their letters to Egypt, Suppiluliumas had arrived on the plains of Aleppo to receive in

22. Ibid., 17.132 (pp. 35ff).   24. EA 53.
23. EA 51.

state the submission of all North Syria. "Then Nikmaddu, the king of Ugarit, did obeisance to the king's sons and to the chiefs, and gave them gifts of gold, silver, and copper . . . and he repaired to Alalakh in the presence of the Sun, the Great King, his lord."[25] Soon all the heads of state in Syria were hastening north to pay their respects to Suppiluliumas. One loyal Egyptian governor wailed "all the servants of the king my lord have gone away to Khatte!"[26] When Akizzi was invited to follow suit, he quotes himself as replying "'I am a servant of the king, my lord, the king of Egypt!' And I sent and spoke the same to the king of Khatte." It was not long, however, before such a forthright statement brought reprisals. Qatanum was overwhelmed by Hittite forces, Akizzi disappears, and all of North Syria passed for the next 170 years into Hittite possession.

It is difficult to explain Akhenaten's apparent inactivity in the face of this threat to his friends. True, the Amarna letters give us but one side of the picture: we do not possess the replies Akhenaten or General Maya may have written to the Syrian rebels. In them cogent enough reasons may well have been couched. Perhaps the consensus at Akhetaten was that any force of "king's archers" which was dispatched to Syria could have provided only token assistance to a cause that looked doomed from the start. To meet the Hittite challenge with any prospect of success would have meant mustering an expeditionary force of 10,000 or more; and that Akhenaten was not yet prepared to do. Not to send troops, however, would be tantamount to discrediting Egypt in the eyes of friend and foe alike; but Akhenaten either did not appreciate this danger, or was ready to risk it. Right or wrong, however, the lasting impression left with the peoples of the Levant was that the new pharaoh would never "march out," and was most reluctant to allow his army to do so.

Perhaps another element in the foreign situation that contributed to Akhenaten's reluctance to mount a major counteroffensive in the north was the rumor of insurrection within the confines of the empire. As noted in Chapter 2, the practice of taking rulers' children to Egypt and indoctrinating them with Egyptian ways produced an intensely loyal group of native regents; but it often drove a wedge between them and their own people, over whom they exercised governance on behalf of Egypt. Rib-addi of Byblos, Abdi-khepa of Jerusalem, or Abi-milki of Tyre revelled in their faithfulness to the

25. Schaeffer, *Le Palais Royal*, 17.340 vs. 22ff. (p. 50).

26. *EA* 196.

Egyptian cause, but never cease to plead for Egyptian garrison troops to help put down uprisings within their own bailiwicks. In the rough and tumble of Levantine politics, where Egyptian imperial control was minimal, it would be only a matter of time before some clever opportunist sought to capitalize on the tendancy toward factional strife in the Phoenician cities of the coast.

This threat had already, late in Amenophis III's reign, materialized in the amorphous principality of Amurru on the upper Orontes and in the Bekaa valley. This territory, with the state of Kadesh, constituted the northernmost of Egypt's inland dependencies, and its loyalty to the suzerain could never be taken for granted. During the later years of Amenophis III a disreputable chieftain named Abdi-Ashirta had sprung to prominence here, and had attempted to increase his political stature by forcing a claim to the governance of part of the coast around Sumur, the headquarters of the Egyptian administration in the area. Awakened from his lethargy by the indignant calls for help from loyal vassals, Amenophis III eventually mounted a small punitive expedition up the Phoenician coast, apprehended Abdi-Ashirta, and put an end to his brief career. But the family continued strong in Amurru. Although we know little about their background, it is probable that the clan belonged to the autochthonous population of a remoter district, untouched by Egyptian civilization. At any rate, Aziru, the son of Abdi-Ashirta who soon assumed leadership of the family, enjoyed the strong support of the *khupshu* class, the rural farmers in most of the Syrian cities. In addition, his social origins got for him the sympathy of the ᶜApiru, a class of gypsylike renegades who hovered on the fringes of the urban society of the Canaanites. To these he seemed so close in his thinking and methods that he was often called an ᶜApiru by his detractors; but, whether true or not, the name-calling never deterred him from using the ᶜApiru to accomplish his ends. It may have been in an attempt to undercut Aziru's power base in the Beka'a that Akhenaten deported numbers of the ᶜApiru to Nubia.[27]

Emerging probably after the first Hittite incursion into North Syria, Aziru lost no time in renewing pressure on the Egyptian headquarters at Sumur to recognize him. Akhenaten chided Aziru for making threatening moves toward Byblos which was responsible for the general oversight of

---

27. On Canaanite society in the Levantine cities of the empire, see M. Heltzer, *The Rural Community in Ancient Ugarit* (Wiesbaden, 1976); on the ᶜApiru, see M. Greenberg, *The Hab/piru* (New Haven, 1955); R. de Vaux, *JNES* 27 (1968), 221ff.; M. B. Rowton, *JNES* 36 (1977), 181ff. On Aziru, see H. Klengel, *MIOF* 10 (1964), 76ff.

Sumur; but Aziru's quick reply was "from old time I have been devoted to the servants of the king, my lord. But the chief men of Sumur have not admitted me." Forthwith Aziru blockaded Sumur, and when the city could hold out no longer the Egyptian governor opened the gates to Aziru, and then hastily retired to Egypt. Aziru destroyed the city, and Egypt's nerve center on the coast was gone.

Months went by and the city remained a ruin. Akhenaten wrote Aziru requiring an explanation why it had not been rebuilt. Aziru replied that he wished to be made a governor, and had not rebuilt Sumur because his fellow rulers were hostile to him. This may well have been the case, for all his actions whether by intent or not had had the effect of creating hostility. Nevertheless, it was scarcely an excuse. Aziru had already come to agreement with many fellow rulers, and had signed treaties with Arvad, Sidon, Kadesh, and Ugarit. Those who, as faithful to Egypt, opposed his moves, were quickly removed. The most notorious case was that of Rib-Addi of Byblos, who for perhaps fifteen years had dispatched report after report to the Egyptian capital, warning of the danger in allowing the Abdi-Ashirta family to escape justice. Rib-Addi was forced to watch helplessly as Aziru took the outlying towns and villages of Byblos. Eventually he was expelled from his own city, and fell into the hands of Aziru, who put him to death.

The expected rebuke came shortly from Akhenaten and it was strong.[28] Aziru's "sins" were listed, including his merciless treatment of the aged Rib-Addi, and the demand was reiterated that Sumur be rebuilt. Aziru had dispatched eight shiploads of boxwood with hostages to Egypt, undoubtedly hoping this would placate Akhenaten for the time being; and this move was astute, for pharaoh, who for several years had been demanding that Aziru present himself in Egypt to answer charges, now relented. Aziru was given a year's grace. In an unguarded moment in the same letter Akhenaten let slip the motivation of his northern policy: "you (Aziru) know that the king does not wish to be hard with the land of Canaan." The sequel shows that Aziru took this to be a sign of weakness.

Aziru used the Hittite presence in North Syria (to put down the revolt there) as the excuse for not coming immediately to Egypt; and he had the audacity to entertain Hittite envoys, which infuriated pharaoh. But if Aziru thought he could try Akhenaten's patience indefinitely he was mistaken. The Egyptian administration was still strong enough to enforce its orders,

28. *EA* 162.

even in central Syria, and soon Egyptian envoys arrived to accompany him to Egypt. Although it cannot be proven with certainty, it is attractive to suppose that the great reception of foreign tribute in year 12 was organized around the arrival of Aziru in Egypt.

We know nothing about how Aziru comported himself at his trial in Egypt; but even though absent from Syria, he could still effect his Machiavellian designs at long range. Reports began arriving from four Egyptian vassals in Amki to the effect that Aziru's friend and ally: "Etakkama, the man of Kadesh, has gone at the head of Hittite forces, and has set the cities of the king, my lord, on fire."[29] Confirmation came from Ilu-rabih, the new vassal in Byblos, who was incensed that Aziru could continue to commit crimes even after the king had interviewed him: "Look, Aziru committed a crime when he had an audience with you, a crime against us! He has sent [his] men to Etakkama, and he has smitten all the lands of Amki, the king's lands; and now he has (even) sent his men to take possession the lands of Amki!"[30] Perhaps for this reason Akhenaten detained Aziru indefinitely in Egypt. How long his stay was is not known with certainty; but it was long enough to give rise to such rumors as: "Aziru will not return from Egypt," and Aziru "dwells in Egypt."[31]

Aziru was in fact eventually released, though whether before or after Akhenaten's death we do not know. No sooner had he regained his patrimony than he renounced his alliegiance to Egypt (possibly on learning of Akhenaten's passing), and became a vassal of the Hittites. Suppiluliumas welcomed him to the fold, and praised him for his steadfastness. The subsequent vassal treaty, which luckily survives, imposes on Aziru an annual tribute of 300 shekels, and forbids an independent foreign policy toward Egypt, Babylon, or the Hurrians.[32]

In my view Aziru was one of the few that had seen through Akhenaten completely. A wily and resourceful tribesman, the equivalent of an inner-city street fighter, Aziru had appreciated the limits inbreeding and sophisticated living had placed on a ruler whose background was wholly different from his own. Though able to employ brutal though effective expedients in politics, Akhenaten refused to apply himself to the necessary organization required to send forth an efficient expeditionary force. Though able to draw up a hard-hitting indictment, pharaoh relented too easily. A recluse with a

29. *EA* 176a.
30. *EA* 140.

31. *EA* 169.
32. H. Freydank, *MIOF* 7 (1960), 356ff.

single fixation, pharaoh was apt to grow tired of the extended periods of concentration necessary to pursue a consistent foreign policy. Having to deal and bargain with people unnerved him; for he was essentially a timorous man. His only irrevocable resolve pertained to his cultic program, not to his treatment of his territorial vassals. All these traits Aziru had understood, and they probably filled him with contempt. His defection was as much due to his loathing of the person of pharaoh as it was a surrender to *force majeure* represented by Suppiluliumas.

CHAPTER TWELVE

Symbiosis: The Reign of Tutankhamun

The cult of the unique sun-disc and the iconoclasm it entailed was too in-alienably stamped with the persona of Akhenaten to survive him long. It was not the sort of cult another could champion; for the "sonship" of Akhenaten vis-à-vis the Disc his father was an intensely personal relationship. It is questionable whether his family and members of his coterie fully understood, or even wished to understand, the king's thinking in this regard. In any case the negative aspects of his concentration on "Oneness" were not appealing. Nor were they practical. The people at court in Akhetaten may well have basked in the warmth, sophistication, and luxury that inevitably attends the political capital of a state; but the vast majority of the population throughout the state were left with nothing. Sources of revenue were cut off, and therefore temples, daily cult, and pageantry, which for nearly 2,000 years had given meaning to life, were impossible. As long as the founder lived they would continue to get nothing.

But let us imagine the founder in the 17th year of his reign, which was to prove his last. For any head of state wishing to secure the future existence of the regime the events of the recent past had not been propitious. Four of his six offspring were dead, a plague had ravaged the land, and two weak boys stood in line for the throne, one already appointed, the other a youngster born after the onset of the revolution. Old Ay, the military commander and amanuensis, still survived, as did the erstwhile holder of the title "Great King's Wife," Nefertity. In addition, in the reliefs a host of faces appear: elegant ladies, undoubtedly distant relatives of the king, who could trace their ancestry back to Amenophis III, and deferential courtiers and ministers, bowing low—all forever unknown thanks to the contemporary practice of naming only the immediate royal family. It is a surfeited, weak, and pliable group of sycophants whom we see displayed here before us, tied neither to the army nor the civil service. Was Akhenaten expecting *them* to provide the main support for his protégé Smenkhkare?

The sequel suggests that neither expectations nor even firm policy existed! When Akhenaten died, suddenly we may well presume, the ship of state swung rudderless for three years. We hear of tentative moves on the part of the erstwhile co-regent and now king, Smenkhkare, to honor once again the imperial Amun. He then dies, and the mood changes. There now seems a firm resolve to remain in Akhetaten, although few if any exquisite reliefs come from this short period at the beginning of Tutankhamun's reign. Yet at the same time, and after a hiatus of thirteen years, construction work is set on foot once again at Thebes (Pl. 12.1) as additions are made to the older temples Akhenaten had constructed. The style is fine "late Amarna," and mention is made of Akhetaten, the old queen mother, and the young granddaughter.[1] But the rigors of the old monotheism are maintained: no gods but the Disc are mentioned, no cultic acts nor mythology are tolerated. Yet at the same time mighty acts of war are being planned of a nature similar to the imperial feats of old. And, most significant of all, early in his reign the young king took, or was given, the Horus-name "Propitiating the Gods."

This hesitancy and vacillation terminated in the third year of the reign with the decision to leave the new city. The king and his court certainly moved, though some part of the population probably remained behind. One cannot help wondering, in the light of the attested presence of Nefertity in

1. Redford, *JARCE* 10 (1973), 93; 12 (1975), 11ff.

12.1. Sandstone block from a dismantled structure of Tutankhamun at Karnak. The name of the building occurs on the right in the epithet of the god of whom the king is said to be beloved, viz. "the Mansion of Neb-kheperu-re in Thebes" wherein the god is said to be residing. Tutankhamun's Horus-name and double cartouche were once inscribed on the left and in the center respectively; but after his death these were carefully shaved off with the result that the surface of the stone was lowered. The corresponding names of Ay were then carved in the appropriate spaces, but these too were erased almost beyond detection with the coming to power of Horemheb. Such accommodation of the reigning pharaoh at the expense of deceased ancestors on standing monuments is characteristic of ancient Egypt.

the early years of the reign, whether it was not her death that put an end to the period of indecision and gave freer rein to those who could fashion a more consistent policy. Be that as it may, the king's presence once again in the Memphite region brought him back from the dream-world of Amarna to the reality of abandoned temples and the remnants of Egypt's glorious past.

It also placed more power in the hands of a man who was rapidly becoming the *éminence grise* of the regime. We have had occasion earlier to glimpse the figure of the shadowy Ay, flitting through the new residence city, always close to the person of the king. All that we know of his origins is contained in the biographical statement in his Amarna tomb: "I was one favored by his lord daily. My favors increased year by year inasmuch as I was extremely competent in His Majesty's opinion; so he doubled my perquisites for me, like the number of the sands. I was at the head of both the princes and the common people. . . . I was a truly correct person, one in whom was no greed. My name [i.e., reputation] reached the palace because I was useful to the king and obeyed his teaching, and performed his laws. . . . I was competent and a man of good character . . . contented and patient . . . who followed the *ku* of His Majesty as he had commanded, as I listened unceasing to his voice."[2] His titles, "battalion commander, general of chariotry, fan-bearer on the king's right hand, king's scribe," evidence an origin in the military and the exalted status he had achieved by the close of the reign. We have opined above that he was a son of Yuya and Tuya, and therefore a brother of Queen Tiy; but strangely he refrains from boasting of his avuncular relationship to Akhenaten. Though it is somewhat stereotyped, there is no reason not to accept the tenor of the above statement: he probably was a competent, docile servant, who was close to the king and somewhat awed by his discourses. Nonetheless he was a practical man. With Akhenaten gone, and his own advancement under Tutankhamun to the purely honorary rank of "eldest king's-son," he must have seen no reason to continue the charade. Much of the course charted during the new reign was undoubtedly of his design.

The essence of the changes of the third year was toleration, rather than censure and condemnation. No temple of the Sun-disc was closed, their reliefs hacked out, or their priesthoods disbanded and slaughtered. There was no sudden *damnatio memoriae* of Akhenaten, Nefertity, and those associated with them. Indeed, for ten years the cult of the Disc continued to exist, if not thrive, in the centers where it had first begun: Thebes, Memphis, Heliopolis. But there was now a major and significant difference: the Sun-disc was no longer *sole* god. Individuals were once again free to use the names of the older gods with impunity, and the king and queen themselves led the way with a politic nod in the direction of the reinstated power: "Tutankh*aten*" the king's birth-name, became "Tutankh*amun,*" while "An-khesen-pa-*aten*" turned into "Ankhesen*amun.*"

The opening of the old temples and the reinstatement of the ancient pantheon was a move based publicly on the doctrine that Egypt's woes

2. *Urk.* IV, 1998.

stemmed directly from its ignoring the gods, and in turn the gods' abandonment of Egypt. Tutankhamun's official edict of reform summed it us as follows:

> Now His Majesty appeared as king at a time when the temples of gods and goddesses from Elephantine as far as the Delta marshes had fallen into ruin, and their shrines become dilapidated. They had turned into mounds overgrown with [weeds], and it seemed that their sanctuaries had never existed: their *enceintes* were (crisscrossed) with footpaths. This land had been struck by catastrophe: the gods had turned their backs upon it. If (ever) the army was dispatched to the Levant (*Djahy*) to extend the borders of Egypt, they had no success. If (ever) one prayed to a god to ask something of him, he never would come at all; if (ever) one supplicated any goddess likewise, she would never come at all. Their hearts were weakened in their bodies, (for) they had destroyed what had been made.[3]

The motif of this pericope belongs to a standard rationalization of the "Time of Troubles," known from the morrow of the Hyksos expulsion until the Libyan dynasties. Usually couched, as here, in the form of a retrospective upon a foreign occupation of the land, the motif often ascribes the current state of society to the rupture in relations between men and gods. No more fitting protocol could be found for the edict, for the propitiation of the gods was what the policy change was all about. Tutankhamun's first efforts at a restoration of the *status quo ante* were significantly directed toward the reopening of temples and their cults which his father-in-law had shut down. The economic role of the national shrines could be ignored no longer. "Now when His Majesty was in his palace which is in the 'House-of-ʿOkheperkare (Thutmose I)-like-Re-in-Heaven,'★ he was wont to administer the land daily, and His Majesty used to take counsel with his heart in seeking all sorts of effective ways and looking for useful means (to benefit) his father Amun (for example) in fashioning his august image of real electrum. He went beyond what had formerly been done, and fashioned his father Amun on carrying poles thirteen (cubits long), his holy image being of electrum, lapis, [turquoise], and various costly stones; now formerly the majesty of this august god had been (carried) upon poles eleven (cubits long). He fashioned the august image of Ptah-south-of-his-wall, Lord of the Life

3. *Urk.* IV, 2027ff.

of the Two Lands, of electrum [on poles] eleven (cubits long)."[4] Refurbishing the cults and images of "his fathers, all the gods" seems to dominate Tutankhamun's thinking throughout his reign. In texts from his celebrated tomb he is called "he who makes monuments which come into being immediately for his fathers, all the gods; he has built their temples anew, he has carved cult-images of electrum, and replenished their supply of bread-offerings upon earth"; and again, from texts of the same provenience, he is the one who "spent his lifetime making images of the gods, so that they daily give him incense, libations, and offerings."[5] In a similar vein the royal lackey charged with carrying out the restoration of temples, one May, says: "I purified Egypt for their lords (i.e., the gods). I was the king's spokesman for refurbishing the temples and for carving the images of the gods. I was the one that entered the 'Gold-Mansion'* in order to appease their forms (i.e., the divine statues)."[6]

Of prime interest is the stress laid on the manufacture of new cult-images. It will be remembered that in the partly preserved speech of Akhenaten from the tenth pylon both the images of the gods and the standard manual of cult paraphernalia are both mentioned in a passage with a decidedly derogatory tone. Tutankhamun's intent clearly arises as a counterblast to this iconoclasm, at once both practical and theoretical. Many statues must have been pilfered and otherwise desecrated (though not necessarily by official decree) once Akhenaten's will had been made known; and Tutankhamun's decree of tolerance must have disclosed the crying need for new icons and images. At the same time his policy was a strong affirmation that gods did indeed *dwell* in a certain sense in replicas of wood, stone, and metal.

The reign of the young king from his Memphite seat constitutes a sort of twilight zone between the rigors of iconoclasm and the full sway of pluralism, in which the Sun-disc enjoyed a symbiosis with the other gods. Thus this decade throws up such oddities as representations of the king, still called "Tutankhaten," worshipping Amun;[7] or the texts from the Amarna desert chapels in which the offering formula calls Amun "Lord of heaven, he who made the earth . . . the unique one."[8] Such worthies as Penbuy and Ptahmay, both proud to display their offices in "the House of the Sun-disc," nonetheless have no qualms about supplicating Amun, Ptah, and other de-

4. Ibid.

5. *Urk.* IV, 2053f.

6. *Urk.* IV, 2165f.

7. *Urk.* IV, 2062.

8. Gunn, *City of Akhenaten,* 1: 92ff.

ities.[9] The king can refer to "his fathers all the gods," and mixes up Amarna and pluralist jargon on the furniture that followed him to the grave: "son of Amun, offspring of Kamutef, whom Mut lady of heaven, reared and suckled with her (own) milk, whom the lord of Karnak created to rule what the sun-disc encircles, bequeathing to him the throne of Geb, the excellent office of Atum . . . image of Re, ELDEST SON OF THE SUN-DISC IN HEAVEN."[10] The worship of the Sun-disc may have been played down, but army regiments continued to display a disc on their shields and to be called by some such name as "the regiment, 'Beloved of the Disc.'"[11] And while hymns to Amun were newly sung, they have a decidedly "Atenist" flavor: Amun is "the holy initiate in the Mansion of the *Benben* . . . dazzling and brilliant the master of brightness, whose sun-rays inundate all lands. . . . Hail to thee, who shines in his disc!"[12]

While we moderns are struck by the collocation of sun-disc rhetoric side by side with traditional phrases, for the ancients it was the reinstatement of Amun and the old pantheon that was startling. It may be wrong to conjure up a party with "vested interests," an "Amun priesthood," waiting in the wings breathing fire and slaughter against the innocent "Aten-worshipers." There was no such professional clergy to speak of in the 14th century B.C., and many an erstwhile servitor in the Karnak Temple of Amun may have been pressed into service by the new cult. But the economic and social aspects of the situation could not be ignored: the temples of the gods had to be reopened. And since Amun had been the chief object of overt persecution by Akhenaten, in the present reversal of fortune, it was Amun, the "king of the gods," that stood to gain most.

New appointments to the sacredotal ranks abounded. A new hierarchy was inducted for the temple of Amun along with secular officials to oversee the estate of the god. Indeed, such royal interest was being shown in Thebes that Tutankhamun was even said to have "founded the city anew." If we are to believe the wording of the royal edict, pharaoh chose all the appointments to the priesthood from the ranks of reputable citizens: "he (the king) inducted ordinary priests and prophets from the children of local princes, each one the son of a notable person, whose name is (well) known."[13]

9. *Urk.* IV, 2083; B. Löhr, *SAK* 2 (1975), pl. VI 2; VII.

10. *Urk.* IV, 2052, 2054f. 2057.

11. T. G. H. James, *Corpus of Hieroglyphic Inscriptions in the Brooklyn Museum,* Vol. I (Brooklyn, 1974), no. 424.

12. A. M. Bakir, *ASAE* 42(1942), pls. 4–6.

13. *Urk.* IV, 2029.

At the same time pharaoh saw to it that the temple incomes were restored and in many cases increased. "All the imposts of the temples have been doubled, tripled, quadrupled in silver, gold, lapis, every kind of august costly stone, royal linen, white linen, fine linen, olive oil, gum, fat, etc. . . . His Majesty, l.p.h., has consecrated male and female slaves, women singers and dancers, who had belonged to the staff of the king's house. Their expense is charged to the palace, to the treasury of the Lord of the Two Lands." In other words, as an act of piety, the king is disbanding the court of voluptuaries that had surrounded Akhenaten, and out of their number is supplying, at his own expense, the choirs and ritual dancers for the temples.[14]

There is another aspect of Tutankhamun's reign that proved to be a harbinger of what was to come. In abeyance, if not outright disfavor, for almost fifty years, the image of the "sportsman-king" was once again consciously cultivated by the young king. The "strong-man" pharaoh was imbued with the spirit of imperialism, the sort the king of the gods Amun had put forward and nurtured. No monarch attempting to restore the *status quo ante* could afford to ignore it. And the adolescent pharaoh was only too eager to step into this role. We see him, in a traditional motif, out hunting in his chariots, or charging in the same vehicle a horde of fleeing enemy. Is the military once again about to provide the ideal of masculine attainment?

14. *Urk.* IV, 2030.

CHAPTER THIRTEEN

Egypt and Khatte: A Tale of War and Peace

Much had transpired in the lands on the periphery of Egypt's sphere of influence since the disastrous denouement of Akhenaten's reign. The dream-like quality of life at Amarna for the ancients who lived there made the outer world seem far away and unreal. But sadly it was all too real; and to its reality Tutankhamun awoke suddenly.

The single most important political event in West Asia during the 14th century B.C. was the overwhelming victory of Suppiluliumas over Tush-ratta. In the wake of the Hittite king's triumphant march through Syria, Mitanni began to crumble, Tushratta was assassinated, and his dynasty shattered. When the dust settled, the entire plain of central Mesopotamia had become a power vacuum, bordered on the northwest by a "superpower," Khatte, and on the east by the newly liberated state of Assyria. A much-attenuated principality of Mitanni survived between the Khabur and the Euphrates, but it was wholly subservient to Khatte. Shattiwaza, one of the surviving sons of Tushratta, fled after his father's murder, and after many peregrinations went to Khattusas,★ whence, as a protégé of the Great King, he returned to Wassukani★ as a Hittite puppet. The vast majority of central and eastern Mesopotamia was taken up by the state of Khanigalbat,★ ruled over by a fragment, perhaps a cadet branch, of the dynasty of Tushratta. These kings tried to placate Assyria, but now found themselves coming increasingly under Assyrian control. The result was a confrontation, along a wavering line that ran somewhere close to the Khabur, between the Hittite and Assyrian spheres of interest.[1]

It is not at all surprising that Egypt should have considered her own and Assyrian interests identical. Khatte, after all, had wiped the empire of Tushratta off the map, and ipso facto had compromised Mitanni's close ally, Egypt. It mattered not at all that Suppiluliumas had, in his march through Syria, carefully avoided states whose rulers were vassals of pharaoh: the brother-in-law of the Egyptian king had been assaulted, defeated, and murdered. Egypt could not but look on Khatte as an enemy (Fig. 2).

It will probably never be known to what extent, in the ensuing international mêlée, Tutankhamun was free to shape the foreign policy of his time. Ay was conspicuous in the inner cabinet, and as a soldier he may have had a powerful say in Egyptian strategy. But I can only plead a sixth sense if I suggest that, away from Amarna, Tutankhamun rapidly became very much his own man. In the Syrian campaign on which he was just about to embark, one can easily sense the mind and spirit of a very young man, self-concious and aware of his roots, who desperately wants to live up to the standard set by his earlier ancestors.

Ashur-uballit I, a slightly older contemporary of Tutankhamun, had ascended the throne of Assyria very late in the reign of Akhenaten, just barely in time to initiate correspondence with him. One of the letters surviving from the Amarna cache mentions his desire for good relations, and whether or not Akhenaten had time to answer before he died, Tutankhamun most certainly warmed to the offer.[2] What happened next has all the earmarks of concerted action, earlier agreed upon by both parties. The strategy involved a simple, two-pronged attack; Assyria would strike west across the Euphrates, while Egypt would attack from the south down the basin of the upper Orontes. If successful, such a plan would have wrested all of Syria

1. On Mitanni and Khanigalbat, see D. B. Redford, *LdÄ* 4:149ff.

2. A. K. Grayson, *Assyrian Royal Inscriptions,* 2 vols. (Wiesbaden, 1972), 1:47ff.

from the Hittites. Sadly for Egypt, success did not attend this daring venture. At first, however, things seemed to go well. The Assyrian forces had no difficulty crossing the Euphrates, and succeeded by the suddenness of their attack in bottling up the Hittite governor of Syria in his headquarters. At the same time the Egyptian army crossed the recognized frontier of its empire on the upper Orontes and made its way toward Kadesh, its old nemesis. Kadesh, a vassal state of Tushratta late in his reign, had been won over to Suppiluliumas during his great Syrian campaign. This rankled the Egyptians, who always felt that this strategic city should belong to them, if not to some friendly power. The forces of Kadesh were forthwith driven back, and the city besieged.[3]

The attack had clearly taken the Hittites by surprise. Suppiluliumas himself was occupied in punitive action in a remote quarter of Asia Minor when it occured, and was unable to deal with the matter in person. He did, however, act quickly. Two forces were at once dispatched, one to counterattack the Assyrian incursion, the other to relieve Kadesh. The Assyrians were confronted and forced back across the Euphrates, while the Egyptian besiegers, perhaps hearing of the Hittite advance, broke off the investment and retired south. In the wake of the retreating Egyptians, the Hittite forces refused to stop at Kadesh, and on one of the few such occasions in the history of Egypto-Hittite relations, they crossed the frontier and attacked the cities of the Amki, at the headwaters of the Orontes, part of the Egyptian empire. After an uncertain, though short, period of time a second attack was mounted on the Amki, and Egyptian prisoners were even taken back to Khatte.[4]

Of these serious reverses nothing was said in the Egyptian sources, our information coming wholly from the Hittite archives. Back home beside the Nile the campaign was represented as a success. Surviving *talatats* show parts of scenes with Egyptian chariots rolling over the corpses of helmeted Hittites and an Asiatic city (Kadesh?) under attack. On the south face of the large pylon at Karnak, tenth in the standard numbering, adorned with colossi of Amenophis III, a traditional head-smiting scene was carved, with the requisite line of vertical ovals containing the names of "conquered" places, each surmounted by the torso of a bound Asiatic captive. Most of the names

3. H. G. Güterbock, *JCS* 10(1956), 92ff.
4. A. R. Schulman, *JARCE* 15(1977), 43ff.

are general—"Upper and Lower Retjenu, the Hau Nebu (the Aegean)"—but one, Takhsi, denotes a district just northwest of Damascus through which the Egyptian army must have passed on its way to Kadesh.[5]

It must have been fairly soon after the return of the Egyptian army from Syria that Tutankhamun died. The Hittite annals record his passing at about the time of their attacks on the Amki, and represent the Egyptian populace as being thrown into a panic by the double tragedy of military defeat and loss of a leader. It has been suggested that foul play was involved, but, although conceivable, there is no proof whatever of such an assertion.

It is extremely difficult to assess fairly the reign of Tutankhamun. His was the double misfortune of having followed almost immediately upon the heels of the most controversial figure in Egyptian history, and of having been cut off suddenly in his prime. In addition, the unbelievable richness of his undisturbed tomb has so dazzled us that it is hard to think of him as a human being. It has also so distorted our vision that, apparently, some of us are prepared to believe anything about the man—that he was really a black, or a problem drinker, or one able to impose a curse on violators of his tomb. Let it be said once and for all that such notions, by whomever voiced, or undeservedly honored by whatever screed, are unadulterated clap-trap with no support at all in the meager evidence we possess. In reality Tutankhamun was a very young man and quite probably slightly bewildered. Born into a world in which the iconoclasm of the heretic already held sway, he had never known at first hand the traditional Egypt of cultic pluralism and the conservative canon of artistic expression. His early death deprived him of an opportunity to show what he could do if given a chance, but the embryonic policies we discern suggest a not ill-conceived program, albeit plagued by rash counsel. On the battlefield he may well have been outgeneraled by an older and more skillful adversary; but at home he still commanded the manpower and organizational skill to erect large and imposing monuments.

Sadly, he possessed no heir to whom he could bequeath the regime. The one offspring we know of, Ankhesenpaaten-minor, undoubtedly died young, and no other relative of any collateral branch of the family had apparently survived. On the eve of his demise the major heirs of power were three: Ankhesenamun, his widow, aged roughly twenty-two years; the aged

---

5. To be published shortly in the *Brunner Festschrift*.

13.1. Architrave block from the building of Tutankhamun mentioned in pl. 12.1. The text refers to the Beautiful Festival of the Valley, a celebration held yearly in the spring when Amun crossed to western Thebes to visit the mortuary shrines of the ancestors and to "rest in his temple." The lower line refers inter alia to "Nubians" and "the tribute of every foreign land," possibly an allusion to the activity in the south and north which marked the closing years of Tutankhamun's reign.

Ay; and a young, promising lieutenant general in the north, called Horemheb. As pointed out above, while Tutankhamun still lived Ay had wrung from him the appointment as vizier and "king's eldest son," a sure indication that Tutankhamun, willy-nilly, had recognized his mentor as his heir. In concert Tutankhamun and Ay had begun to erect buildings, one of which, a columned court in the temple of Amun, is attested by surviving architraves and pillars (Pls. 12.1, 13.1). On certain scenes Ay is shown standing discreetly behind Tutankhamun, a considerable honor for a private person.[6]

On Tutankhamun's passing there were no ostensible signs of quarreling. Ay acceded to the throne without contest, and is depicted performing the obsequies at the deceased pharaoh's funeral. The joint building program was continued at Karnak and Luxor, and construction plans were laid for other memorials throughout the land. One, a large stele and shrine, was cut high

6. R. Saad, *Karnak* 5(1975), 93ff.

up in the eastern cliff in the Nile Valley just north of Akhmim, possibly not far from Ay's home town. In sum, the stereotyped royal iconography betrays no sign whatsoever that all was not well in the royal court.

But the sober Hittite annals certainly do. From the sequel it is clear that Ankhesenamun, who had followed her young husband to the grave and watched while Ay usurped the role of funerary celebrant, did not approve of the new configuration of power. In spite of Ay's formal assumption of pharaonic rule, the bereaved queen seems not to have been suppressed, and continued to enjoy a certain freedom of action. In fact, in a formal sense only, graphic art at times even united her with Ay as his consort, a union belied by the gross disparity in their ages, perhaps as much as forty years! There can be no doubt that Ankhesenamun had little use for Ay, and it may be that she lived in Memphis apart from Ay who may have been occupied with affairs in Thebes (an hypothesis that would more easily account for her ability to act independently). Clearly Ankhesenamun had not in any way relinquished the rights to political power she felt were hers. But now she lacked a party of support within her own country, so thoroughly had the dynasty to which she belonged been discredited; and any assistance would have to come from abroad.

In Syria, in the wake of his advance forces which had beaten back the Assyrians and Egyptians, Suppiluliumas the Great King came to view the field of battle. Only one city continued to withstand the Hittites, the fortress of Carchemish on the Euphrates, and this Suppiluliumas duly invested. While the siege was in progress a lone Egyptian messenger reached the Hittite camp. How he had managed to slip out of Egypt, or negotiate the considerable tract of dangerous, sometimes hostile, territory between Gaza and the Euphrates, was a mystery; but he came bearing a letter from "the queen of Egypt" to Suppiluliumas. As recorded in the Hittite annals, the letter read as follows: "My husband has died. A son I have not. But to thee, they say, the sons are many. If thou wouldst give me one son of thine, he would become my husband. Never shall I pick out a servant of mine and make him my husband. . . . I am afraid!" This candid glimpse of the real political situation inside Egypt probably astounded Suppiluliumas as much as it does us. For once the timeless stereotype of pharaoh as all-powerful master of himself and the world is swept aside, and we perceive fleetingly a divided court peopled by terrified human beings who know their own weaknesses. The Hittite annals, drawn up by Suppiluliumas's son Mursilis II, represent the king as saying, upon receipt of the letter, "such a thing has never happened before in my whole life!"[7]

Suppiluliumas was, however, too astute to jump at the opportunity and too imaginative to let the initiative slip from him. So he dispatched an ambassador to Egypt to investigate the situation. As the subsequent course of events indicates, Ankhesenamun was able to entertain and impress the ambassador, who clearly had no inkling that Ay was already king. For if the signs of Ay's kingship, or Ay himself, had been present, the Hittite envoy would never have returned so favorable a report to his master. Once again the only hypothesis that will wholly explain these facts is one that assumes Ay to have been occupied and physically present in Upper Egypt for the first year or so of his reign, while Ankhesenamun resided in the manner of regent in Memphis.

Suppiluliumas had obviously been skeptical regarding the queen's offer, and had verbally communicated his suspicion of deception to his ambassador before sending him off. When the ambassador returned to the Hittite homeland the following spring, having faithfully conveyed to Ankhesenamun his master's feelings, he brought back an Egyptian plenipotentiary Hania, and a petulant letter from the queen. "Why didst thou say, 'they may deceive me' in that way? Had I a son would I have written about my own and my country's shame to a foreign land? Thou didst not believe me. . . . He who was my husband has died. A son I have not. Never shall I take a servant of mine and make him my husband. I have written to no other country . . . so give me a son of thine: to me he will be husband, but in Egypt he shall be king." Suppiluliumas could not let the opportunity to humiliate the Egyptian emissary go. He brought out a copy of the treaty he had signed with Egypt, and must have gloated as he pointed out to Hania how the Egyptians, and not he, had contravened its provisions: "I myself was friendly, but you suddenly did me evil. You came and attacked the man (i.e., king or ruler) of Kadesh whom I had taken away from the king of the Hurri-land (i.e., Tushratta of Mitanni)." But with this one Parthian shot, Suppiluliumas relented and complied with Ankhesenamun's wish: one of his sons, Zidanza, was sent off to Egypt.[8]

The confused events of the next few years center upon the figure of the lieutenant general Horemheb, one of the most enigmatic power-wielders of

7. Güterbock, *JCS* 10(1956), 96ff.
8. Schulman, *JARCE* 15(1977), 43ff.; *idem, JNES* 38(1979), 177ff.

the New Kingdom, and the man who was destined to terminate once and for all the attempts of the surviving member of the 18th Dynasty to salvage the situation. No extant text tells us of Horemheb's early career, or even of his place of birth. The fact that his name is compounded with "Hor," i.e., Horus, the falcon-god, has caused some to look to the 16th township, where "Horus of Hebnu" was the local deity. But this is nothing more than a guess. It is very doubtful whether he was ever at Amarna. "Pa-aten-em-heb" has been suggested as the form of his name at Amarna (whence "Hor-em-heb" by later suppression of the "Sun-disc"); and the bearer of that name from Amarna tomb #24 has been singled out as Horemheb as a young man. The title, however, shows Pa-aten-em-heb to have been quite a different worthy.[9]

The earliest unequivocal attestation of Horemheb is from the beautiful tomb he erected in the memphite necropolis at Sakkara. Torn asunder in the last century to provide fragments of exquisite relief for collectors, the major decorated pieces from this tomb are now to be found scattered among museums from New York to Berlin. The excavations of the Egypt Exploration Society under the direction of Dr. Geoffrey Martin have, in the past few years, succeeded in relocating what remains on the original site, and have provided additional relief scenes.[10] To judge from the style of decoration, the tomb dates late in the reign of Tutankhamun, and was in process of decoration under Ay, when, a fortiori, a courtier would be buried near the Memphite residence. (The fact that, in it, Horemheb already is called "heir apparent" [iry-p't]militates in favor of decoration during Ay's *floruit*, although some of the events pictured may be earlier.)

From the evidence of the tomb, the following picture emerges regarding Horemheb's career. About the middle of Tutankhamun's reign Horemheb springs to prominence with a posting in the north of Egypt. His titulary betrays a military training: he is a "royal lieutenant" (var. "lieutenant of the entire land"), with responsibility for foreign affairs. It was probably he that Tutankhamun selected to lead a punitive campaign in Nubia, to coincide with the appointment of a new viceroy of the southlands, Huy. The latter's tomb shows in more traditional style the investiture scene and the gay flotilla of vessels carrying the new appointee south to his command; but it is the vivacity and "naturalism" of the late Amarna style of Horemheb's tomb

9. J. Vandier, *JdS* (1967), 80.
10. G. T. Martin, *JEA* 63(1977), 13ff.; 65(1979), 13ff.

that more accurately conveys the spirit of the occasion. The text on one of the blocks from the Memphite tomb describes Horemheb as being "sent as royal messenger to the limits of (the region wherein) the sun-disc shines, and when he came (back) festival was made for him. . . . No land could stand before him, for he despoiled them in but a moment. His name was noised abroad . . . after he sailed north. When His Majesty [himself] appeared on the throne for the reception of tribute, and the [tribute] of South and North was brought in, the Heir Apparent Horemheb was standing beside the th[rone], th[anking] god [for His Majesty]."[11] The reliefs give prominence to this Nubian venture which, in all probability, was nothing more than a minor punitive campaign or policing action. The captives are shown seated submissively in rows, being dragged forward or being beaten. The frustration of years of defeat seems to work itself out in an indulgence of brutality which finds as ready and faithful a recorder in the unknown sculptor as modern war crimes do in the reporter-photographer.

Horemheb next appears as a "chief overseer of the army," the equivalent of our "field marshal" or "five-star general." At a gala celebration, recalling the lavish pomp of Amarna days, he is decorated with rewards of gold, and presents his captives to the king. One wonders whether it was he, in concert with Amenemone, another field marshal of the time, that led the abortive attack on Kadesh. The tombs of both men—Amenemone's was also in the Memphite region—depict Asiatic captives brought back to Egypt; though Horemheb's reliefs have the distinction of depicting a group of submissive, though irate, Syrian princes.

Ay had no (surviving?) natural offspring to succeed him, and it was perhaps expected that he would choose Horemheb. Both men were from the military; and Horemheb was untainted by the Amarna heresy. He was energetic, imaginative, and responsible, and clearly had the nation's interest at heart. Horemheb's appointment as "heir apparent," whether it came at this time or after the "Zidanza affair," signaled a change in the internal affairs of Egypt: the army had taken over. Never again would a scion of the great Thutmosid family, the 18th Dynasty, sit upon the throne of Egypt. Disillusioned by their ineffectual handling of domestic and foreign situations, the army now determined to keep a tight hold on the body politic. Even priests at times are now chosen from the army!

11. Sir A. H. Gardiner, *JEA* 39(1953), 3.

This was the axis of power that confronted the small party of unsuspecting Hittites as they approached the Egyptian frontier bringing Zidanza to his nuptials: an aged king who must by now surely have known what was afoot, and a military "strong-man," waiting in the wings. What happened next was evidently an act of state, authorized by the highest repository of legal power in the land, namely pharaoh himself; but we do not actually know if Horemheb was in any way directly involved. Zidanza was murdered as soon as he set foot on Egyptian soil, and Ankhesenamun disappeared.

The repercussions could easily have been predicted. Suppiluliumas flew into a range when news of Zidanza's assassination reached him, and at once planned military action. Again Hittite forces descended upon the Egyptian frontier in the Antilebanons, and laid waste the cities of the Amki. Our sources present a spotty and confused picture of the fighting. Apparently the Hittites were engaged by the Egyptian army, and both sides took prisoners, but the hostilities gradually petered out and both sides broke off without any major conclusion. The Hittites eschewed involvement any further south than the headwaters of the Orontes, not so much because of the distance, but rather because of the presence of Egypt in these reaches and pressing political problems closer to home. For to the Hittites the Kaska-hordes to the north of the capital, the kingdom of Arzawa to the west, and the "Hurri-lands" to the east across the Euphrates demanded far more attention and were more profitable to exploit than Syria on the south. Add to these factors of geography and politics the advanced age of Suppiluliumas, and there can be little wonder that the Hittites did not force the issue. Egypt was given a brief respite from hostilities and a reprieve from embarrassment. Ay could claim to have lived up to his Horus-name, "Smiter of the Asiatics," and his generals could proudly display scenes of their battles in their tombs without fear of contradiction.

CHAPTER FOURTEEN

Epilogue

Several months into his fourth year the aged Ay finally died. He had had carved for himself a rock-cut tomb near that of Amenophis III, in a lateral valley close to the Valley of the Kings at Thebes; and this he presumably occupied in death, in close proximity to the man who may have been his brother-in-law. Curiously, the tomb is decorated *inter alia* with a scene of the king fowling in the marshes, a motif similar in spirit to scenes of the "secular" repertoire of high Amarna times. But that is the last gasp of the anti-cultic spirit of the iconoclast: the new heir to power knew nothing of Akhenaten and his movement.

The Reformer

"Horus, Might Bull: Ready in Plans; Favorite of the Two Ladies: Great in Marvels at Karnak . . . King of Upper and Lower Egypt, Djeser-kheperu-re, Ruler of Truth, He-whom-Re-has-chosen, the Son of Re, Horemheb"—this was the heir to the kingdom, and this was the titulary by which he broadcasted his credentials, plans, and aspirations. There were no rivals: the surviving claimants of Thutmosid descent were not in the running. For the time being there was no war: the Hittites were occupied elsewhere and in any case suffering from the plague. Horemheb and his coterie of like-minded military men were able to get on with the task of restoring order to the state.

Horemheb is the one protagonist of the period who has suffered a "bad press." Thanks to Hollywood and the popular literature he has been unfairly burdened with the image of a red-neck or a Machiavelli, neither of which bears the slightest resemblance to the man. It behooves the careful and intelligent reader to bypass the river of unrelieved nonesense spouted by the contemporary novelist—the poverty of his style should not make that difficult in any case—and concentrate wholly on the evidence which in text and monument has come down to us. If this is done, a strikingly different Horemheb will emerge. Not only will his origin and participation in the Amarna court of Akhenaten fade from the realm of probability, but also his postulated role as "man behind the arras" in Ay's reign will grow increasingly unlikely.

Before he came to the throne Horemhab was a docile general who worked for his lord; afterwards, he became an energetic, down-to-earth manager who brought the country back to its senses. This does not exclude an imagination and a sense of the dramatic. At the outset of his reign, and in keeping with the exhiliration everyone sensed in the air, Horemheb conceived a triumphal procession to Thebes at one of the major festivals. Horus, his own patron god, led the flotilla upstream to the Southern City, and made the necessary "introduction" to Amun. All went according to plan: Amun-Re received Horemheb with joy, ushered him into the "palace" and then and there, in the "company" of seven major deities, placed the crown and other regalia upon him. Outside in the bright sunlight, before the wondering gaze of the Theban citizens, Amun embraced Horemheb as his son, and officially proclaimed him king. No act could better have signaled the end of the Amarna period and the beginning of an orderly and auspicious reign.[1]

Horemheb's major efforts were directed toward eradicating bureaucratic corruption and eliminating disorder which sadly had proved to be the only immediate bequest of the period of heresy. After his coronation he is said

1. Sir A. H. Gardiner, *JEA* 39(1953), 3.

to have made a grand tour of inspection. Like any good pharaoh his first thoughts were of the gods. "He shaped all their images in number more than before, increasing the beauty in that which he made. Re rejoiced when he saw them. . . . He raised up their temples, he fashioned 100 images, all their 'bodies' being correct, and (encrusted) with every splendid costly stone. . . ."[2] The end of the Amarna Age had witnessed a lapse into grave-robbing on the part of the Theban populace: Thutmose IV, for one, suffered the desecration of his tomb and mummy. These Horemheb restored, and reorganized the necropolis workers into gangs.[3]

Out of the king's wrestling with corruption in the army and civil service came the most important document of the reign, the great Edict of Reform. Probably delivered early in the reign, the edict is known to us in a single copy published on a stele north of the 10th pylon at Karnak.[4] Although one-third of the text is now lost, more than enough remains to permit substantial reconstruction. The king's aims appear to have been two: to stamp out lawlessness on the official level by the imposition of harsh penalties, and to reform the judiciary. The penalties are decreed in a series of pericopes (which we might have organized into paragraphs) in which a specific crime is described with its consequences, officially condemned, and assigned a particular type of punishment. Roughly speaking, the crimes fall under three heads: 1) extortion practiced by tax-collectors, 2) the connivance of royal inspectors, and 3) lawless acts by the soldiery. Under the latter are mentioned the extortion of goods and services from the peasants, outright robbery, and cattle-rustling. The penalties always involved the restitution of lost property, but in many cases it also entailed mutilation: the dishonest taxman or army sergeant could look forward to having his nose cut off and a permanent exile to Sinai! (Interestingly, in the Ptolemaic period, 1,000 years later, the Sinai frontier was still the place of exile for noseless malefactors!)[5] In order to attack the problem at the root, the king wisely remitted the taxes of the peasants, and the ancient tax on mayors and town councils, and reinstated the practice of treating treasury officials to a monthly banquet at royal expense.

But Horemheb was probably proudest of his "housecleaning" in the Department of Justice. Through the text there runs an undercurrent of aversion toward the opportunists of the Amarna Age who had lacked either

2. Ibid., pl. II.
3. H. Carter and P. Newberry, *The Tomb of Tuthmosis IV* (London, 1904), figs. 7–8.

4. *Urk.* IV, 2155ff.
5. Strabo xvi. 2. 31.

pedigree or integrity. Hear the king himself: "I trod through (the land), both march and interior, seeking men. [I sought out princes] of sound speech and good character, who know how to judge human nature, who obey the words of the palace, the laws of the Porte. I promoted them to judge the Two Lands to the satisfaction of Him who is in the [palace]. I placed them in the great cities of Upper and Lower Egypt, each of them being keen of hearing. . . . I set the regulations before them, the laws in their journals. . . . I instructed them with respect to the Way of Life, I led them to Truth. I taught them as follows: do not fraternize with people, nor take a bribe from a person (for) there is no point to it. . . . It is the prophets of the temples, the mayors of the interior of this land and the lay-priests of the gods who shall constitute any court . . . to adjudicate the citizens of all the cities."

Nothing tears the mask from the Amarna Age like the Edict of Reform. The picture conjured up is not like the beautiful relief scenes at Karnak or Akhetaten. Gone are the elegant ladies and gentlemen, bowing low before a benign monarch beneath the Sun-disc, his father; in their place emerge starkly an army allowed to run riot, a destitute peasantry, and corrupt judges. It may be maintained that these conditions could only have prevailed at the close of the period of heresy, but the evidence opposes any such defense. The withdrawal and the subsequent isolation of the head of state and his court, which clearly brought on the anarchy, must be laid to the charge of Akhenaten himself.[6]

Return to "Orthodoxy"

Already before Tutankhamun died, and increasingly under Ay and Horemheb, texts of religious import had begun to adopt a harder line toward the monotheism of the preceding generation. A didactic tone of admonition is clearly discernible as attempts are made to counterblast the effects of the heretic's erroneous teaching. "The Two Lands are illumined by (Re's) two eyes," sings the psalmist; "*it is not the sun-disc* that appears to those who are in heaven, but the 'head' which has reached to the sky," words that conjure up the mythological concept of some sort of Cosmic Man.[7] The sun-disc

6. Whether Akhenaten ever traveled himself outside the bounds of Akhetaten is a moot point, though he clearly wished to be buried there (W. Westendorf, *GM* 20[1976], 55ff.). One cannot discount the possibility of an occasional excursion to other parts of the country, but the discontinuance after year 5, at Thebes and elsewhere, of all building activity, strongly suggests that the new city had become his favored and perhaps sole residence.

7. A. Piankoff, *BIFAO* 62(1964), 215.

is by no means eliminated from the cultic jargon—how could it be, for it is too immanent a power—but it is once again subordinated as only a manifestation of deity: Amun "is the one that made the sky and lighted it with stars, who made his seat in it *as the sun-disc.* . . . [as for him] who praises thy (Amun's) spirit, the sunlight shines on his limbs, [his] eyes see thee, his body is filled with Truth, (for) I know that thou livest upon it and feedest upon it."[8] Here, in language redolent of Akhenaten's concepts, is a strong affirmation that it is Amun as the sun-disc, and not the latter alone, that sheds light, truth, and favor upon a worshipping world. Again and again the doctrine is stressed that the sun-disc is nought but the "body" or visible manifestation of a transcendent deity, be it Amun, Re, or Osiris; there is nothing in the sun-disc alone to warrant exclusive worship. "The King of the Gods (Amun) is a (true) god, one who takes cognizance of one who is cognizant of him, who favors him that serves him, and protects him who follows him. He is Re, *his body is the sun-disc.* . . ."[9] Noteworthy too in all this is the veiled warning: Amun favors those that favor him! The sun-disc's demotion to the rank of one of the many modes of manifestation of the hypostasis of a great god is everywhere emphasized. The offering formula refers pointedly to libations and offerings "to Re-Harakhty, *to his sun-disc, to his body*"[10] and Osiris, the god damned to extinction by Akhenaten, is not only brought back into the fold, but is now linked with Re. "Thou (Osiris) hast arisen as Re in the horizon, *his sun-disc is thy sun-disc,* his form is thy form. . . ."[11] In all these passages the point being made is that the sun-disc is not a god, unique and without equal, but only a mythological symbol. It is no accident that the morrow of the Amarna Age witnesses the sudden appearance of a plethora of mythological "books," often inscribed in royal tombs, which reestablish with a vengeance the reality of the plurality of divine powers in universe and underworld.[12]

Perhaps we moderns might catch the true sense of what was going on in this theological polemic were we to imagine a fanatical Christian priest denying Christ, the Trinity, and the saints in favor of the Cross. The latter, which in normative Christianity had functioned as a symbol of salvation through which Christ's saving grace was bestowed upon the world, would

8. N. de. G. Davies, *The Tomb of Nefer-hotep* (New York, 1933), pl. 34.

9. *Urk.* IV, 2177f.

10. *Staatliche Sammlung ägyptischer Kunst in der Münchner Rezidenz Hofgarten* (Munich, 1970), pl. 35–36.

11. E. Drioton, *ASAE* 43(1943), 36, fig. 2.

12. A. Piankoff, *MDIAK* 16(1958), 251.

now be exalted and deified as sole god and heavenly father! If one can grasp the tone and implications of such a lunatic aberration, one can perhaps appreciate why these "theologians" of the Post-Amarna period were at pains to eradicate this error by a return to "sound" teaching.

It was Horemheb that finally closed the temples of the Sun-disc. As noted above, these had been allowed to function side by side with the reopened shrines of the gods. The twelve years Akhenaten had spent at Akhetaten had witnessed a suspension of all construction and decoration of sun-shrines at Thebes, Memphis, Heliopolis, and elsewhere; but under Smenkhkare and Tutankhamun decoration had resumed, probably at every site, in a beautiful "late Amarna" style. But this eleventh hour attempt to decentralize was doomed. The new administration had suffered the effects of the centralized monotheism, and cared nothing for it; Egypt had tasted of iconoclasm and had found it wholly wanting. The cult of the Sun-disc had been established as the *substitute* for the plurality of older cults; it was logically impossible for it to *co-exist* with them. In destroying the sun-temples Horemheb was not simply removing buildings in the way of new construction, or using their stones as a substitute for freshly quarried masonry, as some would have us believe. He was in fact doing away with the only surviving symbols of the total failure of the royal house he had supplanted.

Not one block was left upon another at Akhetaten. Walls were torn down to their foundations, mud-bricks pillaged, and steles and statuary hopelessly smashed. Thereafter the ruins provided a quarry for over a century, most of the known blocks gravitating across the river to Hermopolis where the Ramessides used them extensively; but some ended up as far away as Abydos, over 100 miles to the south. The fate of the sun-temples at Memphis and Heliopolis can only be imagined; the one at Memphis was undoubtedly torn down. Today *talatat* are found scattered throughout Old Cairo and the Delta.

Return to Thebes

They returned to East Karnak sometime during the first decade of Horemheb's reign, but not with the intent to worship or celebrate a jubilee. New buildings were arising on the periphery of Amun's complex which would at once obliterate the sun-temples for all time and use their blocks for masonry fill in cores and foundations.

The four major shrines were still standing, though somewhat dilapidated. The wreckers found as they approached that at Karnak, just as at Akhetaten (now largely abandoned), vandals had hammered out some of the reliefs here and there. The faces of the queen had often been hacked with hammer and chisel; less often had the king's visage been so treated (Pls. 4.5, 7.17, 14.1). Cartouches, even those of the Disc, had often been erased, and occasionally the sun-arms had been slashed. Curiously, from time to time the representation of a priest or servant had been chiseled out, as though the identity were well known, even though a caption was lacking. None of the erasures, however, had been carried through with consistency, and in the main the vandalism was confined to those parts of the wall that could be reached from ground level without the aid of a ladder. Without question, then, the evidence does not point to desecration officially sponsored and effected by government agency.

The dismantling was not haphazard; like any wrecking crew, this one pursued methodically a preconceived plan. First, any mud-brick construction within the $Gm \cdot (t) \cdot p^3 \cdot itn$ was demolished and the rubble flattened. Then the legs of the colossal statues around the outside of the court were smashed, and the upper parts of the images allowed to fall forward on their faces into the courtyard. Next, the roofing blocks of the colonnade were taken off and thrown into the court, and the piers demolished one by one. The dismantling of the talatat-wall, with its still-fresh reliefs, followed immediately, section by section. As mortar had occasionally been used in the interstices, the wreckers used percussive force at times to dislodge the blocks. These were taken down outside the wall, in the five-meter-wide stretch of beaten earth between the stone wall and the mud-brick temenos wall; and, as more and more talatat were cast to the earth, a layer of shattered fragments and sandstone grit began to build up. The north wall was the first to go, and we must imagine a steady stream of workmen, each bearing a talatat, moving between East Karnak and the construction site of the second pylon and the Hypostyle Hall. By the time the demolition had progressed to the south side, the ninth pylon was in process of construction; and it is there that our beautiful processional scene from A-quadrant eventually was to slumber for thirty-two centuries.

What was left on the ground was no longer of any value. Steles, offering tables, and the lesser statues which remained were smashed almost beyond recognition. The beautiful blue-painted pottery, which had comprised part of the institution's kitchenware in its halcyon days, was smashed and swept

14.1. *Part of a large matched scene (TS 165) showing the king in the blue "war"-crown and holding the crook and flail, proceeding from his palanquin into the temple. The fans which dispel the heat and at times shade the monarch are visible at the rear. While none of the texts has been tampered with, vandals have dealt a couple of hammer blows to the king's face.*

into a heap on the west side. Some few large blocks were simply left where they lay, being too much trouble to move.

And finally there came the great conflagration. In the excavations of the A, B, and E areas on the south and west side of the court we were early intrigued by the presence of sloping layers of alternating orange, black, and gray, descending from the direction of the *temenos* wall on the south, over the robbed-out foundation trench of the *talatat*-wall, over the fallen colossi, and finally dissipating themselves on the floor of the court. Explanations were as numerous as the number of people who had seen the striations with their own eyes; but the solution eventually came with the help of my colleagues in the Department of Chemistry of the University of Toronto. Tests (neutron-activation and thermoluminescence among others) run on the orange layers proved that they were made up of decomposed mud-brick that had been secondarily fired. The thin black stria, which alternated with the other colors at regular intervals, were ash mixed with mud, undoubtedly the charred remains of the beds of reeds which, in ancient Egyptian brick walls, were placed between every two or three courses. The *temenos* wall must have been set ablaze with combustible material and, on the south side at least, the whole sent crashing down over the colonnade and into the central court.[13]

As Horemheb's engineers laid the foundations for the two additional pylons on the south of Karnak, the shrines of *Tni-mnw* and *Rwd-mnw* came down also. The latter's masonry in part found its way into the foundations of the ninth pylon, along with blocks of 12th Dynasty date; while *Tni-mnw* lent its dismembered blocks to the upper portions of the same pylon. Amenophis III's southern gate, parts of whose walls were now carved with offending scenes of the heretic king, was dismantled on the spot, and immediately re-erected as the (present) 10th pylon, with new facing masonry concealing the hateful reliefs.

Some of the Karnak material was carried far afield. Large quantities of *Rwd-mnw* blocks gradually found their way to Luxor where, seventy years later, Ramesses II was to use them in his great pylon. *Gm·(t)-p³-itn* fragments went northeast to Medamud, eight miles distant, and scattered blocks still turn up from time to time in villages up and down the Nile.

One day the foreman who was directing the work of demolition at the *Gm·(t)-p³-itn* appeared, as usual, with his baton of office. Maybe he waved

13. F. Widmar, *JSSEA* 11(1981), 279ff.

the wand too vehemently at his men; perhaps he struck a lazy worker. Whatever the reason, the stone applique with the cartouche of Horemheb carved on it fell from the tip and was lost in the debris. The foreman may never have realized it was gone; but we found it, in June 1978, among the *talatat* in quadrant E. Horemheb had unwittingly put his signature to the destruction.[14]

To legitimize his succession, Horemheb may have married Mutnodjmet, sister of Nefertity, but there was no public acknowledgement of any legacy from Amarna. Modern scholars sometimes debate whether Horemheb terminates the 18th Dynasty or inaugurates the 19th; the controversy is a pointless quibble. Already with Ay the Thutmosid family was discredited and defunct. The reigns of the four kings from Akhenaten to Ay, amounting to thirty-one or thirty-two years, were added to the official reign of Horemheb, who now appears with a fantastic fifty-nine years. In the king-list his cartouche follows immediately that of Amenophis III, and on the monuments his name is incised everywhere over that of Tutankhamun. If Akhenaten must be referred to in subsequent records it is always by a pejorative circumlocution: a court transcript has occasion to mention "the reign of that damned one of Akhetaten," and a death certificate is said to have been dated in the "9th regnal year of the rebel. . . ."[15] All that lingered in the oral tradition of Egypt, the collective historical memory of the people, was a confused recollection of people afflicted with plague, expelled to the quarries, their temples closed, and subject to a renewed attempt by "foreign rulers" to get control of Egypt. Akhenaten and his family had become "nonpersons."[16]

14. D. B. Redford, *ROM Archaeological Newsletter,* no. 195 (Aug. 1981).

15. A. H. Gardiner, *JEA* 24(1938), 124.
16. See Krauss, *Das Ende der Amarnazeit.*

CHAPTER FIFTEEN

"The Beautiful Child of the Sun-Disc"

One of my fervent desires in my teaching or writing of ancient history is that the novice or reader will be confronted time and again by the factual evidence, as much or as little as it is. Read the scholar's or the novelist's romanticized version of the story and enjoy it fleetingly—then discard it, and turn to ferret out the truth.

Enough, I hope, has been brought forward in the preceding pages to show that the historical Akhenaten is markedly different from the figure popularists have created for us. Humanist he was not, and certainly no humanitarian romantic. To make of him a tragic "Christ-like" figure is a sheer falsehood. Nor is he the mentor of Moses: a vast gulf is fixed between the rigid, coercive, rarified monotheism of the pharaoh and Hebrew henotheism, which in any case we see through the distorted prism of texts written 700 years after Akhenaten's death. Certain affinities have long since been pointed out between the hymn to the sun-disc and Psalm 104, and the parallels are to be taken seriously. There is, however, no literary influence here, but rather a survival in the tradition of the northern centers of Egypt's once-great empire of the *themes* of that magnificent poetic creation.

If we pass in review the hard facts we have adduced above, and, in the absence of facts the circumstantial evidence, we then catch a glimpse of *this* pharaonic figure. A man deemed ugly by the accepted standards of the day, secluded in the palace in his minority, certainly close to his mother, possibly ignored by his father, outshone by his brother and sisters, unsure of himself, Akhenaten suffered the singular misfortune of acceding to the throne of Egypt and its empire. We have no idea who or what influenced him in his formative years; but he was not brought into contact with his father's court, nor is there any evidence that he spent time at Heliopolis. As a result he nurtured a fear and aversion to his father's coterie of gifted administrators and the noble families from which they had sprung; and his apprehension was extended even to those foreign potentates with whom his father had been on intimate terms. There is evidence to suggest that he was a poor judge of character and a prey to sycophancy. Though he was apprehensive about his own lack of resolve, he nonetheless espoused a lenient policy toward his northern provinces which deterred him from acting unhesitatingly in the Asian sphere. Not being gifted as an administrator, Akhenaten was willing to leave the running of everyday affairs, both foreign and domestic, in the hands of military and civilian intermediaries, while he pursued his program of cultic reform.

Akhenaten, whatever else he may have been, was no intellectual heavyweight. He failed to comprehend, (or if he did, to appreciate) the true role and potential of cultic mythology, possibly seeing in it a means of concealment rather than revelation of the deity. Maybe he was reacting to the sophisticated cynicism of the age, just as Luther did in the 16th century A.D.; but if so he was surely guilty of identifying the aberrations of the system with its essence. For myths are the building blocks of any religion, even Judeo-Christianity. Though they come to us as the often crass impedimenta from an early and slightly embarrassing stage in our intellectual development, myths nonetheless pose the challenge of reinterpretation on a higher plane and integration one with another to provide a new and consistent view of the supernatural. Ancient Egyptian, like modern, theologians rose to this challenge, and such documents as the Memphite Theology★ and the New Kingdom hymns to Ptah and Amun are philosophical treatises of the highest achievement. What did Akhenaten substitute for them, once he had declared them anathema? Nothing! If mythology (in the broadest application of the term) is the only means of divine revelation, apart from the vision of the mystic, then what Akhenaten championed was in the truest sense of the word, atheism.

For the icon he devised, that spiderlike disc, could never be viewed as "god." What it was Akhenaten tells us plainly enough: the Disc was his father, the universal king. Significant, it seems to me, is the fact that, on the eve of Amenophis III's passing, the king who sat upon Egypt's throne bore as his most popular sobriquet the title "The Dazzling Sun-disc"; on the morrow of the "revolution" the only object of veneration in the supernal realm is king Sun-disc, exalted in the heavens and ubiquitously termed by Akhenaten "my father." I will not pursue the implications of this, though they appear to me plain enough.

That Akhenaten possessed unusual ability as a poet is, I think, self-evident. For him nature itself, in all its forms, displayed sufficient fascination; the gratification to be had in ruminating on imponderables paled by comparison. Although many images are derivative, the great hymn to the Disc stands out as a major, almost "positivist," statement on the beauty of creation.

I strongly suspect Akhenaten also had a flair for art, sculpture, and design, although this might be harder to demonstrate. The startlingly new expressionism that bursts on the scene in the second year of the reign probably owes more to the monarch's tastes than to those of his artists; and, in the light of the well-known drafting ability of Thutmosid kings, it would be difficult to deny that the king also had a hand in working out the details of the new canons. To me it is the art associated with his program that remains Akhenaten's single most important contribution.

Beautiful though they may be, the Amarna reliefs reveal one of the most displeasing characteristics of the way of life Akhenaten held up as a model, refined sloth. Can the king engage in no more strenuous activity than elevating offerings? True, he rides a chariot; how often does he walk? Time and again we glimpse him lounging, completely limp, in a chair or on a stool. He is seen eating and drinking at a table groaning with food, occasionally interrupting his indulgence to lean languidly from the balcony and smile weakly at some sniveling sycophant in the court beneath. Is this effete monarch, who could never hunt or do battle, a true descendant of the authors of Egypt's empire? The court over which he presides is nothing but an aggregation of voluptuaries, bent on personal gratification, and their opportunist followers.

If the king and his circle inspire me somewhat with contempt, it is apprehension I feel when I contemplate his "religion." In Egypt the sun may well be a reliable and beneficent power, but it is nonetheless destructive, and mankind seeks to hide from it. If Re must be worshipped, let there be a refuge of shade close at hand! Both Karnak and Akhetaten become infernos from March to November. Yet the monarch—with relish it would seem!—not only selected these unholy sites for his use, but insisted on the simple open shrine, with no roof and very little shade, in which to honor his father! As one stands on the baking sand of the vast Amarna amphitheater, one cannot help but sense a sinister quality in all of this.

Not content with the subjection of his own body to the rays of his father at every waking moment, the autocratic ruler demanded everyone else follow suit! A fascinating letter found in the Amarna Tablets from the king of Assyria tells us this, and thus opens a new vista on Akhenaten's mental state. Ashuruballit I, eager to open relations with Egypt, now that Mitanni had been weakened, sent a delegation to Akhetaten; but they must have returned saying something like this: this pharaoh must be crazy! He holds his audiences, meetings, and ceremonies entirely in the sun, and keeps everyone standing in the heat! This occasioned the following remonstrance from the Assyrian sovereign to Akhenaten: "Why are my messengers kept standing in the open sun? They will die in the open sun. If it does the king good to stand in the open sun, then let the king stand there and die in the open sun. Then will there be profit for the king! But really, why should they die in the open sun? . . . They will be killed in the open sun!" The vignette here sketched is at once comical and outrageous. The regime was plainly, at this stage, intolerable.

For all that can be said in his favor, Akhenaten in spirit remains to the end totalitarian. The right of an individual freely to choose was wholly foreign to him. He was the champion of a universal, celestial power who demanded universal submission, claimed universal truth, and from whom no further revelation could be expected. I cannot conceive a more tiresome regime under which to be fated to live.

GLOSSARY

Akh-menu: name used for sacred buildings from the Middle Kingdom, in the form "(King X) is one excellent of memorials." The most famous example is the columned hall of Thutmose III on the east side of the Amun temple at Karnak.

Akkadian: language of the eastern branch of the Semitic family of tongues, spoken in the Tigris-Euphrates valley from the 3rd millennium B.C. and, during the time of Akhenaten, used as a diplomatic language around the Levant.

Alalakh: city in north Syria, capital of the state of Mukishe.

Arsaphes: lit. "he who is upon his lake," name of the ram-god worshipped in the Fayum district of Middle Egypt.

Athribis: city of the tenth Lower Egyptian township, situated toward the apex of the Delta, c. thirty-five miles north of Heliopolis.

baker's ratio: the quantity of loaves of a certain kind (i.e., content of flour) which can be made from one oipe (q.v.) of meal.

Baky: fortress in Nubia, on the east bank of the Nile, c. sixty-five miles south of Elephantine.

Boghaz Keui: modern name of the site of the capital of the Hittites in central Asia Minor.

Chief Lector Priest: (Egyptian, "he who carries the book-roll") the priest charged with keeping and pronouncing the cultic formulae and recitations accompanying divine service.

Coele-Syria: Hellenistic term, usually applied to the southern reaches of Syria, between the coast and Mt. Hermon.

deben: ancient Egyptian measure of weight, approximately the equivalent of ninety-one grams.

Deir el-Bahari: (lit. "the northern monastery"), medieval name for the terraced temple of Hatshepsut on the west bank at Thebes.

determinative: hieroglyphic sign, placed at the end of a word, and indicating broadly the category to which the word belongs.

Drah abu'l naga: modern name of that part of the Theban necropolis that stretches north from Hatshepsut's temple at Deir el-Bahari.

epagomenal days: the five days at the end of the civil calendar in ancient Egypt, designated as the birthdays of the five gods Osiris, Isis, Seth, Nephthys, and Horus.

Fenkhu: term used by the Egyptians for the coastlands of the eastern Mediterranean, the later Phoenicia.

"gas-pipe" trench: a longtitudinal unit of excavation, approximately three by ten meters, which makes possible close scrutiny of stratification and then, if desired, a "peel-back" of layers.

Geb: earth god of the Egyptian pantheon, son of Shu and father of Isis and Osiris. Geb was the "heir" of the gods, through whom passed the right of universal dominion.

god's-father: term for a particular grade of priests in the upper echelons of a temple staff; also used to designated the paterfamilias of a royal dynasty, or the king's father-in-law.

Gold Mansion: craftsmen's workshop, where the cult images of the gods and other sacred equipment were manufactured.

hamseen: (Arabic, "fifty") a dry and oppressive wind that blows in Egypt and North Africa, traditionally for fifty days, in March and April.

Hathor: perhaps originally the female personification of the king's palace, by the New Kingdom the goddess of love, beauty, and femininity, at home in Dendera in the 6th township of Upper Egypt.

ḥm³ gt-*stone*: probably carnelian.

House of ʿOkheperkare: residential installation in the Memphite region built by Thutmose I and occupied from time to time by his descendants over the next 150 years.

Hyksos: (lit. "foreign rulers") a term applied widely by ancient Egyptians to any heads of state of alien extraction; most commonly used to designate those Amorite kings who subdued and ruled Egypt c. 1665 to 1557 B.C., who constituted Manetho's 15th Dynasty.

IFAO: Institut français d'archeologie orientale; the French Institute at Cairo, devoted to archeological, linguistic, and historical studies in Egypt.

Intermediate Period: term applied to two periods of Egypt's history when weak kings brought on economic hardship and anarchy; the first c. 2180–2050 B.C., and the second c. 1778-1550 B.C.

itr *of sailing*: linear measure of approximately 10.5 km., or 6½ miles.

Khanigalbat: geographical and political term for the Tigris valley north of Assyria and the eastern part of the Mesopotamian plain; in the 15th and 14th centuries B.C. part of the Mitannian empire, and occasionally used in royal titles in place of Mitanni.

Khatte: the Hittite kingdom of central Asia Minor (modern Turkey), with capital at Khattusas (q.v.).

Khattusas: capital of Khatte (q.v.), the modern Boghaz Keui (q.v.).

Khnum: the ram god of Elephantine, in the southernmost township of Upper Egypt; noted for his activity as a god of creation.

Khopry: a solar deity, worshipped at Heliopolis and elsewhere, under the form of the scarab beetle (*kheper*), and identified as a form of Re.

ku-*shrine*: general term for any mortuary installation wherein the spirit of the deceased (*ku*) was worshipped and served.

Kush: geographical term used increasingly from the Middle Kingdom on for the Sudanese lands south of the second cataract on the Nile.

Late Period: Dynasties 21 through 24, c. 1070–712 B.C., a period of weak government dominated by Libyan elements resident in Egypt.

Malqata: (Arabic, "place of picking up;") modern name of the site on the west bank at Thebes where the palace of Amenophis III stood.

Mari: city on the middle Euphrates, center of a prosperous kingdom c. 2000–1700 B.C., famous for the tens of thousands of texts recovered by excavations of the palace archives.

Memphite Theology: theological treatise of uncertain, though very ancient, date, known from a copy made around 700 B.C., which posits the god

Ptah as the hypostasis of life and thought, as well as the basis of existence, throughout the cosmos.

Min: ancient god of fertility and ancestor worship, revered at Coptos north of Thebes; often shown in ithyphallic form.

Napata: ancient Nubian city, east of the Nile, within the great bend of the Nile in the Dongola reach. An administrative center under Thutmose III, it later became the residence of native Sudanese kings.

Nekhbit: tutelary goddess of Upper Egypt, depicted as a vulture; worshipped at Elkab in the third township of Upper Egypt.

New Kingdom: Designation of the period of the Egyptian Empire, encompassing Dynasties 18 through 20, c. 1600–1070 B.C.

Nine Bows: the traditional enemies of pharaoh (mainly foreign ethnic groups), often depicted as literal bows beneath the king's feet.

Niya: city in north Syria adjacent to swamps stocked with elephants, not far from the later Apamea.

nomarch: governor of a township (Greek "nome"). Usually appointed by the king, in times of weak central government the office often became hereditary.

oipe: dry measure, roughly equivalent to a half bushel.

Old Kingdom: Designation of the period encompassed by the initial eight dynasties of Egyptian history, c. 3100–2200 B.C., the age of a strong centralized monarchy at Memphis and extensive pyramid-building.

Osiris Heqa Djet: form of Osiris (lit. "ruler of eternity"), worshipped especially in a small shrine erected for him at East Karnak, c. 730 B.C.

Pre: the name "Re" with prefixed definite article, a form common in the later 18th and 19th Dynasties.

Ptah: (lit. "the opener"?) township god of the Memphite district, with special associations with creation and kingship. q.v. Memphite Theology.

Qufti: native of the town of Quft (ancient Coptos), just north of modern Luxor; noted for their training by Sir Flinders Petrie in the art of careful excavation, Quftis are much in demand as specialized diggers.

rekhyet-*birds*: lapwings, with wings pinned back, used as a heraldic device in art to represent the common people.

Saite Dynasty: term applied to the 26th Dynasty (664–525 B.C.), because of its origin in the city of Sais in the Delta; a period of archaizing and reverence for ancient models.

Sea Peoples: coalition of sea-roving peoples, with piratical instincts, originally at home in the Aegean and the Ionian coast of Asia Minor, who bore down on Western Asia and Egypt during the period c. 1220–1190 B.C., and ushered in the Iron Age.

Sekhmet: lioness-headed goddess of slaughter and pestilence, often associated with the fiery heat of the "sun's eye."

Shasu: broad generic term for the nonurban, seminomadic tribes of West Semitic-speaking peoples who occupied the Negeb and other steppe regions of Palestine and Syria.

She-that-faces-her-Lord: name of that quarter of ancient Thebes occupying the west bank directly opposite Karnak.

shōmu: the season of harvest (summer) in the ancient Egyptian calendar.

Shu: god of atmosphere and air; son of Atum, the creator, and father of earth (Geb) and sky (Nut).

Sile: border fortress on the northeastern frontier of Egypt, facing the Sinai desert.

Southern Heliopolis: occasional appelative of Thebes, less frequently of Hermonthis.

suk: covered street, market.

Sun-folk: provisional translation of Egyptian *ḥnmmt*, epithet of the Egyptians as a race.

Taharqa: third king of the 25th Dynasty, reigned 690-664 B.C.; of Sudanese origin and birth, he did much to restore Thebes and the temple of Amun. He was expelled from Egypt by the Assyrian invasions.

Takhsi: district in Syria, north of Damascus.

Taroy: Sudanese region of uncertain location.

Thoth: the scribe of the gods, associated with wisdom, learning, writing, and the arts; closely linked with the ibis or the cynocephalus baboon, worshipped principally at Hermopolis, opposite Akhetaten.

Thutmosids: the family and descendants of Thutmose I, used in this work as the equivalent of the 18th Dynasty.

Turin Canon: papyrus of 19th and 20th Dynasty date, containing on the verso a copy of the kings of Egypt from Ptah, the founder and creator of the land, down to the Ramessides (probably). It is the only true king-list to have survived from pharaonic times.

12th Dynasty: royal family of southern origin who held sway c. 1995–1778 B.C., and who reunited Egypt after civil war. Their prosperous administration gave Egypt a classical age.

22nd and 23rd Dynasties: families of Libyan extraction who held the kingship from c. 930–712 B.C.; a period of relative weakness and isolation.

Ugarit: a major city and state on the Mediterranean coast of Syria, just south of the mouth of the Orontes. The royal archives, recovered through the excavations of the French, have shed a flood of light on the history, culture, and religion of Syria c. 1500–1200 B.C.

Upper Retjenu: common but vague Egyptian term for the uplands of Palestine and Syria.

Wady Tumilat: shallow torrent bed, or depression, leading from a point just east of Bubastis eastward to the Bitter Lakes on the eastern side of the Delta; an entry point for bedouins and the route Egyptians took to the turquoise mines of Sinai.

Wassukani: the capital of Mitanni, to date not located.

SUGGESTED READING

Those wishing to pursue an "in-depth" study of the Amarna Period can do no better than to consult the bibliography compiled by Edward K. Werner in the newsletter of the *Journal of the American Research Center in Egypt* (nos. 95, 1975; 97/98, 1976; 101/102, 1977; 106, 1978; 110, 1980; and 114, 1981). Here they will find a complete listing of all works that have appeared within the last generation, anywhere in the world and in any language. The present purpose is to list only the general works in English.

The best general introductions to the period are those of Cyril Aldred, *Akhenaten Pharaoh of Egypt: A new Study* (London, 1968), and *Akhenaten and Nefertity* (Brooklyn, 1973), the latter being the catalogue of the exhibition of Amarna art at the Brooklyn Museum. The same author has also contributed the chapter on the Amarna Age to the most recent edition of the *Cambridge Ancient History*.

For the excavations at Amarna (Akhetaten), see W.M.F. Petrie, *Tell el-*

Amarna (London, 1894); T. E. Peet et al., *The City of Akhenaten,* 3 vols. (London, 1923–1951); J. Samson, *Amarna, City of Akhenaten and Nefertity* (Warminster, 1972); with profit one might also consult the interim reports which, between 1919 and 1939, appeared almost annually in the *Journal of Egyptian Archaeology* (published by the Egypt Exploration Society). The private tombs at Amarna are the subject of a six-volume publication by N. de G. Davies, entitled *The Rock-tombs at Amarna* (London, 1903–1908); the royal tomb has been treated by G. T. Martin in *The Royal Tomb at El-Amarna* (London, 1974).

Relief scenes from Amarna are published by J. D. Cooney, *Amarna Reliefs from Hermopolis in American Collections* (Brooklyn, 1965); G. Roeder and R. Hanke, *Amarna-Reliefs aus Hermopolis,* 2 vols. (Hildesheim, 1969 and 1978).

The work of the Akhenaten Temple Project is still in process of publication; see R. W. Smith and D. B. Redford, *The Akhenaten Temple Project,* Vol. 1: *The Initial Discoveries* (Warminster, 1977). For the excavations, one should consult the interim reports of the present writer in the *Journal of the American Research Center in Egypt* 14 (1977), 9ff.; *Expedition* (Summer, 1977), 33ff.; *Scientific American* 239, no. 6 (Dec. 1978), 100ff.

For the cult of the sun-disc, one might consult articles by the present writer in the *Journal of the American Research Center* 13 (1976) and 18 (1981).

Rather more research has been devoted to the close of the Amarna Period. One might begin with Aldred's useful article in the *Journal of Egyptian Archaeology* 43 (1957), 30ff. On the so-called tomb of Tiy in the Valley of the Kings one might consult the articles by Sir Alan H. Gardiner, H. W. Fairman, Aldred, and R. G. Harrison in the *Journal of Egyptian Archaeology* 43 (1957), 10ff.; 47 (1961), 25ff.; 41ff.; 52 (1966), 95ff. The new theory on the person of Nefertity has been propounded and elaborated by J. R. Harris in *Acta Orientalia* 35 (1973), 5ff.; 36 (1974), 11ff.; 38 (1977), 5ff., and by J. Samson, *Journal of Egyptian Archaeology* 63 (1977), 88ff.

Egypt's foreign relations at the close of the period can be investigated by consulting the pertinent chapters in the *Cambridge Ancient History* (Vol. 2), supplemented by K. A. Kitchen, *Suppiluliumas and the Amarna Pharaohs* (Liverpool, 1962).

There exists no good compendium in English translation of Amarna texts; but reliable renderings of certain selections will be found in the following: J. B. Pritchard, ed., *Ancient Near Eastern Texts Relating to the Old Testament*[3] (Princeton, 1969); W. K. Simpson, ed., *The Literature of Ancient Egypt* (New Haven, 1973); M. Lichtheim, *Ancient Egyptian Literature,* Vol.

2: *The New Kingdom* (Berkeley, 1976). The Amarna Letters may be read in the somewhat inferior translation of S.A.B. Mercer, in *The Tell el-Amarna Tablets,* 2 vols. (Toronto, 1939): while Hittite texts may be perused in Pritchard, *Ancient Near Eastern Texts,* or H. G. Güterbock, *Journal of Cuneiform Studies* 10 (1956), 41ff.

INDEX

General Index

A-quadrant, 92, 94, 110, 112, 115, 228ff.
AB-quadrant, 105, 117
Abdi-Ashirta, 200f.
Abi-milki, 199
Abu Gurob, 125
Abydos, 227
AC-quadrant, 117
AD-quadrant, 117
Aegean Greece, 34, 193, 214
Africa, 34
Ahmose, 9, 11, 13, 15, 30, 151, 160
Akhenaten, 141, 144, 146f., 148, 164f.,
    168, 171f., 198f., 201, 207, 223, 225,
    232ff.; anathematization of, 231; as poet,
    234; daughters of, 148, 186f., 189, 205;
    death of, 193, 205; foreign policy of,

194f., 201f.; image of the Disc, 179;
interpretations of, 4; meaning of name,
176; sister of, 192; and Smenkhkare, 188,
204; titulary of, 149; worship of, 180,
190
Akhetaten, 142, 147ff., 150ff., 165f., 175,
    177, 179f., 193, 199, 205, 225;
    destruction of, 227f.; lack of inscriptions,
    191; tombs at, 187, 235; wharves, 194
Akh-menu, 96
Akhmim, 36, 217
Akita, 194
Akizzi, 167, 198f.
Alalakh, 32
Aleppo, 14, 40, 197f.
Alexander the Great, 3, 88

altar scribe, 159

Amarna, 111, 148, 179, 185, 206, 212, 219, 223, 225; age, 189f., 192, 225f.; art, 205, 219, 222, 227, 234; blocks from, 147; desert chapels at, 209

Amarna Letters (Tablets), 40, 79, 148, 166f., 213, 235

Amenemhet ("Surer"), 49ff.

Amenemone, 220

Amenophis I, 9, 11, 13, 17

Amenophis II, 17, 19, 27, 31f., 160, 163

Amenophis III, 28, 34f., 150, 159, 161, 164ff., 168, 171f., 197, 200, 205, 214; at Amarna, 148; death of, 54; jubilee reliefs of, 125, 132; *maru* of, 149; marriages of, 36; palace of, 44; pylons of, 45, 60, 62, 71, 230; sickness of, 52; son of, 163; title of, 35; tomb of, 222

Amenophis IV: accession of, 57; aping his father, 130; appearance of, 58, 63; building program of, 71; colossi of, 83ff., 89, 102, 104, 228, 230; change of name, 141; criticism of, 139, 165; daughters of, 71, 79f., 82, 138; education of, 59; political weakness of, 167; titulary of, 133f. *See also* Akhenaten

Amenophis, son of Amenophis III, 37, 59

Amenophis, son of Hapu, 47f., 51, 132

Amenophis (chief steward), 49, 51

Amenophis si-se, 161

Amki, 202, 215, 221

Amorites, 15, 17, 39

Amun, 11, 17, 37ff., 42, 47, 49, 51, 59, 65, 67, 86, 89f., 99, 130, 149, 158, 179, 189, 205, 208, 216, 223, 233; closing of temple of, 175; cult of, 158ff.; enclosure wall of, 91, 96; erasure of name of, 141f.; first prophet of, 160f.; name, banning of, 176; nature of, 162; reinstatement of, 209f.; royal attributes of, 162; second prophet of, 160f.; son of, 13; and sun-disc, 226; temple (house) of, 27, 44, 95, 97f., 159; universalism of, 163

Amun-re, 97, 105, 171, 223

Amurru, 26, 167, 196, 200

Amurtaeus, 88

Anat, 28

Anatolia, 15, 23, 195

ancestors, royal, 13

Anen, 59, 151

Anii, 180

Ankhesenamun, 207, 215, 217f., 221

Ankhesenpaaten, 79, 150, 190, 193, 207

Ankhesenpaaten-minor, 193, 215

annals, Hittite, 214f., 217

anthropomorphism, 175f.

antiquity, delight in, 52

Antef, 11

Anubis, 51, 175

ʿApiru, 200

Apiya, 151, 194

Apophis, 176

"Appearing in Truth," 38

archbishop, 51, 60, 160f.

archery, 31, 38

archives, 148

Armenia, 196

armor, 27

army, 21f., 139, 152, 170, 193; Nubians in, 194; officers of, 144, 152, 220

aromatics, 27

Arrapkha, 32

arrows, 127, 130

Arsaphes, 90

Artaxerxes III, 88

Aryan-speaking, 15

Arvad, 201

Arzawa, 36, 221

Ashurbanipal, 87

Ashur-uballit I, 213, 235

Asia, 26, 214

Asiatics, 16, 19, 23, 28f.; princes, 193

Assyria, 14, 212ff., 217

Assyrian invasion, 87

Astarte, 28

Aswan, 9, 24, 39, 95f., 101

Asyut, 101

"Aten," 170

atheism, 234

Athens, 3

Athribis, 47

Atum, 157, 162f., 171, 210

Avaris, 15

Ay, 132, 150ff., 177, 180, 205ff., 213, 216f., 218ff., 221f., 223, 225, 231

Aziru, 167, 200ff.

B-area, 230
Ba'al of Memphis, 28
baboon, 175, 178
Babylon, 14f., 34, 40, 52, 167, 187, 202;
    king of, 37; princesses of, 36
Bahr Yussef, 142
Baky, 38
banquet, 224
barracks, 148
battalion commanders, 152, 207
battle, love of, 17
bedouin, 29
beekeepers, 135
beer, 134f., 144
Bek, 63
Bekaa, 26, 200
"benevolences," 16, 193
Berlin, 219
Beth-Shan, 26
blindness, 130
blood brotherhood, 29
bnbn-stone, 60, 72ff., 138, 146f., 166, 210
Boghaz Keui, 168
bones, bovid, 90, 101
Book of the Dead, 176
boundary steles, 23, 142, 144, 165
bouquets, 134f.
bows, 27
boxwood, 201
bridge, 145
"broad hall," 63, 159
"broken cornice," 75, 145
bronze, 45
brotherhood, 40ff.
Bubastis, 125, 130
Buhen, 39, 194
bulls, 117, 175
Burnaburiash, 187
butchers, 117
butler, 23, 60
buttresses, 146
Byblos, 18, 32, 34, 187, 196, 199–202

Canaan, 25ff., 167, 201
Canaanites, 3, 9, 19, 25, 28, 34, 200
caption texts, 70

captives, 193, 220; females, 78
Carchemish, 18, 217
carrying chair, see palanquin
cartouches, 110f., 141, 178, 228
cattle, 24, 26f., 135, 144, 149, 180
cedar, 26
cenotaphs, 11
censer, 122, 132, 180
chamberlains, 132, 151
charioteer, king's, 151
chariotry, commander of, 151f., 207
chariots, 22, 27, 130, 142, 147, 214, 234
Chemistry, Department of, 230
Chevrier, H., 67f., 83–86, 89, 108ff.
chief lector priest, 111, 134
chief stewards, 49, 151
"child of the harem," 22, 164
choirs, 211
Christ, 226, 232
Coele-Syria, 196
colonies, 16
colonists, 24
colonnade, 78, 102, 116f., 128, 228
columns, 145
conflagration, 230
copper, 26, 31, 45, 199
co-regent, 188, 191, 205
coronation, 125f., 188
cosmogonies, 157f.
costume, 102
courtiers, 93, 111, 119, 122, 128, 132, 134,
    138, 144, 179, 187
court ladies, 79
"court of the great ones," 126f., 130
Crete, 34, 40
Cross, 226
cult images, 126
Cusae, 100
Cyprus, 26, 34, 40, 195

dais, 79, 126, 130, 193
Damascus, 19, 25f., 194, 196, 215
dancers, 211
David, 3
Davis, T., 189
"Dazzling Sun-disc," 35, 171, 234
decorative arts, 176
Deir el-Bahri, 97f.

Delta, 28f., 100, 208
departments, government, 14
deportation, 194
diplomacy, 39f.
Disc, 60, 170f., 173, 175–80, 204f., 210, 228, 234
Divine Worshippers, 86
Djehuty, 160
dôm-wood, 26
domestic apartments, 71, 147, 149
Dongola, 158
double crown, 102
draft lists, 22
Drah abu'l naga, 98
durbar, 186

E-area, 230
E-quadrant, 117f., 122, 231
East Karnak, 83, 85f., 88ff., 96, 100, 107, 144, 227f.
ebony, 26f., 36
Edfu, 159
Edjo, 126
EE-quadrant, 117f.
Egypt Exploration Society, 219
electrum, 26, 32, 45, 142, 208f.
Elephantine, 43, 60, 208
elephants, 19
Elijah, 3
Elkab, 43
Emramesha', 99
engineers, 151
Ennead, 171, 176
ergastulum, 159
Esdraelon, 18, 26
Etakkama, 202
eunuchoidism, 63, 82
Euphrates, 15, 18, 23, 196, 212ff., 217, 221
Eusebius, 39
"Eye of Re," 170

faience, 145
Fairman, H. W., 176
falcon, 187, 192
famine, 99
fan-bearers, 126
fans, 111
Favorite, 187, 192

FE-trench, 109
feasting, 124, 128, 166
Fenkhu, 16
Fertile Crescent, 15
figurines, 90
"fire, sea of," 175
First Dynasty, 125
fishing and fowling, 30
flag-staffs, 111
"flame, house of the," 126
foreign affairs, 15f.
foreigners, 112
4th township, 11
fowl, 144
fowling, 222
Freud, 4
fruit, 144
funerary practices, 176

Galilee, 14, 19, 26
game, wild, 144
gardens, 149
garments, 36
garrisons, 16, 26, 194, 200
Gaza, 26, 29, 217
Geb, 210
Genesis, 3
Gezer, 27, 36
Gilu-khepa, 36, 41, 43, 150
goats, 135
gods, 175, 205, 209; absent from jubilee, 130, 132; failure of, 172; father of the king, 210; reopening of temples of, 207f., 210; word for, 176
god's-fathers, 134f., 151, 160
god's-prophet, 159
god's-treasurer, 159
Golan, 26
gold, 24, 26f., 36, 41f., 45, 166, 186, 199, 211, 220; mines, 34, 50
"Gold Mansion," 209
governor, 26
granaries, overseer of, 48f., 151
grave-robbing, 224
"great house," 126f.

Hammurapi, 14f.
Hania, 218

Hapuseneb, 160
Harakhty, 173, 186
Harakhty-Atum, 162
Hare township, 139
harem, 72, 134
Harris, J. R., 191
harvest, 48, 125
Hathor, 90, 130
Hatnub, 139
Hatshepsut, 18, 24, 60, 97, 161, 164
Hazor, 14, 25
head-smiting scene, 62, 78, 138, 214
"heart," 157
Hebnu, 219
Helck, W., 187
Heliopolis, 22, 43, 59, 138f., 147, 149, 152,
    173, 180, 207, 227, 233; cosmogony of,
    157; cult of, 73
henotheism, Hebrew, 232
heralds, 14, 22
Hermopolis, 140, 147, 157, 227
high priest, house of the, 97; of
    Neferkheprure, 111; of the sun, 111, 135,
    152, 166
Hittites, 15, 32, 34, 40, 186f., 195, 197f.,
    201f., 213ff., 217, 221, 223
Horemheb, 65-68, 71, 92, 216f., 218ff.;
    coronation of, 223; edict of reform, 224,
    227, 230f.; in king-list, 231; tomb of,
    219f.
"horizon," 139, 144, 165, 186
Horus, 32, 35, 127, 152, 163, 219, 223
hostages, 22, 25f., 201
hour priests, 159
"House of Rejoicing," 63, 135, 144, 146f.
houses, orientation of, 98
hunting, 30f., 36
Hurrians, 3, 15, 34, 202, 218, 221
Huy, 151, 219
Huya, 150
Hyksos, 14f., 30, 100f., 208
hymns, 127, 170f., 175, 177, 210, 233
hypostyle hall, 67, 83, 228

Ibhat, 38f.
icon, 148, 173, 175, 209, 234
iconoclasm, 158, 169f., 173, 204, 209, 215,
    227

Ikhernofret, 99
Ilu-rabih, 202
image(s), 208f., 224
Imhotpe, 48f.
impalement, 194
incense, 132, 134, 144, 180
induction, 161
intermarriage (royal), 40
Ipuwy, 49
Isaiah, 3
Ishtar, 42, 52, 54
Itj-towy, 49
ivory, 26f.

Jerusalem, 199
jewels, 186
Jordan valley, 14, 26
jubilee, 79, 94, 111, 116, 118, 122ff., 130,
    136f., 139, 148, 165, 173, 227
Judeo-Christianity, 233
Justice, Department of, 224f.

Kadashman-enlil, 40f.
Kadesh, 18, 196, 200ff., 214f., 218, 220
Kadesha, 28
Kamutef, 210
Karnak, 44, 66f., 83, 85, 87, 92, 96, 100,
    130, 145f., 147, 173, 176, 180, 185, 191,
    210, 214, 216, 225, 230, 235
Karoy, 36
Kaska, 221
Kassite, 40
Kawa, 194
Kenamun, 32
Kenisa, 23
Khabur, 212
Kha'emhat, 48, 51
Khanigalbat, 213
Khartoum, 23
Khatte, 15, 167, 195-99, 212, 214
Khattusas, 213
Khay, 151
Kheruef, 49-51
Khnum, 43
Khonsu, 65, 90, 125
Khonsuemhab, 160
Khopry, 43, 163, 171
kilt-wearer, 159

king, childhood companions of, 22
kings, relations among, 40f.
king's barber, 23
"king's children," 130, 161
"king's ornaments," 22, 79
"king's peasants," 130
king's personal staff, 22
king's scribe, 47, 207
"king's son (of the southern lands)," 14, 24
kingship, divine, 178f., 181
kiosks, 72, 111, 122, 149, 186
Kiya, 150f., 186ff., 190–92
"knights," 25
ku-shrine, overseer of, 159
Kumidi, 26
Kush, 24, 177

lapis lazuli, 26, 45, 208, 211
Lauffray, J., 67, 96
laws, 225
lead, 26
Lebanons, 18f., 26, 196
lector priest, 159f.
Letopolis, 43
letters, exchange of, 40
Levant, 187, 199, 208
libation, 122, 132, 144, 180, 226
Libya, 186
Libyans, 72, 208
limestone, 145
linen, 211
lions, 38
livestock, 135, 186
loanwords, Canaanite, 28
Luther, 233
Luxor temple, 45, 66, 71, 216

Maanekhowtef, 151
Ma'at, 171
Madu (Medamud), 11, 66, 71, 230
magnetometer, 107
Mahu, 151
Malqata, 51
Mani, 42
manorial system, 14
"Mansion of Menmare Sety Merenptah," 91
Mari archives, 14

marriage, dynastic, 20
Martin, G., 219
Maru-aten, 149
matriarchy, 164
May, 209
Maya, 152f., 168, 199
mayors, 24ff., 135, 151, 224f.
meat offering, 90
Megiddo, 26; battle of, 18
Meketaten, 79, 186, 190
Memnon, 43, 45
Memphis, 3, 9, 21, 28, 37, 43f., 49f., 59, 97, 126, 134, 139, 151, 153, 159, 162, 175, 194, 206f., 209, 217ff., 227; theology of, 157, 233
Men, 63
Menkheper, 50
Menkheperre, 91
merchant fleets, 34; Syrian, 28
Meretaten, 79, 187f., 190ff., 193
Meretaten-minor, 193
Merimose, 38, 50f.
Meryptah, 161
Meryre, 132, 134, 152, 166
Meryre (II), 150
Mesopotamia, 130, 196, 212
metalwork, 27
Middle Kingdom city, 96ff.; destruction of, 98, 100; enclosure wall of, 98; society in, 159
military activity, justification of, 16
military at court, 72, 152
milk, 134f.
Min, 36
minerals, 24
mining, 48f.
Min-montu, 160
Minmose, 26
Mitanni, 15, 17–20, 34, 36, 40f., 52, 195ff., 212, 218, 235
Mnevis-bull, 149
monotheism, 158, 176, 205, 225ff., 232
Montu, 31, 44f., 62, 90, 97
Montuhotpe, 11, 97f., 100; mortuary temple of, 159
Moses, 3, 232
"Most Select of Places," 97
Mukish, 197

Mursilis I, 15
Mursilis II, 217
musicians, 119
Mut, 44f., 62, 65, 85, 90, 97f., 141, 210
Mut-nodjmet, 150, 231
Mycenaean pottery, 193
myths, 169, 177f., 205, 233f.

Nag el-Fokkani, 89
Naharin, 19, 32, 36
Nakht, 148, 151
Nakhtmin, 50, 194
Napata, 19
Napkhururiya, 166f.
Nebamun, 161
Nebmare, 35, 38, 43, 164
"Nebmare-the-Dazzling-Sun-disc," 49
Neby, 161
necropolis, 144, 165
Nectanebo I, 83f., 89, 96
Neferhotpe I, 99
Neferkhepru-hir-sekheprer, 151
Neferkheprure, 72
Nefer-neferu-aten minor, 149
Nefer-neferu-re, 149
Neferperet, 23
Nefersekheru, 49, 51
Nefertity, 23, 78f., 104, 138, 147, 150f.,
    186, 188, 190–93, 205, 207; death of,
    206; titulary of, 134
Negeb, 18, 29
Neha(?)-em-pa-aten, 152
Nekhbit, 43, 126, 175
neutron-activation, 230
Ne-woserre, 125
New York, 219
Nikmaddu, 197–99
Nile, 135, 180
Nine Bows, 163
Nineveh, 52
ninth pylon, 66, 83, 115, 134, 228, 230
Niya, 19, 197f.
nomarchs, 159
"north city," 145
north palace, 148f.
Nubia, 16, 24, 26f., 32, 43, 72, 139, 186,
    193f., 200, 219
Nubians, 39, 93, 99

Nukhashshe, 197f.
nurses, 149f.
Nut, 171, 175

oath, 25
obelisk, 62, 74, 146
offering prescriptions, 134ff.
offering scene, 72, 82, 147, 174
offering stands, 72
offering table, 70, 122, 146, 228
offices, 148
officials, coterie of, 164f.
oil, 26, 211
oral tradition, 231
orchestra, 119, 129f., 147
Orontes, 18f., 196f., 200, 213f., 221
Osirian cycle, 130
Osiris, 141, 175f., 226; temple of, 96, 159
Osorkon II, 125
oxen, 180

Pa-aten-em-heb, 151, 219
palace, 111f., 115–18, 130, 145ff., 171
palanquin, 94, 111f., 119, 126; bearers, 93,
    115, 119
Palestine, 14, 18, 26
Panehsy, 48
"Pan-grave People," 101
panther, 27
Parennefer, 60, 132, 135, 151
Patriarchs, 3
Pawah, 148
"Pax Aegyptiaca," 39
Paynehsi, 148
Penbuy, 209
Pentu, 151
Pericles, 3
Persian rule, 88
Peru-nefer, 28, 32
pharaohs, worship of, 24
Phoenicia, coast of, 18f., 26, 200
phyle, regulator of, 159
physician, chief, 151
piers, 105, 110, 145, 228; bases, 92
pigeons, 134f.
plague, 187, 205, 223
police, 72, 151, 161
pottery, 228; kilns, 87

POWs, 22f., 27f.
Pre, 60
prehistoric, 125
priests, 93, 111f., 130, 132, 134, 138, 152, 159f., 179, 220, 225, 228; houses of, 148; mortuary, 160; solar, 160
princesses, 36f.
prisoners, 23
processional scenes, 82, 94, 111, 116, 119, 127
prophets, 159f.
Psalm 104, 232
Ptah, 32, 37, 43, 130, 161, 175, 208f., 233
Ptahhotpe, 180
Ptahmose, 51, 161
Ptolemy Lagus, 88
Punjab, 15
pylons; of *Gm(t)-p³-itn*, 105, 111f.; of *Ḥwt-bnbn*, 75, 145; at Karnak, 66f.
pyramids, 11, 72; pharaohs, 97

Qatanum (Qatna), 14, 25, 167, 198f.
quarry, 43, 227
quartzite, 147

race, 126f., 130; course, 126
Ramesses II, 43, 66, 86, 89, 91, 96, 168, 230
Ramesside: kings, 227; pottery, 91
Ramose, 49, 51, 59, 132, 134, 151f., 161
Ra-nefer, 151f.
Re, 17, 33, 59, 72, 134, 162f., 169ff., 179, 186, 224, 226, 235
rebellion, 17
red crown, 126–28
Reharakhty, 20, 60, 62, 67, 71, 74, 163, 173, 177, 180, 226
rejuvenation, 125
rekhyet-birds, 178
relief-scenes: defacement of, 228; matching of, 70, 82; sequence of, 85, 110f.
reporter, 159
Reshef, 28
residential area, 148; buildings, 96
Retjenu, 214
revenues, diversion of, 142
rewards, 23, 165f., 193, 220
Rib-addi, 199, 201

Roman period, 91
Rome, 3
"Royal Road," 145, 148
royal secretary, 47
"royal sitting," 111

Saad, R., 67
sacred standards, 93, 126, 130, 134
Sadeinga, 43
Sai, 39
Sais, 135
Saite period, 86f., 108
Sakkara, 219
Samson, J., 191
Sangar, 32
Sat-amun, 37
Satepenre, 149
scarabs, 42f., 171, 176, 194
scribe of recruits, 47
scribes, 159f.
Sea Peoples, 40
Second Cataract, 38
second pylon, 83, 127, 228
"Secret of the Two Partners," 127
sd-festival, 51f., 62f., 71, 124ff., 132, 135, 138, 148, 152, 178, 186, 193
sedan chair, 132
Sehtepibre-onkh, 180
Sekhmet, 100
Selkit, 130
Sema-behdet, 60, 139
Semna, 38f.
Senu, 47
Senwosret I, 11, 97, 159
Senwosret III, 14
servants, 72, 118
Service des antiquités, 67
Seth, 127
Shasu, 29
Shat-meru, 38
Shattiwaza, 212
Shaushatar, 4
shawabtis, 176
Shechem, 3
sheep, 135
shields, 27
shipyards, 26
shrine-openers, 160

Shu, 102, 186

Shutarna II, 36, 41

Si-bast, 23

Sidon, 201

Si-hathor, 99

Sile, 29

Silsileh, 60

silver, 26f., 36f., 136, 186, 199, 211

Sinai mines, 49, 224

sinusoidal wall, 111f., 116

sistrum, 79

skirmishers, 39

slaves, 27f., 211

Smenkhkare, 188f., 191ff., 205, 227

Sobek, 48

Sobekhotep, 161

Sobekhotpe, 48

Sobekhotpe II, 99

Sobekhotpe III, 99

Sobekhotpe VII, 100

Sobekmose, 48

Socrates, 3

Soleb, 43

Sol-invictus, 4

south, products of, 24

Southern City, 21, 48, 88, 95, 139, 223

Southern Heliopolis, 132f., 135

Southern Opet, 44

speeches, 111, 117, 172

sphinx, 175

sportsman king, 30f.

standard-bearers, 72, 161

statues, 145; fragments of, 109; stelophorous, 171

steles: mortuary, 175; of victory, 39

storehouses, 148

"strongman" king, 30, 37f., 211

Sudan, 19, 24, 26, 36, 38, 50, 86, 194

Sumur, 26, 200f.

sun-barque, 175

Sun-disc, 17, 20, 66, 70ff., 93, 122, 129, 139, 141, 144, 162, 225f.; arms of, 173; child of the, 72, 133, 150, 166, 179, 190, 210; cult of the, 180f., 204f.; didactic name of, 173, 186; father of king, 142, 145, 178; house of, 132, 135f., 144, 146f., 166, 209; iconography, 172f.; as imperial symbol, 170f.; at jubilee, 130; king, relationship to, 149, 179f.; kingship of, 178f., 234; mansion of, 144, 146; monotheism of, 176; mythology, absence of, 169f.; servants of, 151f.; temples of, 68, 71ff., 82f., 142, 207f., 227ff.; universalism of, 177

sun god: as Amun, 162; epithets of, 111, 163; falcon-headed, 62, 67, 173; in mortuary temple, 172

sunshade, 144, 147

Suppiluliumas I, 195ff., 202f., 212ff., 217f., 221

Sutekh, 99

swords, 27

Syria, 14f., 17–20, 25f., 28, 32, 72, 130, 177, 186, 193, 198f., 201f., 212ff., 215, 217, 221; coast of, 197; chiefs of, 166, 220; kings of, 196; princesses of, 36; tongue of, 28; towns of, 27

table scribe, 151

Taharqa, 86

Takhsi, Takhsians, 32, 215

Taku, 198

talatat, 68, 72, 74f., 79, 83, 130, 145, 173, 178, 214, 227f.; debris of, 92f., 109f., 117; early discoveries of, 66f.

Taroy, 38

Taurus, 15, 197

taxes, 4, 24–27, 32, 135, 224

teaching, 179, 227

temple scribe, 159

temples, closing of the, 142, 169, 204

tenth pylon, 66, 83, 172f., 214, 224, 230

Thebaid, 99f.

Theban district, 21

Theban mortuary temples, 27f., 159

Theban plain, 97

Theban rebellion, 88

Thebes, 9, 11, 17, 22, 24, 27, 44, 51, 59, 63, 87f., 97, 100, 137, 139ff., 144, 146, 149, 152f., 159, 162, 171, 175, 179f., 186, 189, 193f., 205, 207, 210, 217, 223, 227; tombs at, 23, 46

Thoth, 32, 43, 47, 130, 140

"Thrones of the Two Lands," 97

Thutmose I, 17f., 45, 97, 159, 208

Thutmose II, 18

Thutmose III, 17ff., 26f., 30f., 34, 62, 96f., 159, 164, 171, 197f.
Thutmose IV, 4, 19, 27, 62, 74, 160, 171, 224
Thutmose, son of Amenophis III, 37
Thutmose (viceroy), 194
Thutmosid kings, 16, 164, 220, 223, 231, 234
Thutmosid profile, 63
Tia, 150
Tigris, 15
"Time of Troubles," 208
titles, military, 22
Tiy, 36, 43f., 50, 52, 79, 148, 150f., 166, 187, 189, 192, 195, 207
Tjanuna, 161
Tjaru, 161
torus roll, 105, 109
town planning, 96
Transjordan, 26
treasurer, 14, 50, 151
treasury, 48, 150, 161, 165
treaty, 40, 195, 198, 202, 218
Trinity, 226
Tripoli, 19
Tunanat, 198
Tunip, 18
Turin Canon, 99
Turkish Hatay, 19
turquoise, 45, 49, 208
Tushratta, 41, 52, 166, 195ff., 212ff., 218
Tutankhamun, 189, 191f., 205, 207–213, 215f., 219, 225, 227, 231
Tutankhaten, 192f., 207, 209
Tutu, 151, 166ff.
Tuya, 36f., 207
Tyre, 25, 34, 199
"Tyrians, Camp of the," 28

Ugarit, 3, 34, 197, 199, 201

Ullaza, 26
universalism, 163, 177, 235
"Upper Egyptian Heliopolis," 95
Upper Retjenu, 26
uraeus, 170, 173, 178
User-satet, 27

Valley of the Kings, 189, 192f., 222
vassals, 40
vegetables, 134f., 144, 180
viceroy, 24, 32, 38, 50, 194, 219
vizier, 14, 24, 49ff., 132, 134, 165f.

Wady Allaki, 24
Wady es-Sebua, 43
Wady Tumilat, 29
wall(s): height of, 82; temenos, 105, 230; of temple, 105
Wassukani, 213
Wawat, 24
weapons, 27
Western River, 135
West Semitic, 15, 17, 28, 100
white crown, 19, 115, 126f., 128
Wiedemann, A., 67
"will of my father," 127
"window of appearances," 119, 128f., 136, 146, 193
wine, 26, 144, 180; jars, 118, 129, 136, 180, 185–89, 191
wood, 24
workmen's village, 148

Yamkhad, 14f., 17
Yuwy-Amun, 23
Yuya, 36, 151, 207

Zagros Mountains, 41
Zidanza, 218, 220f.
Zinzar, 198

Index of Egyptian Words

iw⁶yt, "permanent armed forces," 22
imw psšt, "tent of apartments(?)," 142
'inw, "benevolences," 51
iry-p⁶t, "heir apparent," 219
it-ntr, "god's-father," 179
itr, 38

⁶3 n pr, "major-domo," 161
w⁶b-priest, 159f., 179
bit-bread, 134f.
pisn-bread, 134
nfr-nfrw-itn, "exquisite beauty of the sun-disc," 79; cf. 186, 188, 191f.

INDEX

Rwd-mnw-n-itn-r-nḥḥ, 63, 71f., 83, 148, 230
Ḥwt-itn, "Mansion of the Sun-disc," 146
Ḥwt-bnbn, "Mansion of the *bnbn*-stone,"
  63, 71f., 74f., 78, 83, 146
ḥmᶾgt-stone, 27
ḥm-ntr, "god's-servant," 179
ḥkᶾw ḫᶾswt, "foreign rulers," 100
smᶾᶜ ᶜᶾbt, "making the great oblation," 180

šw, "light," 180
šbt-object, 130
ḵnyt, "braves," 22
Gm-itn, 139, 146
Gm.(t)-pᶾ-itn, 63, 71f., 83, 94f., 102ff., 111,
  124, 125, 130, 142, 144–46, 180, 228,
  230
Tni-mnw-n-itn-r-nḥḥ, 63, 71, 83, 230
tryt, 25

Index of Akkadian Words

maryannu, 25
Nimmuᶜariᶜa, 35, 41
šākin mâti, "territorial governor," 26

Library of Congress Cataloging in Publication Data

Redford, Donald B.
Akhenaten, the heretic king.
Bibliography: p.   Includes index.
1. Akhenaton, King of Egypt.
2. Egypt—History Eighteenth dynasty, ca. 1570–1320 B.C.
3. Pharaohs—Egypt—Biography. I. Title.
DT87.4.R42 1984 932'.014'0924 [B] 83-22960
ISBN 0-691-03567-9

Donald B. Redford is Professor of Near Eastern Studies at the University of Toronto and Director of the Akhenaten Temple Project. He has also been Director of the East Karnak Excavations since 1975. Professor Redford has published extensively in the fields of archaeology and Egyptology, as well as preparing a documentary film on the Akhenaten Temple Project (*Akhenaten: The Lost Pharaoh*, 1979) and a libretto for an opera (*Ra*, 1982–83).